DOUBLE CROSSOVER

STUDIES IN SPORTS MEDIA

Edited by Victoria E. Johnson
and Travis Vogan

*For a list of books in the series,
please see our website at
www.press.uillinois.edu.*

DOUBLE CROSSOVER

Gender, Media, and Politics
in Global Basketball

COURTNEY M. COX

**UNIVERSITY OF
ILLINOIS PRESS**
Urbana, Chicago, and Springfield

© 2025 by the Board of Trustees
of the University of Illinois
All rights reserved
Manufactured in the United States of America
1 2 3 4 5 C P 5 4 3 2 1
♾ This book is printed on acid-free paper.

Cataloging data available from the Library of Congress

ISBN 978-0-252-04657-5 (hardcover)
ISBN 978-0-252-08868-1 (paperback)
ISBN 978-0-252-04788-6 (ebook)

For Ronald and Gaylen Cox,
the best coaches I could ever ask for.

Contents

Acknowledgments

Basketball is a team sport, albeit one where individuals can shine while playing their position. I am indebted to all the teammates that have made this project possible. I am so very grateful to my parents, Gaylen and Ronald Cox, the driving force behind every success I've experienced to date. Thank you for your unconditional love and support—I can never begin to describe what you both mean to me. I am also thankful for all the extended family members who supported me throughout this process, with special thanks to my Dallas and LA fam: Uncle Ken, Vonda, Granny 3, Auntie Rhonda, Grandy, Bri, Lauren, Michael, Aunt Susan, and Uncle Ted.

To my amazing friends, colleagues, and comrades who have held me down over the past ten years of this process: Brooklyne Gipson, James Sutton, Sama'an Ashrawi, Perry B. Johnson, Kate Miltner, Philana E. Payton, Jasmin A. Young, Marissiko Wheaton-Greer, Stefania Marghitu, Becca Johnson, Nick Busalacchi, Antar Tichavakunda, Rachel Kuo, Amira Rose Davis, Matt Bui, Cerianne Robertson, Evan Brody, Alvin Wyatt, Brittaney Belyeu, Rhian Rogan, Kwame Garrett-Price, Andrea Holman, Marcus and Angelica Brent, Justin and Elena Iglehart, Andrew and Chelsé Lilly, Aris Hall, and Preston Wilson. Thank you for reading portions of this project, sending memes, helping me through moments of anxiety or doubt, and believing this could someday be a book. To the amazing group chats that fueled me from graduate school and beyond: the Squaaaaaaad, Elevated and Hydrated, Girrrrrlllfriennnnddssssss, Public School Book Club, Terraza Squad, Anti-Chardonnay Chardonnay Club—I appreciate all of you so much.

This book would not exist without the intellectual contributions and embodied knowledge of the participants who so graciously shared time and space with me. I hope that this project makes every athlete and advocate of women's basketball feel a bit more seen and heard. Special thanks to Cierra Burdick, Nneka Ogwumike, and Sydney Colson for their constant support and assistance throughout it all.

This book emerged out of my graduate study at the University of Southern California. My time at Annenberg included a fantastic qualifying exams and dissertation committee: Robeson Taj Frazier, Sarah Banet-Weiser, Christopher Holmes Smith, Nayan Shah, Safiya Noble, and Ben Carrington. These brave souls saw the best in the very early, very rough versions of *Double Crossover* and pushed me to think bigger and expand further than I thought possible. Since then, I've had the incredible opportunity to build with the good folks at the University of Oregon's Indigenous, Race, and Ethnic Studies (IRES) Department. An enormous thank you to this amazing group of scholars who have made the work more critical and expansive in its understanding of how race, gender, and nationality inform participants' lives: Charise Cheney, Brian Klopotek, Laura Pulido, Lynn Fujiwara, Ernesto Javier Martínez, Jennifer O'Neal, Lana Lopesi, Abigail Lee, Cera Smith, Alaí Reyes-Santos, Michael Roy Hames-García, and Sharon Luk. I am also so grateful for finding UO fam outside of IRES in Kirby Brown, Rachel E. Weissler, Angela Addae, Aris Hall, Celena Simpson, Ana-Maurine Lara, Isabel Millán, and Yvette Saavedra.

I have also benefited tremendously from the intellectual community outside of UO, including the University of Illinois Media and Cinema Studies Department, the American Studies Association Sports Studies Caucus, and the International Association for Communication and Sport. I am especially grateful for Jenn McClearen, Samantha N. Sheppard, Noah Cohan, Yannick Kluch, David J. Leonard, M. Aziz, and Rudy Mondragón.

A lot of life happens when you're writing a book. I am thankful to Dr. Agnes Oh, Zankhana Smith, and Lawanda McGee for their guidance and care. I am beyond grateful for Dr. Chanda Reese and her team at OSF Healthcare—you're the real MVP.

Thank you so much to Chimene Tucker, Miriam Rigby, and Lauren Goss for all your assistance and support. Librarians and archivists are truly the foundation of my intellectual curiosity and growth.

My deep appreciation goes to the Oregon Humanities Center (OHC) for the intellectual community activated from the moment I stepped on campus and their financial support in completing this book. Thank you to all the incredible people at the University of Illinois Press, especially Danny Nasset, Mariah Schaefer, and Megan Donnan. My sincere, complete appreciation goes out to Travis Vogan and Victoria E. Johnson for believing in this project early on and allowing me to join a fantastic series. I am so very humbled by the kind words and strategic guidance offered by the anonymous reviewers for this book—I will forever cherish your warmth and wisdom. I am also indebted to Mary M. Hill for getting this book in tip-top shape as my copyeditor and to Twin Oaks Indexing for their help in offering a fantastic index for readers.

I also extend my gratitude to the many coffee shops that have supported this project with strong Wi-Fi, even stronger coffee, and solid outlet offerings. Big shout-outs to Cafe Mak, the LINE LA, Highly Likely, Nature's Brew, Cafe Dabang, The Boy & The Bear, Sisters Coffee Company, Farmers Union Coffee Roasters, and many more for letting me camp out until the words felt right.

Prologue

Cheryl Miller is on her way to Congress. Unfortunately for her opponents, she happens to have a bit of a home court advantage. Three groups—the House Committee on Education and Labor, the Subcommittee on Civil and Constitutional Rights, and the Committee on the Judiciary—convene on a spring morning at the Kinsey Auditorium in Los Angeles, California, mere walking distance from where Miller led the University of Southern California women's basketball team to back-to-back national titles (1983–84) and not too far from the Forum in Inglewood, California, where she captained Team USA's first gold medal in women's basketball during the 1984 Summer Olympics.

That day, less than a year after cutting down the collegiate championship nets and standing atop the Olympic podium, Miller seeks a different kind of victory. Following the passage of Title IX of the Education Amendments of 1972, the US law designed to prohibit sex-based discrimination within educational settings, several challenges to the bill emerged. In 1984 the Supreme Court case *Grove City College v. Bell* determined that Title IX did not apply across the entire higher education landscape. In this instance, Grove City, a private religious college, did not receive institutional federal aid and refused to submit documentation of compliance with the bill.[1] However, given that its student body received governmental assistance in the form of grants, the question of what constituted federal aid sent the case to the highest court in the country. With the Supreme Court ruling in favor of the college, Title

IX's precarious status troubled gender equality advocates concerned about the law's continued erosion.

In response, a 1984 press conference and demonstration in Washington, DC, featured athletes and advocates of equity in sport—including Miller—who spoke out in support of the Civil Rights Act of 1984, an amendment that would rectify the *Grove City* decision by prohibiting discrimination to any recipient of federal financial assistance.[2] The bill passed in the House of Representatives but died in the Senate, failing to become law. The following year, joint hearings across the country debated the Civil Rights Restoration Act of 1985 as a reparative response to the rollback of Title IX, including the one held this spring day in Los Angeles.

Before Cheryl Miller offers her statement, Augustus F. Hawkins, chairman of the Committee on Education and Labor, addresses her. "Some of us have watched your sports activities. . . . I hope that you are more at ease before this committee than you have been in some other activities," he says, referencing her unrelenting, aggressive style of play. "It can be a little tougher on the court than it is here," Miller replies.[3]

In her statement, Miller recounts her journey through sports and succinctly addresses the effects of Title IX on her basketball career, noting her predecessors who sold baked goods to finance their uniforms and travel. She then laments that the fight to retain key rights across educational and other public service sites persists. "I would like to make one thing clear," Miller says. "The *Grove City College* decision spells disaster, and not just for women athletes. The *Grove City College* decision cuts back the rights of minorities, disabled persons, older people, as well as women."[4] Here she connects the Title IX struggle to the everyday experiences of marginalized folks within the United States:

> I understand that Senator Dole has introduced a bill that would restore the protection in education alone. I am deeply disturbed by that. *I am not only a woman, I am a Black woman.* The Civil Rights Act of 1964, which was also limited by the *Grove City College* decision, is primarily responsible for ending racial segregation in hospitals, social service agencies, and housing, as well as education. Under the Dole bill, I would be protected from discrimination in college, but not in the hospital. I fail to see the justification that all federally funded discrimination is tolerable. . . . I am not a lawyer, as you can see and as my record has spoken. I am

not knowledgeable about all the fine points in the law. I only know that after the *Grove City College* decision, I have less rights than I had before.[5]

Here Miller articulates the stakes of these legislative shifts, connecting her own positionality in advocating for the Civil Rights Restoration Act of 1985. Even as the chairman's condescending comment attempts to limit Miller's contribution and decorum to her on-court prowess (I read his "more at ease" comment as a remix of "stay calm"), her political engagement shifts the conversation from one of gender equity in sport to a broader discourse in how systemic oppression impacts her life off the court ("protected from discrimination in college, but not in the hospital"). Her declaration, "I am not only a woman, I am a Black woman" cements this, making plain the role of race and gender as categories that structure how she moves through space.

This is a book about basketball and its relationship to the world off the court. While I focus on the current hoops landscape through fieldwork conducted between 2015 and 2024, it is impossible to fully conceptualize the problems and possibilities of the sport without predecessors like Cheryl Miller. There is, of course, her illustrious basketball career. At Riverside Polytechnic High School, she led her team to a 132–4 record and over the course of her high school career won a slew of state and national accolades, including Street & Smith High School Player of the Year (twice) and four-time Parade Magazine All-American. Before graduating, she set California state records for single season scoring and career points scored. In college at the University of Southern California (USC), she became a four-time All-American, a three-time Naismith College Player of the Year, and a two-time National Collegiate Athletics Association (NCAA) champion. Her jersey was the first to be retired at USC.

On the international stage, Miller represented Team USA in the 1983 Pan American Games and the 1984 Summer Olympics, leading the United States to gold. Amid the broken records, gold medals, and NCAA championships, what is less referenced in her storied career is her advocacy for full civil rights protections in the 1980s. Too often, Miller is situated solely as a benefactor of Title IX rather than an active participant in its survival. In resurrecting her moment in front of Congress in 1985, I disrupt the idea of Title IX as a "one-and-done" phenomenon, as a reminder that this legislation is a part of a persistent battle for equity in sport and society. That Cheryl Miller, a global figure of sporting dominance at the top of her game, must also take the time to advocate for social change is a dual labor that permeates this book, albeit with new stakes and participants.

Following a series of injuries that would cut her career short, Miller maneuvered into a media career, checking in as a Turner broadcast journalist and eventually becoming the first woman to announce a nationally televised NBA game in 1996. She has also coached at the collegiate and Women's National Basketball Association (WNBA) levels. The sheer dominance of her play on the court and her charismatic energy off it have also made her a popular culture sensation, whether acting in multiple sitcoms, lending her voice to video games, or appearing in various cameos. In fact, even as her brother, Reggie, emerged as a superstar in the National Basketball Association (NBA), he still found himself referenced in some spaces (including one *Seinfeld* episode) as Cheryl Miller's brother.[6]

At the same time, Miller's heightened public persona also led to speculation regarding her sexuality, an obsession often leveraged at athletes within women's sports. That she "clothes herself in masculine regalia" is a concern for those who either reject her self-presentation as a form of homophobia or desperately desire her to "come out" as a lesbian icon.[7] In "Speaking of Cheryl Miller: Interrogating the Lesbian Taboo on a Women's Basketball Newsgroup," Darcy C. Plymire and Pamela J. Forman examine online speculation regarding Cheryl Miller's sexual preference. Whereas their work focuses on how others read Cheryl's body and self-presentation, I found myself constantly looking for Cheryl, locating her in moments like this one in a 1997 *New York Times Magazine* article: "I like to take a long bubble bath and a few moments to reflect. Then I start dressing. I like to wear tailored slacks and a tailored white shirt with French cuffs. The shirt has to be crisp—starched lightly, not real hard. I put on my favorite cufflinks. I put on my suspenders and then a nice tie . . . and then I slip on my trouser socks and favorite Gucci shoes. This gives me the all together look that doesn't compromise my femininity."[8] Cheryl's moment of solitude, of leisure ("a long bubble bath and a few moments to reflect") is coupled with the act of dressing: the crisp shirt, the slacks, the cufflinks, the suspenders, and the tie. For Miller, this style of dress "doesn't compromise" her femininity but rather accentuates it—an aspect I am attuned to far more than what the internet chatter concerning her gender presentation might have to say.

Across each chapter of this book, whether in person, across digital plat-forms, or in media appearances, I continuously sought out athlete perspec-tives and voice. How do they articulate a sense of self? How do they perform gender in ways that cannot be contained through easy narratives or stereo-types? How might we rethink our approach to studying athletes—whether in how they dress, engage in politics, or negotiate their labor around the world? In *Women of Troy*, the HBO documentary delineates the history of women's hoops as BC—Before Cheryl—and AC—After Cheryl. In the chapters that follow, I focus on the athletes of the AC period, aware of the many crossovers that preceded this current moment.

Abbreviations

AAC	American Airlines Center
AAU	Amateur Athletic Union
ACS	American Cancer Society
AIAW	Association for Intercollegiate Athletics for Women
AP	Associated Press
AU	Athletes Unlimited
CBA	collective bargaining agreement
CSR	corporate social responsibility
DEI	diversity, equity, and inclusion
ESPN	Entertainment and Sports Programming Network
FIBA	Fédération Internationale de Basketball
FIFA	Fédération Internationale de Football Association
IOC	International Olympic Committee
LSU	Louisiana State University
MLB	Major League Baseball
MVP	Most Valuable Player
MWSN	Muslim Women in Sport Network
NBA	National Basketball Association
NCAA	National Collegiate Athletics Association
NCPA	National College Players Association
NFL	National Football League
NHL	National Hockey League

NIL	name, image, and likeness
NWHL	National Women's Hockey League
PBC	public benefit corporation
PBL	Professional Basketball League (Russia)
PHI	personal health information
PYM	Palestinian Youth Movement
SEC	Southeastern Conference
UO	University of Oregon
USWNT	United States Women's National Team
WNBA	Women's National Basketball Association
WNBPA	Women's National Basketball Players Association
YMCA	Young Men's Christian Association

DOUBLE CROSSOVER

Introducing the Crossover

The thing about a crossover is that, perhaps more than any other signature dribble move, it relies on trust: a defender willing to trust you, and what they understand about you, and your willingness to deceive them. . . . The main strength of a crossover is that it works best when you are being closely guarded.

—Hanif Abdurraqib[1]

JUNE 1, 2022 | LYON, FRANCE | GYMNASE MADO BONNET

It's my first time in this locker room, but it shares many of the qualities of others I've found myself in since beginning this project in 2015. As I walk in, there are rows of lockers, each labeled with the name of a player for Lyon ASVEL Féminin, a professional women's basketball team in Lyon, France. Inside each stall, an array of jerseys, shorts, and sneakers sits on display. There's also a familiar dampness wafting through the air, a humidity comprised of sweat, used towels, and the steam from the nearby showers. Above the low buzz of the fluorescent lights and the bubbling calm of the hot tub, Cierra Burdick, the team's sole American on the roster, describes how the French style of play differs from basketball in other countries. She's standing in a cold tub, a vertical vat in which she's covered up to her shoulders in chilling water, lamenting the dominance of the Euro step over the open step, two forms of forward momentum on the court. Whereas the open step is welcome within the US context, the Euro step—where an offensive player takes a step in one direction and then quickly pivots with a second step in a different direction—is the preferred method of maneuvering across the court in other countries. The open step, where the step and dribble are in sync, is often called for traveling, a violation within the sport. Cierra sighs as she says, "We started this game and now you want to change it . . . because you don't have the footwork."

The collective "we" references basketball's American origin in the Springfield, Massachusetts, YMCA gym where Dr. James Naismith first tacked up the game's rules in 1891. Naismith's Canadian nationality aside, the sport's constant shift across borders is a testament to both its global appeal and the malleability of the millions of athletes—amateur and professional—who flock to courts each year. The footwork required to successfully maneuver on the court is key for folks like Cierra, a professional athlete who translates her labor around the world and has competed at the highest levels of the game, whether as an NCAA Division I college basketball player at the University of Tennessee under legendary head coach Pat Summitt; on Women's National Basketball Association (WNBA) teams, representing privately owned professional teams overseas; or even at the Fédération Internationale de Basketball (FIBA) Women's World Cup for Team USA's 3×3 squad.

Cierra isn't alone in describing how US players often face additional fouls or traveling calls as they replicate the style of play typical in the NCAA and WNBA. Chelsea Davis, a player who previously competed in Ecuador, Spain, and Romania, runs a YouTube channel chronicling her life abroad, and in one video she uses the spin move, where a player maneuvers around defenders by dropping their shoulder and turning their body in a 360-degree motion while holding the ball, as an example of an evasive maneuver condemned by many overseas leagues. "In America," she says in one video, "you want to use the spin move so you can get from one place to the other. In Europe, if you want to do that, you have to do the Euro step."[2] Whereas the spin move is a legal move in the States, the Euro step is frowned upon by some basketball fans as traveling when executed stateside.

Each maneuver is predicated not only upon how a player moves but also upon who is doing the moving. When I asked another professional basketball player, Rebecca Harris, about the various styles of play she has experienced competing around the world, she told me, "As an American, my movement and my mannerisms are different than Europeans. . . . You are overseas, so we're playing their version of basketball. . . . And once they call traveling once or twice, I picked it up and was like, 'OK, so I can't do this certain movement.'"

Each maneuver—the Euro step, the spin move, the open step—operates as a mechanism of forward momentum even as referees perceive hoopers' movements in different ways. Part of the additional labor required of athletes is adapting their game to each country, learning how to evade both defenders and varying forms of officiating. Traveling, of course, is a key violation here, an ironic naming practice, given the many miles that separate these players from their homes and the game they love.

I begin *Double Crossover: Gender, Media, and Politics in Global Basketball* with a footwork debate for three reasons: (1) it is a good reminder of how much sport changes and is changed by societal shifts and global labor; (2) it tangibly illustrates how athletes struggle to "get from one place to the other" both on and off the court; and (3) it is a key component of the crossover, a spectacular basketball move I use as a metaphor to describe how women and nonbinary athletes maneuver through a sporting industry not designed with them in mind. That Cierra, Chelsea, and Rebecca are aware of the differences between styles of play, how players are officiated on the court, and how they must change their game is but one example of how the athletes of this book navigate their everyday lives. Across each chapter, I chart these navigations through interviews, participant observation, and player-generated media.

The crossover is a basketball move built upon footwork, agility, and deception. It requires feigned commitment in one direction, a brief hesitation, and then a quick lateral shift in the other direction. Aided by an internal rhythm and burst of momentum, it allows the ball handler to bypass the defender and get free, no longer constrained to a fixed space. In the optimal conditions, an athlete who crosses up their opponent would then use the additional space created by this choreography to either pass to a teammate or score on their own.

While not as flashy as a dunk or as violent as a block, the crossover demands rapid lateral movement with seemingly little effort. It also requires a particular sense of poise and control to challenge an opponent's balance, leaving adversaries helpless as they flail, trip, or crash to the ground (referred to on the court as "breaking ankles"). The crossover relies upon an athlete knowing where they are on the court and where they need to go. The well-timed crossover allows a player, who is shifting from one side to the other and following an internal rhythm, to create space for themselves and their teammates, ultimately opening up a clear path to the basket.

Basketball is a vibrant cultural text and set of practices that enable us to examine various shifts and struggles related to labor, identity, and media within today's global sports industry. As the world's second most popular team sport (and the most watched team sport at the Summer Olympics), basketball brings more than 450 million players to the court worldwide and even more inside arenas, in front of TVs, and through streaming devices each year.[3] Both historically and in recent years, the sport functions as a critical site of athlete activism, soft diplomacy, and the proliferation of sneaker capitalism.[4] This transnational facet of basketball, rife with geopolitical impact and economic urgency, makes it a slippery, constantly moving phenomenon, one that Todd Boyd and Kenneth L. Shropshire write is "teeming with issues of race, class, gender, and cultural identity in American society."[5]

At the same time, basketball also operates as a practice of expression, imagination, and emotion as it traverses borders and cultures. Basketball is a performative space at its core—a chest-thumping, high-flying affair. Individuals may stand out as stars, but basketball is a team sport. Bench players react to every play in tandem, with coordinated moves and cheers. An on-court mistake is communicated to teammates through a double pat on the chest—*that was on me.* When an offending player is called for a foul, their performative disbelief can sometimes be worthy of submission for an Academy Award. Embedded within the sport are tangible notions regarding what types of performances reify expectations of certain bodies and dictate the value of athletic labor.

From its early peach basket introduction in 1891, basketball reflected the values of the world outside that now-famous YMCA gymnasium. The mother of women's basketball, Senda Berenson Abbott, brought girls and women to the court within a year of Naismith laying the foundation for men. While the men's game emphasized Progressive Era ideals rooted in a muscular Christianity, early women's basketball within white spaces simultaneously emphasized narrow understandings of womanhood while offering new considerations of strength and resilience that were celebrated so long as they did not disrupt hegemonic norms.[6] As Michael Messner writes in *Power at Play: Sports and the Problem of Masculinity,* modern sport is a gendered institution, one "constructed by men, largely as a response to a crisis of gender relations in the late nineteenth and early twentieth centuries."[7] The structures of sport reflected the fears and needs of a threatened masculinity as empire, technology, and media continuously shifted society.

That basketball is in a constant state of being (re)invented is key to disrupting what Yago Colás calls the "myth" of the game's creation, which is rooted in Naismith's peach baskets of the late nineteenth century.[8] Colás's insistence that we reconsider the oft-cited "birth" of basketball is rooted in the risk of a hoops hierarchy that places these original rules (and players) of the game as the peak (read: right) form of play, whereas the athletes themselves, also capable of moving the sport forward, are at the mercy of the institutions that govern the sport, whether at the local, national, or international level.[9] Given the lopsided racial and gendered demographics of leadership across elite basketball, the fantasy of Naismith's invention highlights the desire that the game, which Naismith created with white, Christian men in mind, could still be exclusively theirs.[10] This becomes particularly important in this book as I articulate the stakes for those outside the purview of the white, male, Christian ideal of hoops history, whether through athletes advocating for racial justice or through the creation of player-driven leagues such as Athletes Unlimited.

One challenge to this hierarchical narrative is the development of basketball maneuvers that emerged after the sport's initial rules were created. One such move, the dribble, signifies the ability to move around the court and evade defenders—a key ingredient of the crossover. Upon seeing it in action, Naismith himself described the dribble as "one of the finest plays, one of the sweetest, prettiest plays in the whole bunch."[11] Colás writes:

> It is hard indeed to find, among basketball's plays, a more appropriate emblem for the game than the dribble—the play that originated as a deceptive breaking of the rules to get free and that came to delight the inventor whose code it broke. . . . The history of the dribble, in other words, shows as much as anything the lack of continuous, essential identity of basketball; it shows it to be *a game evolving in multiple places at different times,* through accidental and deliberate betrayals of its origins that, having been pragmatically tested, only later come to be accepted as valued parts of the game. The dribble, I am arguing, may be seen as a metonym for basketball itself: elusive, heterodox, deceptive, dynamic.[12]

It is important to note that the dribble move was banned in women's hoops in 1910 to slow down the game and prevent it from appearing "too rough." It was later reintroduced slowly with the allowance of a three-bounce dribble in 1961 and the incorporation of continuous unlimited dribbling in 1966. The dribble serves as a reminder of how hegemonic norms and perceived limits of the appropriate have always constrained athletes' bodies and performative potential, especially when those athletes aren't men. The participants that inform this book have mastered this concept. They know the parameters and elude them as they push the game—and one another—forward.

This book considers the social norms and practices that define and regulate women's basketball and centers the alternatives and possibilities cultivated by athletes aware of these constraints. I argue that the participants in this project, operating within a discriminatory system, create new forms of feminist thought developed under various forms of labor that evade temporal and spatial specificity. Amid systemic inequality, they create community and generate new knowledge—new means of maneuvering, wiggling in and out and around defenders, sidestepping opponents, and, as some would say on the basketball court, putting the world on skates.

The Art of the Double Crossover

In each of the sites presented within this project, most of the participants I interviewed and observed are Black women; they comprise the majority of players at the highest level of the game in the United States and feature prominently on professional rosters around the world. As I began interviewing and observing basketball players across demographic markers of race, gender, sexuality, and nationality, I found that Black women and nonbinary athletes experienced the sport differently, not unlike their experiences in other spaces and industries.[13] Tapping into Nirmal Puwar's concept of "space invaders," Letisha Engracia Cardoso Brown denotes the "sporting space invader" as one who "occupies a space (imagined) and/or place (physical) beyond constructed boundaries with respect to sport."[14] Because Black women are deemed to be outside the parameters of white, Western femininity and considered beyond the limits of the appropriate, their perceptions within the sport are a direct reflection of their experiences off the court as well.[15]

In researching and writing this book, I found Aimee Meredith Cox's ethnography of a Detroit shelter for girls and women incredibly useful for thinking through how Black folks (especially those who are not men) move through space once they have been identified as "invaders." In *Shapeshifters: Black Girls and the Choreography of Citizenship,* Cox offers "choreography" as a possibility to describe how Black girls and women move through the various identifications attributed to their bodies—Blackness, femaleness, youth, nationality, and poverty.[16] These categories, Cox argues, serve to remind Black women of where they do and do not belong and how they should or should not be seen—a fixed space. Most importantly, these categories reinforce the potential consequences for stepping outside of the boundaries that serve to define and contain Black women.[17] It is within these various markers that her participants—and the majority of my own—maneuver constantly. Cox writes that we should "use our displacement as a starting point for regeneration and the creation of new lifeworlds and spaces that affirm our collective humanity."[18] Whereas choreography is concerned with the ordering of bodies in space, it can, at its most radical, disrupt and discredit societal expectations by predicting and exploiting them. In doing so, the interlocutors within this book create space for themselves and one another.[19]

This, of course, is nothing new. For Black women taking the court at the turn of the twentieth century, teams like the New York Girls played in front of massive crowds and traveled across the country for games as other leagues developed throughout New York, Philadelphia, and Chicago at the turn of the twentieth century.[20] In *Finding a Way to Play: The Pioneering Spirit of Women in Basketball*, Joanne Lannin writes:

> The Black female athlete living in New York City in the early 1900s knew little of the controversy over rules and roughness that was swirling around the women's game at that time. Living outside of the mainstream, attending segregated schools and their own community clubs, African American women played basketball with the men's rules, and danced the night away after the games.[21]

The sporting silos that emerged under segregation offered few meaningful interactions for interracial play within the women's game. Theodora Boyd is one such exception. She competed in the 1920s at Radcliffe College and became the star player, as indicated in a statement from the college's 1927 yearbook: "I'd like to know just what our athletic record as a class would have been if Theodora had chosen some other college beside Radcliffe. What matters if two or three of the team don't show up? We have Theodora. We don't really need anyone else. At both hockey and basketball she is a very present help in trouble—present everywhere. She seems to draw the ball to her like a magnet. The worse the team is, the better she plays. Three cheers for Theodora!"[22] In the first half of the twentieth century, as the sport took hold across

Black colleges, African American women continued to create a distinct style of play, one subject to critique and conformity even as it significantly differed from that of their white counterparts. Almameta Moore, who competed for Bennett College, one of several Black colleges with women's basketball teams in the 1930s, attributed the lack of interracial competition not only to segregation but also to their style of play. "They were little Southern ladies, that was too rough for them," she is quoted as saying.[23] Her teammate Ruth Glover said, "We were ladies too, we just played basketball like boys."[24] However, as Rita Liberti argues, these women constantly negotiated the limits of what was possible for Black women during this time: "Black women who enrolled as students and athletes in colleges and universities during this period both challenged and yielded to the boundaries of class, race, and gender arrangements in their community. This ongoing process of negotiation is one that exposes a history shaped by multiple and intersecting identities. The juxtaposition of Black women's collegiate athletic experiences with those of Black men and white women, for example, provides further evidence of the varied historical experiences that emerge among particular groups in our culture."[25] Early on, basketball offered new possibilities for Black women to circumvent the constraints imposed on them, whether through practices that allowed them to bypass curfews or through travel opportunities to compete around the country and eventually the world. However, even as these moments provided an entrée into upward social mobility, sport administrators constantly reinscribed rigid notions of what it meant to be a Black female athlete.

Women's basketball expanded significantly in the 1970s at the collegiate level as the Association for Intercollegiate Athletics for Women (AIAW, 1971–83) centered women's college sports before and after the passage of Title IX, the US legislation designed to address gender-based discrimination in educational (and therefore sporting) spaces. Women's basketball became further ingrained within key governing bodies of the sport at the national and international levels as it debuted at the 1976 Summer Olympic Games and eventually became part of the US-based National Collegiate Athletics Association (NCAA). In 1982 the NCAA hosted its first women's basketball championship, a tournament-based postseason I examine in the fourth chapter of this book.

Even as the sport proliferated in the 1980s and 1990s, women's basketball players considered how their experiences significantly differed from the men's game. In her book *Summer Madness: Inside the Wild, Wacky World of the WNBA,* former basketball player Fran Harris writes:

> I've never wanted to be a guy but that doesn't mean that I don't think it has its privileges. Had I been born one . . . I would have played for fifteen years in the league, made multiple All-Star teams, and battled the Indiana Pacers' Reggie Miller for the league's Free Throw Shooting Champion award. I would have had a sneaker named in my honor, The Stroke Master, or something like that. . . . My agent would have secured hefty endorsement deals with McDonald's, Sprint and Gillette. In 2000, I would have retired to a multi-million-dollar broadcasting deal with NBC and smiled daily at my bulging bank account and hefty investment portfolio. But best of all, I would have had the whole wide world right in my capable little hands.[26]

Here, Harris points out the plethora of possibilities for an accomplished men's college basketball player entering the professional realm. As an outside shooter at The University of Texas at Austin, Harris led her team in scoring for three seasons in the lead-up to a perfect season and championship run in 1986. As team captain and conference player of the year, she mirrored the reality for players of her caliber on the men's side:

> But I was born a girl and there was no WNBA when I graduated college in 1986. Nothing for elite women college players to get excited about. Our only option to continue playing was to travel 3,000 miles from home to a team where English was the third language and the women smoked cigarettes in the locker room during halftime. No cable? No shopping malls? No call waiting? No thank you. But I succumbed and left for Italy, as did most of my peers. And while the Italians treated me like the queen I was, I wanted to play on my own soil, in front of people who knew me.[27]

Harris would eventually get the opportunity to compete professionally in the United States with the debut of the WNBA in 1997, over ten years after her college career ended. However, as I argue in the second chapter of this book, WNBA players today still translate their labor to leagues around the world in the offseason, lured by higher salaries and the opportunity to compete beyond the league's summer season.

While new coaching and broadcasting opportunities have emerged for former athletes, there remains a sharp divide in endorsement potential and signature sneaker possibilities for basketball players who are not men. Media coverage and marketing opportunities remain entrenched in normative femininity and are bolstered by empowerment feminism discourses, limiting which athletes are visible in the sport.

Here's what we know: female athletes in general are less likely to be chosen to endorse a product (they appear in only 3 percent of TV ads and mostly as individual athletes, not those on team sports), and when they are chosen, 81 percent are either in suggestive poses or scantily clad.[28] Other important critiques of the marketing of women and sport rely on the juxtaposition of men to reinforce difference and to conform to the idea of a safe, straight, (mostly) white ideal of what a female athlete should be.[29] This often places them adjacent to a male figure in their life such as a husband, boyfriend, or coach to provide visual and textual proof of heterosexuality or the role of men in their success.[30] Women's basketball is full of athletes who challenge this ideal, and to combat this, leagues such as the WNBA often go above and beyond to paint their athletes as mothers, wives, and daughters.

These narrow frames for female athletes, combined with the choice to select the most traditionally feminine/attractive athlete to market a product, continues to set back both progressive politics and profit, given previous research that found no correlation between focusing on an athlete's attractiveness in marketing and increased interest in or attendance at women's sporting events.[31] The difference in treatment and coverage of Black female athletes (even more so than their white or non-Black women of color counterparts) in particular has been documented by scholars who point to either a distinct othering or an invisibility in media coverage.[32] Critical sport scholar David J. Leonard argues that Black female athletes "become commodities or cross-over stars through a sexualizing process. . . . The process of becoming a sexy (female) athlete confers and is the result of their identification with whiteness."[33] The othering of WNBA athletes extends to how much they take home or the accolades they receive, in addition to affecting their visibility as endorsed athletes. Mary G. McDonald understands part of the financial discrepancy to be a cultural one, stating that the stereotypes of WNBA players as "overly masculine and sexually deviant, bodies marked as women of color and lesbians," are also considered "fatal" by marketers due to a fear of difference and the potential to challenge cultural hegemony on and off the court. The diversity (racial and/or sexual) of the sport is seen as an affront to what she describes as mainstream "tastes and sensibilities."[34] Throughout this project, the participants I interviewed and observed grappled with how their labor has been (de)valued within this broader industry compared to that of their male counterparts.

As several scholars argue, the racial politics of the women's game positions it as an alternative to the "showboating" style of men's hoops. This style fuels a global, billion-dollar industry and is often framed as the foundation of superstar athletes no longer playing for the so-called love of the game.[35] Feminist media scholar Sarah Banet-Weiser writes, "The media have recently focused on the idea of women's basketball as representing a 'purer' form of the game—the WNBA apparently demonstrates the way the game 'should' be played. The rhetoric of purity is deeply embedded in a discourse of morality: The female players of the WNBA function as morally superior athletes in comparison to those of the NBA."[36] The constant comparison between the men's and women's games creates a hierarchy yet again of what "real" basketball is and the "right" way to play it. Because of this, the onus falls on women's basketball players to prove themselves on and off the court as worthy of established leagues, equitable contracts, endorsement opportunities, and comprehensive media coverage.

Today, the shifting landscape at the collegiate level, especially athletes' ability to receive compensation for their name, image, and likeness (NIL), exposes these disparities even further. For example, while Black athletes comprised 44 percent of NCAA Division I women's basketball players, Black women's opportunities to profit from their play vary significantly compared to both male athletes and their white female counterparts in the sport.[37] These disparities are compounded when considering how international athletes competing within the NCAA cannot profit from NIL due to the employment restrictions of the F-1 visa, which is how the majority of athletes from outside of the United States are able to compete at the collegiate level.

It is essential to highlight how basketball, racialized as a Black sport, still privileges whiteness, especially in media coverage and endorsement opportunities.[38] In her ethnography of a professional women's basketball team, Jennifer L. Hanis-Martin found that even in a majority Black front office, employees still pursued straight, white, middle-class fans over an audience comprised of minority fans.[39] This bias operates through arena location, promotional materials, and media availability. Throughout my experience with various teams, leagues, and players, I continuously encountered this same disjointedness, where the pursuit of the eighteen-to-thirty-five-year-old white male fan (despite all anecdotal knowledge and market research to the contrary) dominated the approach to selling the sport.

In a feature on WNBA MVP Jonquel Jones, Las Vegas Aces star A'ja Wilson told ESPN that "even though our league is predominantly Black, I think it's hard for our league to push us, in a sense, because they still have to market, in their mind, what is marketable. Sometimes a Black woman doesn't check off those boxes."[40] Even though Jones, a Black woman, was the focus of a feature piece for *ESPN the Magazine,* the media outlet replicated this erasure in their social media promotion for the piece, highlighting quotes by white WNBA players. The article also fails to address ESPN's own role in these disparities as an agenda-setting outlet. In their study of the 2020 WNBA season, Risa F. Isard and E. Nicole Melton found that Black WNBA players received less than half the media coverage of their white counterparts. This gap widens even further when considering how gender presentation factors into the visibility (or lack thereof) of these players.[41] As this research circulated online, it offered tangible evidence to support what many WNBA fans frequently articulate online. To call basketball a "Black sport" even as it remains a space privileging whiteness flattens broader economic and cultural ramifications for athletes today.

These issues also follow athletes as they say farewell to the game. Before the start of the 2022 WNBA season, fans learned it would be both Minnesota Lynx center Sylvia Fowles's and Seattle Storm point guard Sue Bird's last. The two league and Olympic legends received disparate coverage of their sunset seasons, frequently noted by Twitter users within the women's basketball community. When asked about this disparity, Fowles succinctly pointed out that coverage of her final season is merely symptomatic of her entire career: "I don't see why you have to give somebody credit when they've done their job for the last 15 years and been consistent and never gotten the credit. So why now? Because I'm saying I'm leaving? . . . People are like, 'Syl, you deserve it, you've *been d*eserved it,' And I'm like, 'But I never got it.'"[42] The author, Mirin Fader, supports Fowles's stance, listing the many snubs throughout Fowles's career—the magazine covers that never materialized, the league marketing that never happened, and the awards and accolades absent from her trophy shelf.

In centering Black women and nonbinary athletes in this book, I hope to disrupt the broader sports-media nexus that centers white athletes, along with academic research that utilizes famous white athletes as a stand-in for all athletes' experiences. John F. Borland and Jennifer E. Bruening write, "When Black women have been included in research, they have been lumped into one of two categories, women as a whole or Blacks as a whole, never commanding their own category."[43] To remix a key Black feminist text, all of the women are white, all the Blacks are men, but some of us play sports.[44]

When Black women and nonbinary athletes are centered in scholarship, there is an overwhelming focus on how the double jeopardy or dual bind of racism and sexism affects their lives. In this book, I am most concerned with moving forward and building upon this knowledge, delving into how they experience community, pleasure, and agency within the sporting space.[45] Here, I offer work that intentionally lives at the margins with my participants, which bell hooks called "a profound edge."[46] The margins, she wrote, are where the magic happens; they are not merely a site of deprivation but also a site of radical possibility. hooks argued that the margins can operate as a source of creativity and an inclusive space of recovery and resistance. This stance is markedly different from sports scholarship that laments the status of women and nonbinary athletes (especially those of color) without engaging with them directly and considering how they position themselves in relation to power and perform the self. Instead, I continuously ask what it would mean to intentionally reside in the margins, to see, create, and imagine possibilities from these athletes' current standpoint.

Enter the "double" of *Double Crossover*. On the court, it is one of the more elaborate forms the crossover can take—it requires more of a "sell." The double crossover employs a slower lateral cross initially to set up the defender, followed by a second, faster crossover in the opposite direction that immediately creates space in an isolation situation and often leaves a defender looking at best duped and at worst on the ground, flailing. The success of this complicated crossover is dependent upon the range in temporal shift from the first down-tempo cross to the frenetic second one. It also relies on a player's ability to use their vision to "sell" the move to a defender who buys into and commits to where they believe the ball and the offense are going.

In the same way, the athletes who animate this project frequently traverse in one direction, only to rapidly shift to another as they travel, create, engage with media, and build a life beyond the game. In this book, I consider how this duality of race and gender continues to shape athletes' experiences today as they negotiate the terms of their labor, image, and activism through basketball. The ramifications of this system impact labor value, media attention, and overall interest in the sport. These dynamics affect everything from pickup games on blacktop courts to big-time arenas, college scholarships, and draft picks.

To take this even further, in this work I continuously confronted how sport upheld a gender binary that required further interrogation of just how inclusive the term "women's basketball" truly is for those who occupy what feminist media scholar Moya Bailey describes as "the margins of the margins of Black womanhood."[47] In *Misogynoir Transformed: Black Women's Digital Resistance,* she writes, "For those of us on the margins of Black womanhood, 'woman' is not what we name ourselves even as misogynoir colors our experiences of the world."[48]

In a *GQ* article with Layshia Clarendon, the WNBA's first openly trans and nonbinary athlete, they illustrate how basketball (and sport in general) remains a precarious space for trans athletes, especially after sharing the news of their top surgery: "Part of me was really terrified, because I knew how much the binary is very ingrained in all of us. I knew the impact of being like, 'I'm trans and playing in a women's league' and how much that would shake the world up, but the other part of me was naïve in feeling like the women's basketball community is a little niche safe place."[49] For many of the reasons outlined above, women's basketball remains complicated regarding its "safety." Whereas some media members within the sport advocate for the inclusion of pronouns in media guides and full acceptance of trans and nonbinary athletes regardless of their assigned sex at birth, other vocal figures have shunned progressive steps (however small) to challenge the hoops gender binary. Clarendon says, "The binary is changing, and the leagues need to adapt and be flexible. Instead of two binary leagues, I want sports to think of how to make room and expand those leagues and their definitions to include all the people who want to play in them."[50] And while I use "women and nonbinary" in tandem to describe the participants in this project, I remain challenged to broaden my own negotiations of these terms, as some athletes, such as the WNBA's AD Durr, reject the categorization of woman, trans, or nonbinary altogether.[51] In many ways, Durr represents what Legacy Russell writes in *Glitch Feminism:* "A body that pushes back at the application of pronouns, or remains indecipherable within binary assignment is a body that refuses to perform the score."[52] Refusal to perform gender as scripted takes on many forms throughout this book. Whether in their pregame attire, style of play, or pronouns, these athletes cross over leagues, governing bodies, and media organizations, pushing past and daring them to catch up. Russell writes that "when we gender a body, we are making assumptions about the body's function, its sociopolitical condition, its fixity."[53] When the athletes who animate this work refuse expectations of femininity, heterosexuality, and assumptions of she/her, they manipulate the very fabric that drapes so-called women's sports. In this project, I use the term "women's basketball" to signify a sporting designation rather than a catch-all for the athletes within this framework; their positionalities and descriptions of the sport inform this distinction.

Finally, in choosing the crossover as a conceptual framework, I look to decenter the dunk as the pinnacle of basketball performance, a high-flying maneuver too long entrenched in a hoops hierarchy created to minimize the sport when men aren't on the court.[54] In *No Slam Dunk: Gender, Sport and the Unevenness of Social Change,* Cheryl Cooky and Michael Messner write:

> In current narratives about gender and sport, the slam dunk in the game of basketball has for many become the potent symbol that differentiates the men's game from the women's game: Men, so the story goes, play the game "above the rim," acrobatically soaring and dunking; women play the game with their feet "stuck to the floor," relying on the less exciting strategies of passing, screening, and shooting. This difference, in some people's view, is not only what elevates men's basketball over women's; it also explains lower fan interest in the women's game, and by extension, justifies less media attention and lower pay for women players.[55]

Whereas a significant amount of research focused on women's sports is about what athletes who are not men cannot (or do not frequently) do, this book focuses on what they do instead, why it matters, and how it factors into how they see their lives off the court.

Rethinking Sporting Mobilities and Temporalities

Given the markers of race, gender, and nationality that dictate the movements and media of athletes on the court, it is hardly surprising that those markers also shape how (or if) they can move off it. Across each chapter, this book grapples with how sport—and the people within it—travel across space and over time. Who is able to move across borders and leagues, and why? How do athletes and advocates of women's basketball grapple with both the flows of capital and labor and the nonflows, the constraints (whether political, cultural, or financial) that impede global mobility? Ultimately, I hope to contribute to the study of what Raka Shome and Radha Hegde describe as "uneven patterns of global processes" that occur through transnational flows (and I would argue nonflows) of capitalism and culture.[56] In their work, they argue that in the twenty-first century, the rapid pace of movement causes borders themselves to become a contested category, where the local impacts the global (and vice versa) in new and profound ways.

Globalization, of course, is nothing new. Rather, the defining markers of today's version are the intensity, the frenetic pace that can both connect disparate places and expand who can be affected by economies, information networks, and politics thousands of miles away.[57] Movement, for Shome and Hegde, is not merely about the act of booking a flight or boarding a train. Instead, it is about the ability to "move across different spatial registers of power."[58]

Athletic sites have much to add to this area of research, given the high visibility of its laborers, an emphasis on the body, and an entrenched connection to the nation-state. In Globalization and Sport: Playing the World, Toby Miller and colleagues write, "Labouring bodies are the principal objects of sports. They are selected, trained, disciplined, bought, sold, monitored, invaded, celebrated, desired, and despised."[59] These bodies represent the nation (and the corporate) deployed through symbols that reinforce hegemonic ideals of racial integrity, the economy, technology, and gender, among others. This vibrant sporting labor market has created new opportunities not only on the court, pitch, or field but also in offices where lawyers, accountants, and agents gauge global interests and consult athletes on international contracts.[60]

In conducting research through the routes of athletes like Cierra, I discovered that her trajectory represents the very labor translations that Joshua I. Newman and Mark Falcous advocate for including in mobilities literature. In "Moorings and Movements: The Paradox of Sporting Mobilities," they argue that sport allows a dynamic exploration of the time-space compressions of late capitalism bound up in global markets, tourism, and geopolitical ramifications.[61] Specifically, they offer up the concept of "mobility of movement" as an entry point to consider what sport might offer to mobilities studies, where the microlevel movements of making a bucket, for example, can be directly linked to broader social and geopolitical movements.[62] They also note that the sporting body is a "spectacle of mobility," one subject to hypervisibility and privilege compared to other forms of mobile labor.[63]

While the current sporting mobilities literature offers insightful contributions to studies of the impacts of global sport on athletes, fans, and franchises, several gaps remain. Most research focuses on the mobilities of professional male athletes, with entire books dedicated to the global movements of men in this space.[64] C. L. R. James's *Beyond a Boundary* is perhaps one of the best examples of how sport might help us untangle notions of nationality, post/ coloniality, and belonging. In his work, he uses cricket to conceptualize West Indian identity as it relates to race, class, and gender in an important way. Like *Beyond a Boundary* and other texts concerning sporting mobilities, athletes who are not men seldom move from the periphery of the game. At best, they are relegated to the "Future Research" portion of articles and books.[65] In *The Global Sports Arena,* John Bale and Joseph Maguire argue for the study of transnational mobility in women's sports: "The study of gender and sports migration is one direction in which future research must go. Other areas include comparative analyses of the experience of athletes overseas, the ways of adjusting to change, the new perceptions athletes obtain of foreign countries as a result of temporary sojourn and the images they have of the countries they have left behind. Concern with the experiential aspects of sports migration must also be combined with consideration of issues of political economy and of what the process of sports labour migration reveals about broader questions of globalization."[66] The relocating—and dislocating—of sporting bodies is affected by talent, of course, but it is also restricted by what Black feminist scholar Patricia Hill Collins terms the "matrix of domination," where race, gender, and national identity (as well as other identity markers) shape both the ability to maneuver across borders and the reception once an athlete arrives.[67] Audrey Macklin writes that borders are gendered, with limited mobility for women around the world, and gender is bordered, where the boundaries of gender identity remain so strict that "crossing these borders is not called migration, but transgression."[68] In this book, I study the movements of women and nonbinary athletes as they maneuver their labor across countries, attending to the differences intertwined in their experiences.

Crossover Methodologies

I began this project as a graduate student primarily interested in the relationship between new media technologies and sport. My previous life working in sports media guided most of my research as I concerned myself with how sports journalists adapted to the role of social media in their personal and professional lives. At some point, I expanded these questions to professional sports organizations and spent a season with the WNBA's Los Angeles Sparks in 2015. There, I assisted in the launch and execution of a season-long campaign that tapped into familiar marketplace feminism discourses and empowerment logics to sell women's sports. While the daily dynamics of a front office drew me into insightful ethnographic fieldwork, I quickly realized that I lacked the perspectives of the athletes behind the glossy handouts that I circulated in the concourse of the STAPLES Center during home games. In the few moments I shared with the players on that year's roster, I realized two things: the majority of the league's athletes played year-round around the world, and too many dialogues occurred about them rather than with them both in the cubicles I sat in that summer and throughout the literature I read on campus the following fall. What did they think about how the sport is mediated and marketed? How did they see their labor within what we call the sports-media nexus?

To answer these questions, I began interviewing athletes and eventually trekking with them as they moved through online and offline spaces. I often connected with potential participants via Instagram direct messages (DMs) and set up interviews via Skype, Google Hangout, or Zoom.[69] Throughout this project, I constantly contended with how these technologies shifted communicative possibilities, whether through the Instagram posts of professional basketball players or through the Zoom events designed to engage athletes and media members in matters of social justice. Because of the wide-ranging geographies involved within the sport, I did not predetermine my field sites. Like the athletes who inform this work, I operated season to season as teams and leagues emerged and collapsed. This malleability became particularly important in 2020 as the COVID-19 pandemic shifted life—and sport—drastically, with research sites such as the 2020 Summer Olympics and the annual NCAA March Madness basketball tournament entirely off the table and a WNBA season relegated to a restricted, fan-free

environment in Bradenton, Florida. At the same time, these historic moments also shifted the focus of this project to *how* athletes move across
borders and what is at stake when their mobility is limited or altogether
impossible. This moment also allowed for more willing engagement online
using Zoom, a platform that proliferated during the pandemic.

In-person participant observation took place on the court and away from
it in cafés, clubs, restaurants, and homes. Conversations frequently took place
on walks, during train rides, on subways, and in cars that were sometimes
crossing over national borders. Most of the participants in this research are
women in their twenties and thirties who competed as athletes or supported
women's basketball in some capacity (as journalists, employees, entrepre-
neurs, or activists). In addition to conducting participant observation and
interviews, I also analyzed their social media presence (along with affiliated
institutions such as the WNBA, FIBA, or USA Basketball), considering how
each person framed their experiences within the sports industry. This mul-
tisited, multimethodological approach matched the pace of my participants.

Throughout this book, my methodological approach centers athlete voice,
whether in interviews, observations, or content analysis of relevant media.
In *Hood Feminism: Notes from the Women That a Movement Forgot,* Mikki
Kendall writes, "Girls like me seemed to be the object of the conversations
and not full participants, because we were a problem to be solved, not people
in our own right."[70] Aware of this objectification, I constantly negotiated my
positionality during this process, acknowledging shared identities while being aware of the power dynamic of the researcher-participant relationship.
Whenever possible, I privilege their voices and perspectives (whether in
personal communication or media texts) over my observations or the official
statements from leagues or governing bodies.

Care is central to how this research took form across nine years of interviews and fieldwork. Here, I would like to distinguish between what Rosalie
Rolón-Dow describes as aesthetic/technical care and authentic/relational
care. Aesthetic care focuses on the technical aspects of a particular setting.
For example, in basketball, this would be care rooted in a player's performance
or ability to "make it" in the sport—a primary focus on how they succeed in
the space. However, authentic care moves beyond assumptions about who
participants are and what their lives are like and allows for a holistic space
for them to share how the multiplicity of identities they hold shapes their

relationship to sport and society. A critical care praxis, Rolón-Dow writes, "builds on the work of those who have argued that caring theory needs to be politicized and needs to address questions of otherness, difference, and power if it is to be effective in the case of historically oppressed groups."[71]

Participants cared for me as they invited me to stay in their homes, ensured I reached them (or home) safely, or offered emotional support as I navigated my own academic career. In return, I also found myself invested in care as I cooked for participants after a long practice, chatted with their loved ones over FaceTime, helped them through graduate school logistics, or proofread their work as they began their media ventures. These moments shaped my approach to understanding the worlds that athletes and advocates of women's basketball create for themselves, worlds that move beyond headlines or case studies to the realities of their lives. Just as they do within the broader sports-media complex, participants weave in and out of each chapter/setting.

Chapter Overview

Double Crossover: Gender, Media, and Politics in Global Basketball tracks the global, multimodal maneuvers of basketball athletes, coaches, journalists, and advocates of women's basketball as they pursue livelihoods within the game. Like the sport itself, this book is organized into four quarters, with each chapter located in a different hoops context.

The first quarter, "'Betting on Ourselves': The Politics and Ethics of Care in the WNBPA," traces how athletes' demands for more equitable labor conditions set the backdrop for new articulations of social justice activism during the 2020 WNBA season. I center the Women's National Basketball Players Association (WNBPA) and its decision to opt out of an expiring collective bargaining agreement, resulting in a landmark deal between the league and its players. I then consider how the agreement signed in January 2020 grounded the union's social, cultural, and political approach to a tumultuous season affected by both pandemic and protest. Using virtual field observations and a critical discourse analysis of the documentary *144*, I argue that the athletes of the WNBA enact an ethics and politics of care that inform their relationships with one another, their labor, and the process of "doing the work" of activism.

In the second quarter, "Translating Timeouts: The Choreography of Playing Overseas," I follow the game as it traverses across borders and as athletes translate their sporting labor abroad. I focus on the experiences of professional Black American athletes competing outside the United States through interviews (both virtually and in-person) and field observations conducted in 2018 in Russia (Kazan) and in 2022 in France (Bourges and Lyon). Throughout this chapter, I map how these crossovers require athletes to be acutely attuned to each hoop site's cultural, economic, and political specificities. These acts of translation are a direct response to the racialized and gendered logics of performance embedded within their teams both on and off the court. These athletes' ability to adapt to each arena dictates their longevity in the sport.

In the third quarter, "Mission Equity: New Sporting Labor Considerations within Athletes Unlimited," I explore the development of a new "player-centric" sports venture featuring four women's sports: basketball, volleyball, lacrosse, and softball. In examining the 2023 and 2024 basketball seasons in Dallas, Texas, I consider how Athletes Unlimited's status as a public benefit corporation (PBC) impacts the daily operations of the league while creating new opportunities for professional athletes seeking to stay stateside year-round. I also consider how Athletes Unlimited fits into a larger hoops ecosystem of college, WNBA, and overseas athletic labor. Throughout this chapter, I interrogate the complexities and contradictions of an expanding market for women's hoops that seeks to support athlete causes while maintaining corporate sponsorship and innovative media coverage.

In the fourth quarter, "You Can't See Me: Moving Past Misogynoir during March Madness," I situate the 2023 and 2024 NCAA Division I women's basketball tournaments within a broader lineage of college basketball coverage and competition. These end-of-season tourneys are widely celebrated as a sign of the sport's longevity and the promise of Title IX beyond its fiftieth anniversary, but the apex of the collegiate season continuously revealed lingering issues at the intersection of race, gender, and media within the world of basketball. Combining field observations at the Sweet Sixteen, Elite Eight, and Final Four rounds with a close reading of media discourse surrounding March Madness, I argue that key issues of labor, media, and politics persist even as the game itself becomes more popular than ever.

My conclusion, "Overtime: The Game Is Grown," outlines the current shifts in women's basketball and how the crossover might serve as a useful analytic for future research. I also articulate how Black feminist theory and mobility studies offer critical interventions for sport studies scholarship. In doing so, I hope that we—athletes, scholars, and advocates of the game—may collectively find transformative potential in ontological alternatives not immediately apparent but possible one deceptive sidestep at a time.

"Betting on Ourselves"
The Politics and Ethics of Care in the WNBPA

There's never an off day of being Black. Every day you're
always reminded by something small or something big, and
so how you react to that is you either educate or be silent.

—Jewell Loyd, Seattle Storm[1]

On a dark night in Bradenton, Florida, a table holds dozens of clear dispos-
able cups that slowly transform into candle holders as they are filled with
tealights and circulated to masked players. It's August 26, 2020, a day when
sport stopped abruptly again in the United States. While the global spread
of the COVID-19 virus halted US sports in March of that year, professional
athletes across the country withheld their labor that day in August in response
to a police officer shooting Jacob Blake, a twenty-nine-year-old Black man,
seven times in Kenosha, Wisconsin, paralyzing him. Some outlets reported
this collective athlete resistance as a boycott, while others defined it as a
wildcat strike. In lieu of competing in three scheduled games that day, the
players of the WNBA joined together and walked onto the court wearing
T-shirts, some of which individually spelled out each letter of "Jacob Blake"
across the front. On the back, drawn bullet holes served as a visual articulation of the violence he suffered at the hands of that officer.

That night at the vigil, Nneka Ogwumike, president of the Women's National
Basketball Players Association (WNBPA), addressed the union: "Obviously,
today's been quite an eventful day. It's important that we're all gathered here
today outside of what we're here doing—playing basketball. This moment is a
reminder of a nonnegotiable that we had going into this season. So right now
I want to take this moment as a league to recognize all of the reasons why we
were brought here to this season this year. Most specifically, of course, Say Her
Name."[2] In the opening scene of *144*, an ESPN Films documentary focused on

the WNBA's 2020 season, Ogwumike's words signal how this union approached a season marked twice by pandemic and protest. The "nonnegotiable" of the season she mentions here is the ability to organize and advocate for racial justice in the wake of a heightened visibility of Black lives lost to police violence. More specifically, the invocation of "Say Her Name" signifies the league's partnership with the #SayHerName movement to amplify the lives and stories of Black girls and women killed by police and to support the families they left behind.

Throughout this chapter, I argue that the crossover materializes as resistance to the devaluation of Black women's lives and labor. The athletes of this league emphasize the importance of collective organizing, whether through the WNBPA bargaining for a new labor agreement with the league or advocating for Black life under the constant threat of state violence. What makes this form of activism unique in the long lineage of athletes' political engagement is the constant refusal to align with logics that emphasize the individual, working instead to support one another in addition to other organizations and campaigns. Whereas neoliberalism centers the unattached individual maneuvering through the so-called free market and relegates resistance to commodity activism, Aimee Meredith Cox considers alternative ways of knowing and being when she writes that "Black girls should not be objects of critique and/or worry but should be seen as the vanguard of a political movement capable of building and creating what neoliberalism dehumanizes and destroys."[3] In this chapter, I describe how the WNBPA's membership operates as a model of this vanguard as they "build and create" within the sporting sphere (and outside of it). Moments like the vigil reveal the relationship between care, labor, and resistance within this union, a moment within a broader timeline that began with the landmark collective bargaining agreement (CBA) between the WNBA and its players' association in January 2020 and proliferated both on and off the court during the season that year. Using interviews, digital participant observation, and a close reading of ESPN's *144* documentary, I consider how the WNBPA's collective action offers new perspectives on athlete activism and labor organizing.

Documenting Sport On-Screen

Directed by Lauren Stowell and Jenna Contreras and produced by WNBA player and ESPN analyst Chiney Ogwumike, *144* traces how the 2020 WNBA season came together, from the decision to enter a bubble in Bradenton, Florida (affectionately dubbed the Wubble) to the Finals series sweep by the Seattle Storm over the Las Vegas Aces. Like other players, Chiney Ogwumike had to decide whether she wanted to take the health risk of playing during the pandemic. In opting out, she realized the potential of combining her insights as a player and her connections as a media member to create a vantage point for viewers interested in learning more about how the season unfolded behind the scenes. "We did not know what was going to happen in the season," Chiney told Forbes.com. "We just knew that we were going to capture and tell the story of it. And my goodness, it turned into one of the most powerful stories I think we've ever seen in sport."[4]

The recent influx of sports documentaries and docuseries reflects a new market for sports content creation and consumption. In the current media landscape, these documentaries can draw in viewers without the price tag of live sports broadcast deals. They also reflect the "serious turn" of sport, where the spectacle of athletic achievement (or defeat) meets the "discourses of sobriety" described in Bill Nichols's work on documentary as genre.[5] Marina Zenovich, director of several sports documentaries, told the *Los Angeles Times*, "They can be so compelling, and with all the content [needs] from streamers and others, it's become a whole business."[6] In many ways, *144* continues ESPN's successful lineage of sport documentaries, often housed under the ESPN Films label and ranging from *SportsCentury* to *30 for 30* and beyond. The success of these films, frequently driven by nostalgia and the parasocial relationships fans create with their favorite athletes or teams, has created new ways of communicating sport through narratives that move beyond the box score. In an article debating the oversaturation of the sports documentary landscape, Showtime Sports president Stephen Espinoza told the *Los Angeles Times*, "It's not about telling sports stories for the sake of telling sports stories. It's about seeing how we can illuminate the human condition, societal issues, and cultural developments."[7]

Given that the WNBA is comprised of over 70 percent Black athletes, the ways that they are "illuminated" in *144* offer new understandings in how the contemporary athlete is mediated. In *On Racial Icons: Blackness and the Public Imagination*, Nicole R. Fleetwood argues that Black athletes' ability to thrive both within and outside their respective sports is a "recurring source of public drama," one that operates as a "familiar cultural narrative of success and failure played out on various media platforms."[8] She offers two main frameworks for how Black athletes are typically covered: representational politics (as a highly visible representation of the Black community at large) and/or racial achievement (where achievement on the field or court can respond to racist logics). She notes that while we often watch in wonder as athletes execute embodied excellence, the skills and spectacle they offer that evade our own abilities also shape our understanding of (in)equalities and subjugation.

While the sports documentary genre has flourished within the sports-media complex, as several scholars argue, historically there has been a dearth of these films that center the stories of women and/or queer athletes, reflecting the broader masculinist space of sports media.[9] However, with the expansion and proliferation of documentaries across streaming platforms such as Netflix, ESPN+, and Hulu, some shifts in terms of both who is the audience and who can be the subject of a "serious" sports film have emerged in recent years.

As famed film critic and scholar Bill Nichols writes, documentaries are a product of the very institutions and organizations that create them.[10] The partnership between the WNBA and ESPN is important in shaping not only the style and content of the film but also its ability to promote the league and increase investment in the sport, especially through viewership. We see this in the timely debut of the film near the start of the 2021 WNBA season. In the introduction to their edited collection *Sporting Realities: Critical Readings of the Sports Documentary*, Travis Vogan and Samantha Sheppard write that both "ESPN's and Netflix's sports documentaries are as invested in branding these media entities and promoting their other corporate properties as they are in illuminating or critiquing their subjects."[11] For a network like ESPN, creating documentaries related to media properties it owns offers a tandem branding opportunity: viewers can watch live games on their network, and they can experience a "recap" of the previous season as they gear up for the next one. ESPN can create evergreen content while ushering eyes to live sports.

In using a documentary as source material, I acknowledge the film not as a representative of "what really happened" but as a mediated version shaped by the presence of camera crews and edited for narrative impact and time constraints. However, for the purpose of this chapter, *144* offers key insights into the effects of the pandemic and the expansion and co-optation of the Movement for Black Lives in the summer of 2020. Given that attending games in person was not an option for audiences, the film serves as one lens, one angle on how athletes approached the season. *144* employs an observational documentary mode, described by Ian McDonald as "present[ing] real life as close to reality as was possible, and . . . eschew[ing] the temptation to direct the audience to interpret in a particular way."[12] In doing so, the film offers an insider perspective of a season where so much was obscured and contained, striking a balance between game play and what occurs behind the scenes.[13]

About the WNBPA

The WNBA debuted in 1997, tipping off with eight teams and financially backed by the NBA. The following year, on November 6, 1998, the WNBPA became the first labor union comprised of professional female athletes.[14] Tasked with negotiating CBAs, filing grievances on behalf of athletes, and providing relevant benefits and resources to its members across their careers, the WNBPA serves as a critical turning point in the history of US sporting labor. While the union's previous advocacy for higher salaries, additional roster spots, paid maternity leave, retirement plans, and full health insurance benefits paved the way for labor organizing in women's sports, key disparities still plagued the league.

On November 1, 2018, Nneka Ogwumike, president of the WNBPA, penned an article for the *Players' Tribune* announcing that the union would opt out of its expiring CBA with the league and its owners to negotiate for better resources, larger salaries, and improved travel accommodations. In the piece, Ogwumike writes, "Opting out means not just believing in ourselves, but going one step further: betting on ourselves. It means being a group of empowered women . . . not just feeling fed up with the status quo, but going one step further: rejecting the status quo."[15] The "status quo" for the league included constant travel issues. Players dealt with long layovers, were often stranded on commercial flights due to delays or cancellations and found themselves in cramped middle seats. In the offseason, players still found themselves supplementing their incomes with overseas leagues in part due to the revenue-sharing model that afforded only 20 percent of league revenue to players. For those seeking to stay in the States, many found the constraints of the current CBA prohibitive to their career and financial growth. For example, Kristi Toliver began coaching in the NBA during the offseason but could only receive $10,000 as compensation due to "competitive fairness" rules. At the time, Toliver played for the Washington Mystics and coached on the Washington Wizards staff. With both teams under the same ownership group, Monumental Sports and Entertainment, the coaching position was seen as an unfair advantage to recruiting athletes during free agency and retaining star players beyond the league's salary cap.[16] In the name of "fairness," the WNBA inadvertently created a gendered pay gap in the NBA coaching ranks.

Outside of salaries and career opportunities, the WNBPA also struggled to secure consistent, safe venues to compete in each summer. With the construction and renovation of arenas around the country and shared venues with NBA and National Hockey League (NHL) franchises for some teams, WNBA players found themselves the first teams relocated to inadequate facilities. They also received fewer maternity benefits than the girlfriends and wives of their NBA counterparts.[17] Given all of this, Ogwumike connects the status quo of the WNBA with a broader critique of how girls and women are treated across sports and, more broadly, in society. In the article, she gives a shout-out to her fellow union executives, lists some of their concerns, and addresses naysayers who would call her and other players "greedy" or "ungrateful" because of their demands. "It's about what the future of the WNBA can mean to all people," Ogwumike writes. "It's about what the excellence of female athletes can mean in a more universal sense—with enough investment, and resources, and respect. We're opting out of our CBA because of the world we want to live in."[18]

On January 14, 2020, Ogwumike and league commissioner Cathy Englebert joined host Robin Roberts on *Good Morning America* to announce a landmark agreement that not only significantly increased salary maximums but also considered how the league could better care for its athletes. The union negotiated for fifty-fifty incremental revenue sharing with the league, an increased salary cap, individual hotel rooms on the road, and upgraded flight accommodations. The union also made significant advances in parental benefits—a childcare stipend, nursing accommodations, and reimbursement toward adoption fees, fertility treatments, or freezing eggs. The league will also provide counseling and resources concerning mental health and intimate partner violence.[19] While the higher salary cap drove headlines following the announcement, the new CBA also reflects a holistic approach to thinking about care—for parents, mental health, and even athletes outside of the WNBA. During the *Good Morning America* segment, Roberts asked Ogwumike, "What do you think is going to be the message for team sports for women?" She replied, "Interestingly enough, as much as we fight for what we feel we deserve—we know that we deserve—we have women's soccer, we have women's hockey that are looking up to what we are looking to do, so we're really hoping it can set the tone and really create that legacy for women in sports moving forward."[20] As union president, Ogwumike notes here a responsibility not only to the athletes of the WNBA but also to the National Women's Hockey League (NWHL) and the United States Women's National Team (USWNT), among others.

In *Huddle: How Women Unlock Their Collective Power*, CNN anchor Brooke Baldwin connects the labor struggles of these leagues:

> Women in all three sports were paid significantly less than their male counterparts. . . . They were also given shoddier working conditions and benefits and were universally underestimated for their ability to advance their respective sports to future generations of athletes and fans. More than just equity, it was a matter of respect and dignity for these women. Sports leagues and federations not only determine the amount of their athletes' paychecks and the quality of their locker rooms and travel accommodations, they also designate the level of investment to make in their athletes via corporate sponsorships and marketing opportunities.[21]

Baldwin introduces the concept of the huddle, defined as "a moment that brings women together in any time or place—whether on the front lines of a public protest or in a quiet church basement—to provide each other with support, empowerment, inspiration, and the strength to solve problems or enact meaningful change."[22] The huddle is decidedly about collective action and is similar to the crossover in that it is less invested in the outcome as a means of evaluating success. Instead, it is about the process, the approach to what we colloquially call "the work." Baldwin writes, "Sometimes [huddles] are a space where women can simply bear witness for each other, or quietly sustain each other's very survival."[23] Fused by this shared inequality, basketball, soccer, and hockey athletes worked together, or huddled, for years on how to gain public support and organize for better labor conditions.[24] Englebert noted this perhaps when she told Roberts on *Good Morning America*, "[This CBA] redefines what it means to be a professional female athlete today in society, and we're hoping to not just lift women in sports, women in basketball, but women in society."[25]

However, it is essential to note that the process of labor organizing with over one hundred athletes spread across the globe and collective bargaining with leagues and governing bodies is an additional labor ask. Baldwin describes this in *Huddle* following her interviews with leaders across the WNBA, NWHL, and USWNT: "There was much talk of crammed meetings in hotel rooms, late-night phone calls, learning the complexities of legal negotiations and collective bargaining, and keeping up on detailed text chats on top of an already busy training schedule."[26] The often-invisible labor of collaborating, organizing, and negotiating is rarely acknowledged in these hypervisible moments of union success, but in the WNBPA's approach to its CBA, it also set a standard for the pending rupture of the pandemic across US professional sports in the weeks that followed.

Basketball before the Bubble

In many ways, basketball operated as a centerpiece for understanding the severity of the pandemic in the United States. I recall serving as a guest coach during the University of Oregon women's basketball game on February 28, 2020, in the midst of a historic run for a team featuring Ruthy Hebard, Satou Sabally, and Sabrina Ionescu. At the time, UO women's hoops represented the future potential for the sport, given its preseason exhibition victory over Team USA, sell-out crowds throughout the regular season, and its "unfinished business" in completing a title run. In that moment, the college game seemed primed to reach new heights in terms of its popularity and mainstream media coverage. On February 29, 2020, the day after my coaching "stint," the National College Players Association (NCPA) released a statement concerning the virus and college athlete health ahead of the annual March Madness tournament and advocated for spectator-free arenas to prioritize athlete safety.[27] Then, on March 11, 2020, NCAA president Mark Emmert announced that March Madness would be free of fans, a decision made as conference tournaments were already under way.[28] For many, this signaled a significant shift in how the threat of the pandemic was understood within

US sports. That evening, NBA insider Shams Charania tweeted, "Utah Jazz All-Star Rudy Gobert has tested positive for coronavirus. . . . Sources say Gobert is feeling good, strong, and stable—and was feeling strong enough to play tonight."[29] Four minutes later, Adrian Wojnarowski tweeted, "The NBA has suspended the season."[30] Given this development, the NCPA called for the cancellation of all college sports activities, especially March Madness, a decision the governing body of collegiate sports would eventually make.[31] On April 3, 2020, the WNBA officially postponed the upcoming season.

As athletes, teams, and leagues grappled with the impact of a pandemic on a day-by-day basis, journalist Bradford William Davis wrote that sport "reminded regular people that COVID-19 was not a foreign abstraction, but a present threat."[32] The disruption of sports seasons aligned with the disjointed spatial and temporal realities of life under the pandemic. Like many other industries, sport faced key labor questions regarding athlete safety in resuming play. In 144 WNBPA president Nneka Ogwumike says, "There was concern around coronavirus. There was concern around the intricacies of not playing for five months and then being asked to play. There were concerns around the length of training camp. There were concerns around pre-existing conditions, high-risk players to coronavirus. I mean, there were so many concerns."[33] From an organized labor perspective, players had to consider whether the protocols offered by their respective leagues were adequate to prevent the spread of the virus.

Athlete as Essential Worker

In May 2020 Acting Secretary of Homeland Security Chad F. Wolf signed an order that exempted some international professional athletes from previous legislation preventing their entry into the United States. In the official release, he is quoted as saying, "Professional sporting events provide much needed economic benefits, but equally important, they provide community pride and national unity. In today's environment, Americans need their sports. It's time to reopen the economy and it's time we get our professional athletes back to work."[34] The signed order included athletes, staff, team, and league leadership, as well as their spouses and dependents. The exemption in essence made athletes essential workers, a designation defined by the Department of Homeland Security as those who conduct operations essential for critical infrastructure. This official opening of the border to international athletes occurred in the midst of xenophobic policies and discourses that blamed immigrants for the spread of COVID-19 as "vectors" for the virus. Homeland Security not only closed the border to asylum seekers but also deported over forty thousand migrants.[35] At the state level, forty-six states and Washington, DC, created their own definitions of "essential worker," typically including employees within health care, emergency services, childcare, food and agriculture, energy, transportation, media, and service industries. The notion that US citizens "needed" sports and that fans were eager for professional athletes to get "back to work" reveals a semblance of American exceptionalism coupled with the economic value of the sports-media complex.

By May 2020 the pandemic had made vividly clear the economic disparities already baked into American life across racial, gendered, or classed lines.[36] Sport mirrored these disparities, and in *144* WNBA commissioner Cathy Englebert unpacked her thought process regarding taking the 2020 season off entirely: "As we were doing the scenario planning, what I was trying to convince certainly the players on is we cannot be out of the sports landscape for more than twenty months . . . and had we not played and started in May of '21, that's a long time to be out of sight, out of mind."[37] While a lost season would be financially difficult for any sports league, Englebert hints at how devastating the absence would be for the WNBA, a league already relegated to the periphery of mainstream sports coverage.

In June 2020 the league proposed a twenty-two-game regular season set to begin the following month in a bubble staged at IMG Academy in Bradenton, Florida, to assuage the fear of being forgotten. However, part of the proposal would reduce players' pay to 60 percent of their expected salary. Several athletes and advocates of the women's game objected to the salary cuts, including Penny Toler, a former WNBA player, coach, and executive who was quoted saying, "These young ladies, as well as the men in the NBA, are putting their lives on the line to come back. Yes, to earn a salary of course, but also putting their lives on the line because sports do make people better. So I don't feel that any of the women players should be taking a pay cut, even though they're having a 22-game season."[38] Basketball commentator LaChina Robinson is quoted in *144* saying, "Playing basketball in a pandemic looks like this—no mask, no six feet apart. To put yourself in harm's way or increase your chances of getting the virus I'm sure is a scary decision."[39] As athletes and leagues worldwide considered how best to return to the game in this new landscape, the question of who can determine when and how to resume play continued to plague global sport. The economic and political imperative to essentialize athlete labor reflected existing power structures (such as leagues' or governing bodies' existing broadcast rights contracts), and the terms of players' reentry into a season relied upon whether athletes belonged to unions that could advocate on their behalf. In documenting how gender disparities affected athletes during the pandemic, Paul Davis and Charlene Weaving write, "One of the most significant lessons learned with respect to women athletes and women's sport is how COVID-19 highlighted and reinforced inequities—media coverage, funding, sponsorship, opportunity, access."[40] The WNBPA's recent success with the CBA carried over into an agreement to resume play in 2020 with full pay for the abbreviated season.

Bubble as Space

The WNBA's 2020 season tipped off on July 25 in Bradenton, Florida, where athletes lived in a sequestered compound and found themselves subjected to daily COVID testing, frequent games in a compressed schedule, and constant interaction with other athletes. Several members of the WNBPA discussed how the season's grind felt different from previous ones. In *144* Jewell Loyd says, "The mental aspect of it, it's been challenging. Every day, you feel like you're trapped. You feel like you can't leave. And the only outlet you have is basketball."[41] Her Seattle Storm teammate Sue Bird described it this way: "Usually when you're competing against people, you don't have to see them 24–7. You're not eating meals with them and seeing them in the elevator and walking around. It's like constantly 'hey, hey, hey.' Even if you don't know people you feel rude. . . . There's nothing to get you away from basketball, which is tough."[42] The notion of constantly being "in it" within this space also affected how athletes struggled to care for loved ones outside the bubble. This is seen in a particularly poignant scene from *144*, where Natalie Achonwa is making breakfast and reflecting upon a recent incident:

> We have a Ring doorbell so we can see the camera and stuff like that. There was a police officer outside of my house, and my boyfriend was walking down the pathway from our house to the cop car. As soon as the notification came to the app, I'm . . . blowing up his phone like, "What's

going on? Are you okay?" And not because I feared that he did anything wrong, but I feared for, for him. My first thought was, "Did you tell them you're a six-three black man when you called the police?" Because we live in a nice neighborhood.[43]

She pauses for a moment before saying, "As hard as it's been in this bubble, it's also been a privilege to be in this bubble. 'Cause this bubble's probably one of the safest places, from COVID, from interaction with police. So in a sense, this, this bubble has been protection." As athletes grappled with this new environment, they also considered the benefits of this space compared to the turmoil looming outside of their temporary home at IMG Academy. That this space could simultaneously feel like a "trap" and like "protection" illustrates the complexities of this unknown space and the potential impact on athletes' mental health.

Caregiving Inside of the Bubble

Throughout the documentary *144*, care is displayed in a variety of ways. Athletes cook together and host their own culinary-themed nights. Players who are parents FaceTime their children, while those who brought their families into the bubble are seen across the film. For example, Dearica Hamby brought her daughter, Amaya, into the bubble along with her mother. In the film, we see them playing softball together and hear Hamby's voice over their game: "I'm glad that [my daughter is] here to help me. . . . I'm thankful to have her."[44] These moments of joy occur with her daughter even as Hamby ends up battling an injury. There are two readings of caregiving within the bubble. Some scholars argue that for these athletes, the care work involved with children in the bubble represents yet another disparity between the NBA and WNBA. Davis and Weaving write, "Women athletes juggling childcare and their children's health and well-being has been amplified during the pandemic, and such labor has become more visible, reinforcing traditional gender expectations. The asymmetrical arrangements between the women's and men's games—with children and families not allowed in the men's league bubble until the final days—also provides ideological reinforcement of the preceding notion that 'real' sport is [a] male enterprise and women's equivalents [are] the diminutive versions."[45] However, I would like to argue for a second possibility related to care. That family members and partners were allowed in the bubble created care in a meaningful, tangible way. When Candace Parker hugs her daughter after a tough playoff loss, this seems less of a burden and more of a moment of reciprocal care. As players grappled with their role in a broader wildcat strike across professional sport, Tianna Hawkins pauses for a moment with her partner and child outside of the locker rooms as she processes the team's decision. Her toddler son, Emanuel, asks why she's crying. "You wouldn't understand," she replies. Her partner turns to him and says, "They're not playing tonight, OK? Come here, come here." He picks up Emanuel. "There is stuff going on right now that you are a little too young to understand. But it's not your fault, OK? Don't think they aren't playing because of anything you did, OK? It's not you."[46] Hawkins kisses her son, and at that moment, the viewer briefly experiences the balance required for Hawkins to juggle playing, parenting, and protesting all at once. That she must simultaneously process this moment for herself and work through how best to care for her son absolutely represents the asymmetrical arrangements of labor for male and female athletes. Moments later, her teammate Ariel Atkins holds Emanuel as she speaks to ESPN reporter Holly Rowe, and in these two moments, I see the inclusion of families in the bubble as less a di-minutive effect and more a semblance of communal care, a means of being more than an athlete or activist in such a fraught moment. While I see the parallels of additional care work prescribed to women under the pandemic and historically both within and outside sport, I offer this alternate reading via the reflections of the Wubble's athletes, where they share in the burden of care and benefit from having loved ones in a space otherwise sealed off.

Care through Play

The refusal to operate solely through their labor as athletes or in alliance with activists is also part of how members of the WNBPA envision their full humanity—how they care for and love on one another. Care operated in a variety of ways in the bubble and brought me to *The Care Manifesto: The Politics of Interdependence*, a text that considers what radical care might look like as a broader resistance to capitalism: "The practices of care that recognise the complexity of human interactions also enhance our ability to reimagine and participate more fully in democratic processes at all levels of society."[47] In the documentary, one seemingly mundane moment reflects this form of care. Outside their housing facility, the Los Angeles Sparks receive postpractice treatment from the medical staff, including head athletic trainer Courtney Watson. Sparks player Reshanda Gray tells the cameras, "Sorry, y'all, it's a little quiet. Ice baths normally go up. We normally have double Dutch out here."[48] Double Dutch is a jump rope game where two folks each turn two ropes in opposite directions at the same time while one or more participants jump in, and it is considered a cultural tradition among Black girls and women. Robin D. G. Kelley describes double Dutch as a "highly stylized performance" where "the good jumpers perform improvised acrobatic feats or complicated body movements as a way of stylizing and individualizing the performance."[49]

In the next scene, Gray and Watson turn the ropes for Brittney Sykes, who briefly jumps in before getting tangled in the ropes. The viewer hears, "Let the old lady show you," as Watson jumps in, hitting a little footwork and showing off her skills. Then, in a voice-over, Watson says, "We just try to do all of the enjoyment that we can in our villa. We're together every day . . . so we have to keep loving and supporting and becoming as much of a family as we possibly can." As she says this, there is laughter and joy as Gray jumps in, a beautiful if not brief reprieve from the world outside their bubble.

Double Dutch was formalized as a sport by David Walker, a New York detective who established tournaments in 1974. The tournaments became a tradition held annually at Lincoln Center in New York over the next decade. Journalist Danielle Young writes that the American Double Dutch League's iconic city-wide competitions became "a space for young women from urban communities to see that their favorite street sport was world-class."[50] The competition would eventually introduce the world to Delores Brown Finlayson, De'Shone Adams Goodson, Adrienne Adams Howell, and Robin Oakes Watterson, collectively known as the Fantastic Four. The legendary double Dutch team began competing in the late 1970s and eventually won the World Wide Double Dutch Championship. Their popularity increased as they appeared in a McDonald's commercial and the Emmy Award-winning documentary *Pick Up Your Feet* (1981) and as they continued turning ropes around the world.

In a blog post on the annual double Dutch tournament, Stephanie Carter draws a connection between basketball and double Dutch as crucial connectors for Black girls in urban spaces, arguing that both sports "thrived because the community could come together and play games that didn't require much equipment. Children across the country picked up those two ropes and found something more than what was in front of them."[51] In the same way, Kelley considers basketball and double Dutch as forms of "symbolic creativity" that struggle to "carve out a kind of liminal space between work and play, labor and performance."[52] For the Sparks, this interlude blends the play of double Dutch with the seemingly mundane work of rehabbing postpractice. I've repeatedly returned to this scene since the documentary first aired, considering how these fleeting moments of joy coalesce even as athletes face a grueling schedule, an insular space, and the additional labor of organizing work. In many ways, in such a dark summer, Watson and the Sparks engage in what Renee Nishawn Scott calls "light making"—"a methodology for thriving in spite of perpetual anti-Black subjugation in the historic and contemporary context of the United States."[53] She emphasizes that light making not only functions as a strategy to emphasize a sense of self but also is both learned and reproduced through community. This key crossover tactic illuminated the path forward for the WNBPA, whether in the vigil following the shooting of Jacob Blake or in determining their next move as a union.

The Social Justice Council

When the league and the union set a date for July to start an abbreviated season in a bubble located in Bradenton, Florida, they also announced the formation of the Social Justice Council with the intent of "cultivating designated spaces for community conversations, virtual roundtables, and other activations to address this country's long history of inequality, implicit bias, and systemic racism that has targeted black and brown communities."[54] The players were intentional about playing only if the league willingly dedicated time, energy, and financial resources toward key causes and organizations.

In particular, the WNBPA centered Breonna Taylor, a twenty-six-year-old Black woman killed in her home by police officers in Louisville, Kentucky, in March 2020. The WNBPA players placed Taylor's name on the backs of their jerseys, just below their own names, for the duration of the season. "It really hits home 'cause it could have been me," Natalie Achonwa says in *144*. "And that's the hardest part. It's like it doesn't matter. At the end of the day, when I take off this jersey, I'm still a Black woman. So that's where the fight comes from. That's where the passion comes from. Because it could have been me. It could have been my sister. It could have been my teammate."[55] For a league comprised of over 80 percent Black women, establishing a racial justice initiative reflected broader sociocultural concerns and aligned with the priorities of most of the WNBA's players. However, this was not the first time WNBPA players saw themselves in the lives of those killed by law enforcement. In 2016, another summer marked by high-profile cases of police brutality, players rallied together following the killings of Alton Sterling and Philando Castile. Some demonstrated by collectively wearing custom shirts that read "Change Starts with Us," while others opted for black shirts during warmups and only took questions regarding police violence during media availability. In response, the league fined each team $5,000 and issued a $500 fine for each player. At the time, Doug Feinberg of the *South Florida Times* wrote, "The fines seemed to galvanize the players, who [used] postgame interview sessions and social media to voice their displeasure."[56] WNBPA member Tina Charles pointed out, "When we take off our jerseys and we are out there, we could be next. We were able to show our voice. People responding to me said you gained a fan, not because of what I do on the court, but the act I did. We have followers now because of who we are, not what we do."[57] Public outrage at the financial penalties eventually resulted in the league rescinding the fines. However, the activism of the WNBA's players that summer was overwhelmingly absent from larger narratives surrounding athlete resistance. Journalist Scoop Jackson asked,

> How deep does the discrimination, the not treating or considering women in sports as equals, go? CNN presented a video photo essay on its website: "A Timeline of Social Activism in Sports." Of the fourteen photos used in the photo essay, there was only one image that even included women: a pic of US soccer player Megan Rapinoe, taking a knee during the national anthem, prior to a match against Thailand in 2016. That's it. And even then, the inclusion of women as equals as athletes showed a woman following the lead of a male athlete. . . . No protest pics of Maya Moore and the entire Minnesota Lynx team advocating for "Black Lives Matter" or how "Change Starts With Us" surrounding social injustice cases.[58]

Here, Jackson offers a vivid example of how Black women and nonbinary folks slip through narratives of athlete activism, where the erasure of the WNBPA's direct action during the summer of 2016 is subsumed by two other athletes—Colin Kaepernick and Megan Rapinoe—and their solo actions rather than the collective advocacy of entire teams. In *Black Feminist Thought*, Patricia Hill Collins writes that one of the primary means of suppressing Black feminist thought is the depoliticization of Black women's feminist contributions.[59] I argue that basketball operates as another regulatory mechanism to devalue the knowledge production and labor of Black women while attempting to subvert their activist practices for capitalist gain.

As the Social Justice Council began organizing and promoting its cause across social media and mainstream outlets, members also organized Zoom calls with various organizers and political figures such as Valerie Jarrett, Michelle Obama, Stacey Abrams, and Tamika Palmer, the mother of Breonna Taylor, to educate themselves on key issues. In one of the meetings, Sydney Colson says, "We've had an opportunity to hear from and be educated by so many people that I think that we didn't really, we couldn't have foreseen the kind of education that we would be receiving and who it would be from."[60] Zoom, a video communication platform, had already become a communal space for classrooms, meetings, memorials, first dates, and family reunions as COVID-19 numbers rose and people remained quarantined. For the WNBPA, it became an organizing space, and for Sydney Colson, a member of the Social Justice Council, it operated as a tool to connect the union to the ideal expert and cause: Kimberlé Crenshaw and the #SayHerName campaign.

In an interview with Colson, she told me about joining MSNBC via Zoom to represent the union in a segment that fortuitously followed a network interview with Kimberlé Crenshaw, a critical race scholar credited with introducing the term "intersectionality" to denote how one's intersecting identities shape how one experiences systemic oppression. Crenshaw listened to Colson's segment and later reached out to her through the show's producer. "So we got on the phone later that day," Colson told me. "We spoke for over an hour, and it was just, the word I always use is serendipitous. . . . It was really like the perfect, the best thing that could have happened, because then I started pushing to make sure that we had her involved [with the WNBPA]."[61] The Crenshaw/Colson connection resulted in a league partnership with the #SayHerName campaign.

#SayHerName as a hashtag rose to popularity through a series of webinars hosted by the African American Policy Forum—cofounded by Crenshaw—to elevate the experiences of girls and women targeted by police violence, beginning with the extrajudicial murders of Black women and expanding from there. In *Hashtag Activism* Sarah Jackson, Moya Bailey, and Brooke Foucault Welles write that this hashtag and others reflect the creative and political work of care and conversation generated by women of color. They argue that these in-group hashtags "provide critical challenges to feminist and ethnic counterpublics by centering intersectional frameworks and experiences."[62] In partnering with the #SayHerName campaign, the WNBPA and the Social Justice Council held regular Zoom meetings to connect players within the bubble to crucial leaders and voices outside it. I attended one of the calls in July 2020, during which the union invited media members to hear from Colson, Crenshaw, and several mothers of women killed by police. It also featured a cameo at the end with recording artist and actress Janelle Monae, who also partnered with the league that season. Near the beginning of the call, Bethany Donaphin, head of WNBA League Operations, described the approach to creating the council and shaping the season-long commitment to Breonna Taylor and the #SayHerName movement: "When we thought about how to operationally execute a season in the midst of the COVID-19 pandemic, we also had to stop and say we're battling two global crises right now. The other is systemic racism, and how can we conduct a season in a way that honors that and affects change in our society and elevates the platform that the players have and their strong voices." When Sydney Colson spoke about her role as a player and member of the Social Justice Council, she reiterated the fact that the league's demographics served as a critical motivator for players' intentionality in their activism:

> It isn't far-reaching for one of us to be Breonna Taylor, you know? And I think that's the frightening thing and the thing that made this season so much bigger than just basketball. I think a lot has been put into perspective for a lot of players. . . . Every day is not guaranteed that racial injustice is still a huge issue. . . . It was really important to have a lens on women. And it's so impactful to have Professor Crenshaw as part of this conversation. When you think about it, there's no other league that has the intersectionality that we have with 80 percent Black women and also many who identify as LGBTQ+. I think it's really important that we're having really open and honest conversations about what that means, particularly with experts in various aspects of social justice.

Here, while Colson acknowledges the diversity of the league, she also critically notes how the identity politics bound up in the WNBA operate as a launching point for the league's advocacy, which is driven forward by engaging with experts and those most impacted by state-sanctioned violence. Sydney Colson also told the audience that the league's brass had "switched from 2016, where teams got fined for wearing 'I Can't Breathe' shirts and, you know, police walked out of the game in Minnesota. For us to now be in the bubble, where they're allowing us to be the frontrunners and to be the face of the social justice season, I think it shows that they understand the power that we have together, especially in this unique season being all 144 together, that we feel really empowered in this moment and we have something to say." Here, Colson signals how the WNBA office's shift in supporting Black Lives Matter marks the current moment. A 2016 Pew Research poll found that 84 percent of Black adults and 50 percent of white adults surveyed felt that Blacks were treated less fairly than whites in dealing with the police, while 41 percent of Black adults and 14 percent of white adults surveyed "strongly supported" the Black Lives Matter movement.[63] The racial climate of 2020 proved different. The amplified focus on racial violence erupted into the streets via protests, seeped into the election trail, and permeated the news cycle in a renewed fashion. In "White Guilt in the Summer of Black Lives Matter," Lisa Spanierman delved into how white guilt became a mobilizing factor in 2020: "While left-wing critiques of white guilt as paralyzing, defensive, and performative are accurate in many cases, burgeoning evidence in the field of psychology suggests that white guilt may be a socially productive force with reparative potential."[64] She attributes this shift to the election of Donald Trump to the US presidency, coupled with the effects of the pandemic and reinforced by the circulation of Black death through the killings of Breonna Taylor, George Floyd, and Ahmaud Arbery.[65] The phrase "Black Lives Matter"—previously perceived as a controversial stance—became a staple lawn sign, storefront decoration, and email subject line from various corporate entities. It was also stamped across the hardwood of the courts in Bradenton, Florida, as the league competed at IMG Academy. As antiracist book lists, statements, and speaker series ran rampant across the public sphere, this new climate provided opportunities for the WNBPA to direct funds and programming without fear of retribution from the league (a sharp turn from the punitive response of sports leagues to athlete activism unleashed in 2016). In many ways, 2020 marked a significant shift in athlete activism, requiring athletes to be conscious of neoliberal commodity activism that would subsume any resistive potential in their work.

As Crenshaw began her presentation, she noted that the partnership between the #SayHerName campaign and the WNBA reflects a fundamental shift in potential movement work:

> They are all women on the forefront of change, and I'm especially excited about the possibility that we may be on the precipice of a new moment in the way that we talk about anti-Black racism. This is a time, this is a moment, this is a possibility that Black women can be at the center of the discourse rather than being erased from it. The feeling that I had this weekend, watching the tip-off with LA and witnessing the players pay tribute to Breonna Taylor and seeing #SayHerName on full display, it was all a profound moment.

Crenshaw then shared slides that provided more in-depth information regarding the statistics, complete with maps, surrounding Black women and police brutality. She then grounded the extensive institutional violence with photographs of those killed by police, pictured with their loved ones, seen in their full humanity rather than merely reduced to their last moments of life. Finally, she played a video that introduced those in attendance to the "sisterhood of sorrow," comprised primarily of mothers who are left to mourn their daughters' deaths and who then offer advice and care to the "next member" who enters their ranks.

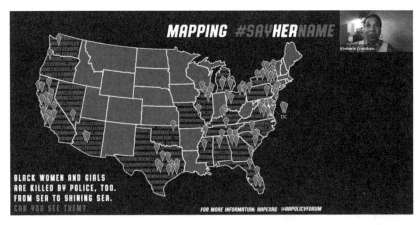

Figure 1. Dr. Kimberlé Crenshaw presents #SayHerName statistics to Zoom participants.

While the video and testimonies from the mothers present during the call confronted media members in attendance with the often unseen aftermath of Black death, the call also directly addressed familiar narratives levied toward police reform, whether in suggesting additional training or in attempting to ascertain the intentionality behind officers' actions.

In sharing with the group how the partnership with the #SayHerName campaign developed, Colson also pointed to the Social Justice Council as a player-led action, a bottom-up approach to athlete activism. During the Zoom meeting she said, "I had been looking for someone for the past week or so to speak to from the #SayHerName campaign. And I wasn't finding who I should contact to make sure that if we were using that hashtag and that phrase either on our courts or on the backs of our jerseys . . . we needed to make sure that we were doing it respectfully and that we were following whatever mission they had with that campaign." Here, there is a sense of the care taken by the players: they did not want to "hijack" the campaign; instead, they sought out a meaningful space in the movement. Colson told me in an interview that "it would be crazy for us to not give her credit and African American Policy Forum credit or to financially help them." This notion is particularly important given the various forms of hijacking of Crenshaw's theoretical contributions to both critical legal studies and feminist theory. The lack of consistent citational practice and the resulting "depoliticization" of intersectionality render it shorthand for market-driven diversity measures packaged as an entrepreneurial endeavor.[66] This does not occur by accident. Rather, Sirma Bilge writes that it is directly aligned with the systematic marginalization of scholars and activists of color in knowledge production: "Neoliberal assumptions create the conditions allowing the founding conceptions of intersectionality—as an analytical lens and political tool for fostering a radical social justice agenda—to become diluted, disciplined, and disarticulated."[67] She denotes this as "ornamental intersectionality," something that the WNBPA's partnership seems to combat. In an intellectual moment when intersectionality is so often quoted without properly citing and crediting Crenshaw or often misused or misapplied, this union serves as a vivid example of intersectional feminism operating outside of the academy as a means of reclaiming some of its core tenets.

The *144* documentary features the Zoom calls as players describe the impact of connecting with the #SayHerName campaign. Colson was interviewed

Figure 2. A still shot of *144* as WNBPA member Satou Sabally participates in the Social Justice Council Zoom call.

inside the bubble, where she says that "for us to speak to the mothers of these families, like on Zoom calls that the WNBA and the Social Justice Council organized, it was really, really overwhelming to hear the grief and the sadness of these mothers sometimes."[68] Rookie Satou Sabally, another council member, is seen behind her computer, logged into a Zoom meeting with those families. Taking part in the calls, she says, "gives it more depth and humanity instead of headlines. Most of the times, you know, the stories of Black women are not spread out. And I feel like it's our duty to be informed about the stories of our sisters."[69]

Here, the Zoom meetings operate as a form of a broader Black feminist practice of witnessing, one that legal scholar Brittany Farr argues "accentuate[s] visibility, encourage[s] reflection, and engage[s] in direct address."[70] There is a duality in this witnessing, where the counternarratives offered by the loved ones of slain girls and women televisually presented on Zoom are not only received by the players themselves but also transmitted to the media members responsible for translating the event for broader audiences. And while the efforts of the WNBPA found support across multiple outlets and favor among organizers and activists engaged in similar work, the union's direct action was not wholly embraced by the league, particularly, one WNBA team owner.

Political Engagement as Care

As the 2020 season took form, the campaign trails for the upcoming US election cycle ramped up at the state and national levels. Kelly Loeffler, co-owner of the WNBA's Atlanta Dream and US senator from Georgia, was seeking reelection, and as part of her platform, she spoke in opposition to the WNBPA's Social Justice Council, the union's partnership with the #SayHerName campaign, and the inclusion of the phrase "Black Lives Matter" on the IMG Academy courts in the bubble. She initially wrote a letter to the WNBA and league commissioner Cathy Englebert asking for the removal of the partnership and suggested instead that an American flag decal be added to uniforms and other team apparel. "The truth is, we need less—not more politics in sports. In a time when polarizing politics is as divisive as ever, sports has the power to be a unifying antidote," said Loeffler. "And now more than ever, we should be united in our goal to remove politics from sports."[71] While a politician and part owner of a professional sports team calling for a separation of politics and sport is indeed ironic, Loeffler's claim that the WNBPA's decision to invoke Black Lives Matter and #SayHerName as divisive and uninformed compelled the Atlanta Dream to respond. In an op-ed for *Vox*, Elizabeth Williams, a member of the Dream roster, writes, "We had not come to promote Black Lives Matter as a team without a lot of consideration and thought, and we now felt like our voice was being used as a prop by our co-owner to drum up support among her conservative base."[72]

Following Loeffler's comments, allyship took two forms throughout the 2020 WNBA season. The first was the solidarity shared across the league as players began actively campaigning for Loeffler's opponent, Raphael Warnock. They invited Warnock to join them in a Zoom call to ask about his platform and goals for the state of Georgia. After agreeing to support his campaign, individual players and entire teams began posting photos wearing "Vote Warnock" shirts, pushing beyond the suggestion to merely "vote," a familiar rhetoric across sports that year and previous election cycles that combines celebrity culture with an apolitical call to make one's voice "heard."

The second form that allyship took was among the league's white players who aligned with their Black and Brown teammates throughout the season. In *144* Breanna Stewart says, "When we say #SayHerName, we're talking about the majority of the women in our league. You know, the majority of the women in our league are Black women, and what happened to Breonna Taylor could have happened to them. You know, it might not have happened to me because I'm white, but that's something that they will always think about."[73] The many moments of solidarity across the league that season, whether in the players' attire, direct action, or partnerships with various causes, operate as a master class in how white women might support women of color (specifically, Black women) in the struggle. In *Hood Feminism: Notes from the Women That a Movement Forgot*, Mikki Kendall shifts the conversation from a position of allyship to the role of an accomplice—a more active form of solidarity that requires difficult conversations and sacrifices over a distanced form of support or care: "Being a good accomplice is where the real work gets done. That means taking the risks inherent in wielding privilege to defend communities with less of it, and it means being willing to not just pass the mic but to sometimes get completely off the stage so that someone else can get the attention they need to get their work done."[74] A key role Kendall identifies for accomplice feminists is "between the white supremacist systems (which are less likely to harm them) and those that the systems are trying to harm."[75] For the WNBPA, this role was on full display as the union took on Loeffler with its campaign in support of Warnock. Sue Bird, who helped coordinate the "Vote Warnock" shirts worn by players throughout the season, also took to social media to advocate alongside her Seattle Storm teammates for Loeffler's opponent. In using her platform, Bird deflected from the misogynoir other players might receive because of their positionality. In an interview with *People*, she said: "[Loeffler] came out against a lot of what the women in our league stand for, I think [it] was emotionally tough for a lot of the women in our league to hear that. But very quickly we started to realize that this was only happening for her political gain. This was something that she wanted. And the more noise we made, whether it was a tweet saying to get her out, that was just playing into her hands."[76] Instead, the pivot to advocate for her opponent removed Loeffler's name from the discourse and increased the visibility of Warnock and his campaign. In *144* Williams says, "We felt a big burden as the Dream players to say something and do something. The pressure was on us. But then it's like, wait, we have our sisters behind us."[77] Even as the early opposition from Loeffler challenged a season and a union already plagued by the pandemic and police brutality, the care employed by the rest of the league's athletes in support of the Atlanta Dream served as a unifying catalyst of care.

Sue Bird
@S10Bird

...

We are @wnba players, but like the late great John Lewis said, we are also ordinary people with extraordinary vision. @ReverendWarnock has spent his life fighting for the people and we need him in Washington. Join the movement for a better Georgia at Warnockforgeorgia.com

5:00 PM · Aug 4, 2020

1,856 Reposts   **206** Quotes   **10.4K** Likes   **28** Bookmarks

◯   ↻   ♡   🔖 28   ↑

Figure 3. Members of the Seattle Storm wear "Vote Warnock" shirts in Sue Bird's tweet.

Care through Organizing

In several moments throughout the film, tensions emerge regarding how best to move forward as a union and as activists. These moments are tense and rife with the messiness of organizing work. Viewers take in how players made the decision not to play following the police-involved shooting of Jacob Blake, how they navigated their labor as a union, and how they interacted with media following this decision. As the August 26 games hung in the balance, players from the Washington Mystics gathered to discuss how they wanted to approach the game. Alaina Coates says, "The thing is, if people are going to speak their voice, they need to stand on their convictions, not say something one minute and then switch it up because everybody else is saying something. Stand on your convictions, stand on what you want." Her teammate Leilani Mitchell responds, "I agree, but then I think other people bring other factors into it that they haven't thought about. . . . Like, were people thinking about 'well, what if ESPN does pull [its broadcasting contract with the WNBA],' and then you have no more money. Are you going to be fine to pay your mortgage? People got bills to pay."[78] Here, the reality of what taking a stand might mean for players' paychecks is brought to the forefront alongside the potential rupture of the league's relationship with a major broadcast outlet. Mitchell is seemingly on board with not playing but also speaks to the fact that everyone may not agree. Moments later, the Mystics meet with the Atlanta Dream, their scheduled opponent. Elizabeth Williams says, "What we do, we do it together." Mitchell, representing the Mystics, says, "I mean, at the end of the day, it's bigger than basketball, and we feel like something further needs to happen."[79] What is instructive here is that the teams sat with all the potential responses to the strike and decided that they wouldn't move forward until everyone was on board. The film shows that after a bit of frantic coordination behind the scenes, players begin to plan their next steps. Williams, representing the union and the Dream, approaches the same cameras and microphones established to capture that evening's game. She reads a statement from her phone:

> After speaking with representatives from teams playing tonight, as well as our WNBPA leadership, the consensus is to not play in tonight's slate of games. What we have seen over the last few months and most recently with the brutal police shooting of Jacob Blake is overwhelming, and while we hurt for Jacob and his community, we also have an opportunity to keep the focus on the issues and demand change. This is the reason for the 2020 season. We will continue to use our platform to speak of these injustices that are still happening and demand action for change. Black Lives Matter, Say Her Name, Say His Name.[80]

Players then walk onto the court and support each other, some wearing shirts bearing social justice messaging, others with the letters of Jacob Blake's name across their chests. Whereas fans may have tuned into ESPN expecting tip-off, viewers instead experienced players' protest in real time, with camera crews and commentators in place shifting from game coverage to narrating the scene unfolding before them. Basketball analyst LaChina Robinson, during the games-free broadcast, says, "This is very personal to them. They have taken on the responsibility in trying to figure out the best way to use their voices. This was their way of putting their arms around their community from a distance."[81] Moments before she is set to represent the Mystics in front of the cameras, Ariel Atkins, with tears in her eyes, is surrounded by her team-mates. She struggles to find the right words to articulate a moment of grief and resistance. "What am I supposed to say?" she asks. "We fucking matter? Stop fucking killing us?"[82] Some embrace her, while others rub her back or touch her shoulder. She eventually emerges and stands beside reporter Holly Rowe, flanked by her team. Rowe says, "You know, this was a long conversation. You were here on the court for quite some time talking with other teams about the decision tonight. What were some of the factors you considered going into this?" Atkins responds, "This isn't just about basketball. We aren't just basketball players. And just because we are basketball players doesn't mean that's our only platform. We need to understand that when most of us go home, we still are Black in the sense that our families matter. Like, we got this little guy right here that we see every day." The camera pans down to Tianna Hawkins's son, Emanuel. Atkins continues:

> His life matters. He needs to know that he can do what he wants to do whenever he leaves his house when he grows up. You know, within rea-son—you don't need to go out there all crazy. But he matters. It's hard to say that type of stuff in these moments. It's hard to be vulnerable in these moments, but if we do this unified as a league, it looks different. Because this league is close to, if not over, 80 percent Black women. We have cousins, we have brothers, we have sisters, mothers, everyone. We matter. I know I matter. We know we matter. I'm tired of telling people that. If you don't know that, if you don't think that, you need to recheck it. And if you have a problem with us saying Black Lives Matter, you need to check your privilege, 'cause yes, all lives matter, including the Black lives we're talking about.[83]

As she concludes, Atkins embraces Emanuel. She also hugs Rowe. Her focus on vulnerability, along with her emphasis on the most vulnerable among them, a young child, seemingly moves the conversation from one that is distant and theoretical to a personal position addressing the familiar rhetoric of "all lives matter."

That night, in a players-only meeting, the union regroups to decide its next plan of action following the wildcat strike. Sydney Colson speaks up: "We have to realize that as Black people we are traumatized, and we are going through PTSD whether we realize it or not because of what we're constantly seeing and being desensitized to, not just Black people but everybody. We need to make sure that we are trying to heal as Black people at a time when it's very hard to do so. I think during this time we need to be telling our people that we need help, 'cause we do."[84] Listening to Colson, I considered how she employed trauma, post-traumatic stress disorder (PTSD), and desensitization to describe the psychological impact of constant witnessing and reaction to this particular form of violence. Therapist and organizer Prentis Hemphill describes oppression as a "concentration of trauma" and echoed Colson's calls to healing in an interview with *The Nation*: "Those wounds, they motivate us to join movement and to become a part of an organization, but at the same time . . . it can also be a way for us to avoid or ignore the wound that got us there in the first place."[85]

The union's executive board began asking representatives of teams scheduled for the following day to check in on their decision on whether to play. Indiana opts out, and during the conversation, rookie Satou Sabally speaks up and asks, "What if the NBA decides to cancel their season? Are we going to have, you know, like the same kind of direction because we're kind of forced to, or are we separate and doing our own thing? Because I think that's important."[86] It's uncomfortable in the room before Sue Bird, a member of the executive committee, responds, "It is important to understand that we are not them, they are not us. If we had cancelled our season, do you think they would have? We're not the NBA. Their impact for what they do—this is just reality. Canceling a season is much larger than if we do it. That's one example of it, but I just think we need to start thinking of ourselves as our own league that makes our own decisions." Without dismissing Sabally's concerns, Bird is instructive in her approach to thinking through what it might mean for the union to develop an independent voice separate from their counterparts in the men's game. Her words connect to an interview I later conducted with Ange-Marie Hancock Alfaro, a political science and leading intersectionality scholar who also worked for the NBA in the 1990s and conducted the foundational research and business model that led to the WNBA's creation. She told me:

I think one thing that I've seen over the past four years is I've really seen them come into a position of their own, right? So it's not that they didn't before George Floyd, you know, take stands and, and have, you know, activism that they were doing. It's not like it just came in May like it did for so many people in May of 2020. But I do think there's a greater comfort level with taking a leadership position, right? So they don't need LeBron's approval . . . or even support, it's "Hey, this is what we're doing. If you wanna get on board, don't scrape your knees on the bandwagon, but this is what we are doing." I've really seen a shift in how they perceive themselves as leaders in this space rather than just, we're out here doing our stuff, and we hope somebody pays attention.

That the players might consider what is best for them rather than succumb to the whims of another league marked another critical moment for the WNBPA that summer. As the union gingerly weigh their options, Courtney Williams chimes in:

I'm just going to be honest and put it all on the table. I came in this bitch so I can get paid. You know what I mean? I feel like Breonna Taylor died, and George Floyd died, and we still came in this bitch and decided to dribble a basketball. That's the decision that we made as a whole. These people died, and we still decided to come dribble a basketball. So now— Jacob Blake—and now all of a sudden we're like, "Let's not dribble a ball no more," like now we just had a crazy big epiphany? To not dribble a ball no more?[87]

Someone off camera begins to interject, "I don't think it's . . . " Williams turns to them: "No shade towards y'all. I'm just saying this is just my own opinion on it, my outlook. I'm just saying, to me personally, like I didn't want to come here. Like I didn't. I feel like to me the shit hit so hard and home, I didn't want to come here. But I came here because I know I got niggas I gotta feed, people eat off me. . . . So I decided to come here. To me, I didn't come here like 'Oh, power to the people, let me come here to make a stance.'" Williams raises her fist and continues:

I could have did that at the crib. You know what I mean. I came here to get a check. So I'm just saying, like yeah it's cool, we can "Kumbaya" all day, all night, but we gotta come up with something, and right now it seems like we're talking in circles. I'm not willing to give up my check, 'cause that's the only reason why I'm here. We decided to come here and dribble a ball and make our voice be heard. So now we decide we don't wanna dribble no ball no more, and now we lose our platform, and now what? Now we're looking like Booboo the Fool. So if we're gonna have a real conversation, let's have it.[88]

In noting the economic imperative driving her decision to enter the bubble, Williams says the quiet parts out loud. She vividly articulates what Fleetwood describes in *On Racial Icons*: "Professional sports and their commoditization of the black athletic body also bring us face-to-face with the psychic and physical violence of the racial state that continually attempts to dominate and manipulate black bodies."[89] Making the choice between the impact of the racial state and the value of one's labor is one that athletes like Williams made before entering the Wubble. There is more at risk aside from a canceled season and lost wages (although Williams notes the importance of what "a check" might mean for those who "eat off [her]"). It's quiet in the room before Nneka Ogwumike, the president of the WNBPA, responds: "I hear what Courtney's saying. We do have to figure out what we're going to do with this time. Because we can't just treat this as a day off. There's people that don't have days off right now. There's people who are dying on their days off. So we have to figure out what we can do as a whole that is actionable rather than just boycotting a game and then coming back and playing and it just being that."

As Williams and Ogwumike see it, suddenly shifting their approach to the season and their cause would be to risk the legitimacy of their advocacy with the Social Justice Council and the weight of their strike. For Williams, there is also the notion of needing basketball to be heard as a mechanism of their collective voice. To continue to refuse to play would result in the loss of a platform. As basketball analyst LaChina Robinson says in *144*, "[The wildcat strike] was not an easy decision for a lot of reasons, some players thinking, 'Let's use this opportunity to play and use this platform and our voices in this space.' Others just emotionally shaken."[90]

At the conclusion of his key text, *Race, Sport and Politics: The Sporting Black Diaspora*, sociologist Ben Carrington asks "whether or not today's Black athletes (and others committed to the present and future of sports) are able to develop a critical consciousness sufficient to the challenges of the twenty-first century." If they are, he writes, there is also the matter of "whether the current corporatization of sporting cultures will allow for the types of oppositional voices that once dared to challenge dominant structures within the sporting Black Atlantic world to be heard."[91] In a moment when antiracist discourses within the United States remained steeped in neoliberal logics of corporate diversity, equity, and inclusion, the push "to be heard" is challenged by the risks built into withdrawing one's labor.

In pointing out an idea from her teammate Alysha Clark, Sue Bird suggests a collective action of all 144 players together. Diamond DeShields then speaks up: "We have one name on the back of all our jerseys. We came here, dedicated the season to getting justice for her and #SayHerName. So why couldn't we just further amplify that on a platform as big as ESPN?"[92] Here, DeShields argues for returning to the original mission of the season, a renewed call to center Breonna Taylor and the other women who lost their lives to police brutality.

Watching the union members maneuver through their emotional response, political engagement, and even potential conflict makes plain the complicated nature of this moment for athletes in Bradenton as well as those in other leagues around the country. More broadly, it illustrates how labor organizing offers the potential for political engagement in dynamic ways. Journalist and activist Ewa Jasiewicz writes, "Strikes are the commons of labor in its most active and social form—that of relationship-making, caring for each other and identifying with each other's needs."[93] The WNBPA's commitment to care and learning from the #SayHerName campaign also informed how the union decided to move forward.

The following day, as players filed into the gym, they all wore shirts that read, "Arrest the cops who killed Breonna Taylor." In opting out of playing that day, they offered a call to action in support of Taylor and her family, asking viewers to take their own direct action and pressure authorities to accountability for her death. In the documentary, Alysha Clark describes how vital this particular moment was for players: "It kind of reset why we're here. I think it got lost because it was just game after game after game, and that's kind of all you were thinking about."[94] WNBPA president Nneka Ogwumike then issued a statement to the attorneys general in Kentucky and Wisconsin demanding accountability for Breonna Taylor and Jacob Blake, respectively. She takes a moment to acknowledge the names of eight other women killed by police and finally addresses the viewer: "If you're watching or listening, and you understand the humanity in the Movement for Black Lives, and you recognize that your voice matters, do not remain idle. Demand that your leaders step up and take real action. Do something today."[95] Arms linked in solidarity, the players stand with the same shirts, solidified by the same message. In the documentary, Tamika Palmer, Breonna Taylor's mother, is interviewed about the impact of this moment and the 2020 WNBA season: "It shouldn't be this hard to get justice. She didn't deserve what happened to her. But without these women, I don't even know where I'd be or how many people would have actually paid attention to what happened. It makes you feel like you can take a breath. You're no longer doing it alone, and so some days I don't have to stand up so straight because of them."[96] This notion of creating a breath of relief or a moment of rest amid the constant weariness and grief she experiences succinctly reflects a bodily metaphor of what it might mean to bring care into the equation of organizing and resistance.

Conceptualizing Care

In documenting a moment plagued by uncertainty and unrest, it may feel counterintuitive to frame the summer of 2020 through care (especially given the carelessness of various institutions during this time). As Catherine Rottenberg and Lynne Segal of the Care Collective write, "The COVID-19 pandemic has dramatically—and dreadfully—exposed . . . not only the violence perpetrated by neoliberal markets, but also our enduring interdependence, while revealing, as well, that vulnerability and our need for care are part and parcel of the human condition. It has laid bare the horrors of neoliberalism and the profound falsehood of its ideal subject the self-sufficient entrepreneurial individual. It has also begun a conversation about care."[97]

During this time, discourses surrounding care offered a rejuvenated focus on mutual aid—a solidarity-based support system comprised of networks to address needs too often ignored by neglectful power structures. The pandemic also inspired employees around the country who were subjected to unsafe and unstable working conditions to organize, whether in newsrooms, warehouses, or coffee shops.[98] Employee demands within these industries often focused on the lack of care provided by corporations, such as access to health care, adequate breaks, and the enforcement of safety protocols. As Kim Kelly writes in *Fight Like Hell: The Untold History of American Labor*, while a variety of industry workers have always been "essential" to daily life, the recognition of their value and humanity (or lack thereof by their employers) spurred calls for organizing. "In 2020 and 2021," Kelly writes, "when the COVID-19 pandemic pushed workers onto the front lines and pushed the economy—and the social fabric of the United States in general—to a breaking point, sick-outs, public calls for support, wildcat strikes, and militant action dominated the labor landscape."[99] In many ways, these organizers (as well as the participants who inform this chapter) are responding to what Kimberly Foster describes as "the terror of being uncared for."[100]

As many have written, care itself is in part devalued due to its association as a "soft skill." I would like to directly address the risk of gender essentialism as I read labor organizing and protest through a care framework, avoiding what Grace Clement calls the "false universalism" of care as "women's work."[101] She notes how the ethic of care is constantly coded as feminine, while the ethic of justice is read as masculine.[102] Instead, I propose that care is expertly intertwined with a clear strategy of intersectional justice. Care operates as an antidote to institutional violence and is defined by the Care Collective as "our individual and common ability to provide the political, social, material, and emotional conditions that allow the vast majority of people and living creatures on this planet to thrive—along with the planet itself."[103]

Care is complicated, especially when we consider the racial and gendered aspects of caregiving—and care receiving—both historically and in this contemporary moment. In virtually every realm, women of color are tasked more frequently with administering care, remain undercompensated for care work, and receive significantly less quality care in health care sectors.[104] What I am proposing here (in line with other scholars) is the dissolution of a mythical binary in which politics are a public act and care is a private one.[105] Joan C. Tronto argues that without a public conception of care, a democratic society is impossible to maintain.[106] Within the WNBPA, care operates as one such antidote: the union resists how its membership is devalued both within and outside their labor as athletes.

Later in the *144* documentary, toward the end of the season, Bird reflects on the bubble experience with her partner, soccer star Megan Rapinoe, and compares it to her WNBA offseasons competing in other countries. "I know when I used to go overseas, as much as I could not wait to get home, the last day was like, 'Oh, this is weird,' you know, because you make it home," Bird says. "And I feel like we're all really good at that because we do play overseas, we know how to make something home. I wonder if it'll feel like that when we leave here. 'Cause you get comfortable."[107] Players' ability to adapt to this landscape is aided by the previous labor requirements to play overseas: "making home" is a required, honed skill for women's basketball players translating their labor around the world. While Bird previously described needing an "outlet" from a basketball-centric bubble, as the season went on, she felt a semblance of comfort, of familiarity in a moment otherwise marked by the unknown. Rapinoe echoes this as she lists the upcoming election, the absence of accountability in the death of Breonna Taylor, and a host of other current events plaguing the news cycle. Rapinoe acknowledges the bubble as a space of reprieve because of the community forged by the WNBPA: "I feel like there's a sense of community here that you might not feel otherwise and then still just being able to be themselves. . . . You see just like the full breadth of a human being going through all of this all the time, and it's kind of been comforting in a way to go through it with everyone else."[108] The comfort she describes here is the care that radiated in key moments that summer.

We see this in the documentary as players in the Bradenton compound watch coverage of the grand jury decision on the officers responsible for Breonna Taylor's death. Alysha Clark is receiving treatment on a training table and watching the press conference on her phone. She is soon joined by Jewell Loyd, who peers over her shoulder as Kentucky attorney general Daniel Cameron announces that only one officer will be indicted on criminal charges of endangerment, not for firing any of the bullets that took Taylor's life but for "recklessly firing his weapon into surrounding apartments."[109] Insulated from the harm of the pandemic but still vulnerable to the constant disregard for Black life (and loss), the bubble operated as a space of care for those coping with the myriad of events that summer. These segments of the film break from the more familiar depictions of athlete life. They are less focused on athletic performance or a buildup to the season finale, instead lingering in the everyday of living in the Wubble. Instead of the standardized voice-over narration, the "voice of God" that explains the scene unfolding or the ritual of an expert voice—typically an academic or journalist—that offers context or opinion, the athletes of the WNBPA are centered as authority.

Care beyond the Election Cycle

Following the 2020 WNBA season, the November election resulted in a runoff race between Kelly Loeffler and Raphael Warnock that would determine which party gained the Senate majority. Warnock defeated Loeffler and became the first Black senator in Georgia. Following the special election, journalist Jemele Hill tweeted, "I don't know who needs to hear this but Reverend Raphael Warnock was polling at 9% when the Atlanta Dream and WNBA players threw their full support behind him and elevated his national profile. Now he's Georgia's first black senator."[110] In another tweet basketball analyst LaChina Robinson quoted an email that she received from Warnock's campaign in August 2020: "'Since players from the @WNBA wore their "VOTE WARNOCK" shirts on Tuesday, the campaign raised over $185K online, added over 3,500 new grassroots donors & grew his twitter followers by 3,500' THE REST IS HISTORY."[111]

Across social media, WNBPA membership celebrated the victory, with Diamond DeShields tweeting, "I couldn't be more proud to be a part of THIS group, THIS year. We made history, we are changing the world. And that's on period. U cannot minimize the impact that we have had on THIS election."[112] In the aftermath of Warnock's victory, alongside other key Democratic wins, many heralded the efforts of WNBA players alongside other Black women such as politician and grassroots organizer Stacey Abrams, who founded Fair Fight Action to advocate for voting rights, and activist and community organizer Nsé Ufot of the New Georgia Project. Collectively, the efforts of these groups led many to use the #ThankBlackWomen hashtag, a popular refrain from the previous election cycle. This hashtag trended in 2017 following Doug Jones's victory over Roy Moore in the Alabama senate election, and the response to it led Abrams to respond, "I'm hopeful that this isn't just a moment, but a pattern of behavior where we're not only willing to say 'thank you,' but are willing to invest in the vision of women of color and black women whose political leadership is absolutely essential for the 21st century."[113] In the same way, political strategist and commentator Symone Sanders was quoted in that moment saying, "Black women have been attempting to save America since the dawn of time. That doesn't mean we should allow the fate of America to be laid at the feet of black women."[114]

While players and journalists recognized the role of the WNBPA, Fair Fight Action, and other organizations in Warnock's success, these events also represented a moment when Black women's value and contributions remained acknowledged *only* within the bounds of their labor. This is echoed by WNBPA member Lexie Brown, who tweeted, "Lol @ the fact we had to literally FLIP

SENATE SEATS to get respected as WNBA players."[115] Throughout the 2020 WNBA season, members of the players association constantly illustrated that their actions—in organizing, in activism, and in their everyday actions with one another during the pandemic—were less about "saving" America, needing to be thanked, or even a demand to be "seen" or "heard." Instead, they consistently centered care for one another and the causes and families they highlighted throughout the season. Their organizing emerged out of a sense of care for the Atlanta Dream roster in the face of the team owner's bigotry, an engagement with her opponent's political aims, and the collective desire to respond with intention. In shifting from a results-oriented lens to a framework engaged in process, I take up Joshua Chambers-Letson's call to examine "a blackened time and space that fosters and facilitates performances of Black care and as Black power."[116] I ask what it might mean that these athletes adhere Breonna Taylor's name to themselves as a movement not of visibility but of care, knowing how the (non)being and (non)presence of Black womanhood operates in both life and death. Through this framework, it might make sense that care emerges from these athletes in moments of rampant viral and racial precarity, that vigils can take place the same day as blatant performances of resistance as players revoke their labor and draw bullet holes on white shirts. This care might then coalesce around Kimberlé Crenshaw's #SayHerName campaign, using digital platforms to amplify the voices of those mothers testifying on behalf of slain Black women whose names remain illegible to far too many. Perhaps at its most instructive, it might be about disagreement, operating in moments of tension where it is hardest to hear one another. In each of these moments, care and/as power create new openings, new possibilities for forward momentum, one season at a time.

The crossover requires a combination of embodied knowledge and dexterity, or what Samantha Sheppard calls "critical muscle memory." For Black folks, the memory of racial violence and collective resistance informs how we move through space.[117] Sheppard applies this primarily to sports films (and other mediated forms), and her work is particularly key in considering the documentary *144* in conversation with technological tools that connected WNBA athletes with scholars and activists during the COVID-19 pandemic. Black athletes in particular encounter sport as a site of racial projection and athletic enclosure that requires work to "get free" as they navigate between sports stardom and the everyday Black experience.[118] Sporting blackness is not merely a state of being but, as Sheppard argues, "an action, mode and modality, or occurrence of bodily expression that is constantly being repeated, reinforced, risked, and revised."[119]

At the same time, a key partner in the crossover throughout this chapter is in the pauses, the moments of hesitation. On the court, the "hesi" is a basketball move where a pause, a fleeting moment, occurs before a rapid pivot in a new direction. Black studies scholar Joshua Myers writes in *Of Black Study* that "hesitation is a creative force. . . . Space must be created to make sure we do not close off other kinds of possibilities. So, hesitation is a moment of both refusal and imagination."[120] This brief stoppage does not prevent progress; instead, it allows for new openings, which Myers argues allow us to "imagine what it is to be on the road to repair, to life transformed by breaking free. . . . To hesitate is to begin to resist one's negation."[121] Following the shooting of Jacob Blake, the hesitation by the WNBPA allowed a regrouping, a key reset that enabled the union to return to its core cause, not merely reactionary but actively engaged in a deep investment to one another and the #SayHerName campaign.

This particular season also highlights the importance of intersectionality not only as theory but also, as political scientist Ange-Marie Hancock Alfaro employs it, as an empirical paradigm. Crenshaw, in responding to how she's seen the concept taken up within some academic spaces, writes, "My own take on how to know intersectionality has been to do intersectionality. . . . I've consistently learned more from what scholars and activists have done with intersectionality than from what others have speculated about its appeal."[122] These athletes' engagement in "doing" intersectionality not only allowed tangible wins during and following the election cycle but also offered a clinic in how feminist practice operates in real time. Chandra Talpade Mohanty writes, "Feminist practice as I understand it operates at a number of levels: at the level of daily life through the everyday acts that constitute our identities and relational communities; at the level of collective action in groups, networks, and movements constituted around feminist visions of social transformation; and at the levels of theory, pedagogy, and textual creativity in the scholarly and writing practices of feminists engaged in the production of knowledge."[123] At each level, both the *144* film and media coverage surrounding the Wubble vividly illustrate how these athletes actively chose to care for one another in their everyday struggles during the pandemic, collectively organize their labor and resources, and partner with Crenshaw and the mothers behind the #SayHerName campaign. In doing so, they relied upon the organization's expertise and embodied knowledge to elevate their platform and educate themselves (and others) as athletes. The 2020 WNBA season reflects Chambers-Letson's work when he writes, "This present, though forged through and against myriad histories of black life's negation, is still rich with the possibility for intraracial sociality, care, and self-recognition among and between black people."[124]

New Collective Considerations

In a different film's opening scene, we see Nneka Ogwumike once again. This time, it's October 2023, and the viewer takes in a collective bargaining meeting of the WNBPA. She's standing in a conference room and tells the committee, "Today's really a huge growth moment. I think about what we were doing in '19 and '20, and we can think about how far we've come from then."[125]

Released in January 2024, *Shattered Glass: A WNBPA Story* is a Tubi-produced documentary that once again illuminates the invisible labor of organizing, the long haul of doing work that may not see the light of day for quite some time. The WNBPA's October meeting took place twelve months before the November 2024 deadline to opt out of its current agreement with the league and begin bargaining for new gains. Surrounded by the WNBPA executive committee, including first vice president Kelsey Plum, executive director Terri Jackson, and AFL-CIO president Liz Shuler, Nneka tells the group, "It's about being on top of our game. . . . It's just all about standing together, understanding what's at the table, and what things could look like in the future and the options that we have. I'm looking forward to the conversation and the revelations that we have today for things that don't just affect the WNBPA and its members."[126] Always thinking in conversation and collaboration, Ogwumike echoes the next steps for a league and union experiencing unparalleled growth and expansion in terms of popularity but still looking for key inroads in revenue sharing and travel accommodations.

With the growing catalog of documentaries on women's basketball and more current and former athletes moving into media spaces, it remains important to continue to consider how athletic labor is depicted on-screen across race, gender, and sexuality, among other identity markers. In offering a documentary centered on activism, *144* offers a response to timelines of athlete activism that exclude the work of female athletes, whether lamenting the "lack" of outspoken athletes or the hypercommodification assumed to be a barrier to an activist praxis.[127] In their work, Jennifer McClearen and Mia Fischer remind us that a lack of mainstream coverage of these athletes and their activism does not mean the content creation isn't happening: "It is thus crucial for sports scholars to pay attention to the venues through which the activism of marginalized women, queer, and trans athletes circulates as well as the type of fans and sports audiences they attract."[128] That *144* and *Shattered Glass* depict queer athletes outside the standardized coming-out narrative or the isolation of queerness within sport is important.[129] That these films eschew the individual journey for a collective identity as a union and as a league is crucial in dismantling the singular neoliberal narrative frequently invoked in the sport documentary genre, specifically in the coverage of queer athletes. What does it mean to watch these documentaries, to consume the political struggles and successes of these athletes?

Fleetwood considers how we are implicated in this system: "We audience members and fans are a crucial party in the contractual agreement that regulates the value and usage of human (and other animal) bodies in athletics. Because of the particular emotional and financial investment of fans in athletics, the racial icon in sports registers differently than in other sectors of entertainment culture."[130] To document these "racial icons" outside the narrow frames of representational politics or racial achievements is to see them as people who are in tears moments before offering powerful words in front of a microphone. To capture their organizing strategies in real time moves beyond historical renderings of "progress" and overdue flowers. In particular, the documentary genre allows for the so-called serious considerations too often left out of bounds. In considering films such as *Fist of Freedom: The Story of the '68 Olympic Games* (1999) and *Salute* (2008), Emily Plec and Shaun M. Anderson argue that sport documentaries "enable the social actors of sport to transcend the entertainment realm . . . through the construction of public memory of their significant political statements."[131] That *144* and other films will contribute to the public memory of 2020 feels crucial given how swiftly so many of the gains and discourses of that year seemingly slipped away in just a few years' time.

In the following chapter, I examine how many of the athletes of the WNBPA approach their labor in the offseason as competitors in professional leagues around the world. Combining media coverage, social media posts, interviews, and participant observation conducted in the United States, Russia, and France, I argue that the very act of translating one's labor is steeped in a series of strategies with geopolitical ramifications.

Translating Timeouts

The Choreography of Playing Overseas

Basketball is universal; however, overseas it's a different game
. . . depending on who you are and what you look like.

—Rebecca Harris

On March 5, 2022, Russian news media released weeks-old footage of Brittney Griner, a professional basketball player, being detained in Moscow's Sheremetyevo International Airport. In the video, Griner is seen placing her belongings on a security conveyer belt, followed by airport employees going through her belongings and eventually requiring her to sign documents before she is escorted away. Since 2015, Griner, a Team USA Olympic gold medalist and WNBA champion, had played in Russia for UMMC Ekaterinburg, contributing to four of the team's EuroLeague championships in 2016, 2018, 2019, and 2021. Like the majority of the WNBA's players, Griner competed internationally to supplement her stateside summer salary. In the ten months of media coverage published during Griner's detainment, many journalists, pundits, and bloggers questioned why Griner and other US professional basketball players competed in Russia and other countries at all. In many ways, the transient careers of women's basketball players reflect what Mark Falcous and Joseph Maguire describe as "sports-related mobilities that occur beyond the gaze of media and frequently at the margins of public discourse."[1] That the central questions surrounding Griner's detainment failed to conceptualize these global flows speaks to how this labor is obscured from mainstream sport.

The video circulated around the world during Russia's most recent invasion of Ukraine, an aggressive military tactic escalating the ongoing

Russo-Ukrainian War, a conflict between the two countries that began in 2014. The historical Cold War tensions between the United States and Russia, coupled with US opposition to the invasion and financial support to Ukraine, weighed Griner's detainment with immense geopolitical ramifications.[2] In 2022 these uneasy political relations extended to basketball once again with the introduction of the Putin Accountability Act in the US House of Representatives, which sought to impose the toughest sanctions on Russia in US history and included oligarchs such as Iskander Makhmudov, owner of UMMC Ekaterinburg, Griner's Russian team.[3]

As Griner awaited trial in a Russian prison, the 2022 WNBA season began and with it a sharp focus on the necessary steps to bring her home. Griner's initials and jersey number were etched across the sideline of each court, and the league and its players created posts urging the White House to advocate for her release; they also wore merchandise bearing her name and image. Outside of the WNBA, merchandise proclaiming "We Are BG" circulated across arenas and social media platforms. The phrase, whether on T-shirts or used as a hashtag, seemingly aimed to humanize the specificity of Griner's experience and keep her plight in the spotlight. However, with every post or picture bearing the phrase, I contemplated how many of those proclaiming #WeAreBG (especially her NBA counterparts) would never face the precarity of their labor in quite the same way.

Griner's identity as a Black, queer, masculine-presenting woman makes her experience unique in a sports-media complex that consistently read her as Other and not sufficiently woman due to both her dynamic performance on the court and her gender presentation off it. This chapter considers how and why US women's basketball players compete abroad, detailing the level of ingenuity and resilience necessary to translate their labor and legitimize their economic and cultural value. In *The Global Sports Arena: Athletic Talent Migration in an Interdependent World*, John Bale and Joseph Maguire argue that these migratory patterns are not new but that the process itself has significantly accelerated.[4] Using participant observation conducted in Russia (2018) and France (2022) in tandem with interviews and content analysis, I consider how these athletes choreograph careers and lives beyond the expectations and constrictions of overseas play. In considering the business of international basketball, I argue that the value and terms of their labor are constantly monitored, regulated, and (when winning) celebrated and desired as bodies representing athletic dominance read through both race and national identity and mediated across various platforms.

Choreographing a Career

JANUARY 11, 2018 | МЕЖДУНАРОДНЫЙ АЭРОПОРТ КАЗАНЬ
(KAZAN INTERNATIONAL AIRPORT) | KAZAN, RUSSIA

I'm standing in the baggage claim area in the Kazan International Airport waiting for my luggage. As the conveyer belt jerks to life, I look around me. Advertisements for American restaurant chains—one for Coyote Ugly, the other for Twin Peaks—include images of women wearing cowboy hats and flannel shirts tied up to their cleavage. I'm fascinated at the thought of these two franchises making it to this small airport five hundred miles from Moscow. As the waiting crowd dwindles, I begin to think the worst—my baggage didn't make it. The conveyer belt halts suddenly; no more bags.

I soon find myself in a small office with a middle-aged woman and a young man in his early twenties who work for the airport. The woman, visibly exasperated by my lack of Russian, attempts to assist me in completing the claim form. Her coworker and I frantically use our translation apps to figure out how to exchange basic information to procure the bag. As we struggle to communicate, it all begins to sink in: *I'm in a new country. I don't speak the language. I don't have any clothes on this continent besides the ones on my back. How am I going to figure any of this out?* For a moment, I experience on the smallest scale what it's like for thousands of athletes who travel each fall across borders, through airports, and into gyms around the world to compete in professional basketball leagues. In doing so, they are constantly asked to translate their lives and labor.

Separated from my luggage on that freezing Russian winter night, I step outside of baggage claim, where Cierra Burdick is waiting for me, a familiar face after over twenty-four hours of travel. Burdick is a professional basketball player I first met during the 2015 WNBA season working for the Los Angeles Sparks. Back then, I trailed behind her, a newly drafted first-round pick, for a preseason media day, ensuring she successfully reached each station: hair and makeup, green screen recordings for the jumbotron, and interviews with local and national media outlets. In between shoots, she shared that she had signed an offseason contract to play for Napoli, a team in the Italian Serie A1 League. Before suiting up for her first WNBA game in the States, she already considered her professional career a transnational one. Burdick and I kept in touch as she played for several teams in the WNBA and internationally in Italy and Israel. Following her 2017 WNBA season with the San Antonio Stars, she moved once more to Kazan, a city in the Russian Republic of Tatarstan to play for Kazanochka, a team in the Professional Basketball League (PBL). After I interviewed her virtually via Skype, she invited me to Russia to observe many of the aspects of her life as an athlete constantly negotiating her life and labor around the world.

At the airport I explain my situation to Cierra. She enters the baggage claim office and attempts to communicate with the two employees, who seem even more confused now that not one but two Black women who cannot speak Russian are in this office. It is just past one in the morning, but Cierra decides to call her team manager in the hopes that she can translate the situation for everyone. After groggily answering the phone, Cierra's manager is kind enough to negotiate the appropriate answers for the airline and arranges to have my bag delivered, should it appear, to the gym.[5]

Back at Cierra's apartment, a spacious one-bedroom condo belonging to her team's owner, I slip into a borrowed T-shirt and basketball shorts; she instantly laughs at my petite frame drowning in fabric. In this moment (and many others that follow), there is a unique insider-outsider relationship between Cierra and me; she appreciates having some semblance of familiarity, given that I am a Black American woman who speaks English and is familiar with so many facets of and figures within the game we both love. At the same time, I am distinctly an outsider, given I am not an athlete; my stature typically renders me at least six inches shorter than the shortest player on the court. Jet-lagged, I wash the only clothes in my possession, hang them to dry, and try to drift off to sleep.

In many ways, Cierra and the other athletes who animate this chapter represent what Seungbum Lee denotes as "unorthodox sport labour migration," a reverse routing of the normative expectation that "making it" involves a roster spot in a US professional league.[6] This "out-migration," Lee writes, suggests that global sport currently operates differently from how it worked in the past.[7] However, this notion of out-migration largely obscures how women's basketball has operated for decades. Whereas male players who choose to play overseas often do so after failing to secure an NBA contract, the top women's basketball players in the United States translate their labor overseas due to a lack of consistent professional opportunities. Even with the longevity of the WNBA, limited roster spots in a twelve-team summer league require some of the best basketball players in the world to board international flights each year to continue their careers.

Off the court, players also must maneuver cultural shifts, varying schedules, and significant time zone differences. This transition is easier for athletes like Rebecca Harris, who acclimated to living around the world at a young age. Harris, who grew up in a military family, began playing basketball when she was three years old in the Philippines and lived in Japan and Germany before moving to the United States for high school. "[Basketball] was the only constant that allowed me to introduce myself to others without having to speak very much," she told me. "And for me, without basketball, it would've been ten times harder. It was already hard. You know, you're the Black kid, the new kid, the Black girl who's an athlete. You kind of stand out in different ways. . . . Basketball did the talking for me. And that was the only constant in my life for so long."

For this reason, it should be noted that not all transnational sporting mobilities are created equal. Joshua I. Newman and Mark Falcous write, "The economic dimensions of labour mobility are entwined with identity politics, where issues of attachment to place, eligibility, and allegiances are significant."[8] The relocating and dislocating of sporting bodies are undoubtedly affected by talent, but they are also restricted by the matrix of domination, where race, gender, religion, and nationality shape both the ability to maneuver across borders and the reception an athlete receives upon arrival. Joseph Maguire identifies five categories of transnational sporting labor: (1) pioneers—those dedicated to growing the game and increasing a sport's popularity; (2) settlers—those who permanently relocate their lives and settle down in a new country; (3) mercenaries—those whose migratory patterns are strictly rooted in employment opportunities that require them to constantly move to new locales; (4) nomadic cosmopolitans—those who translate their labor in order to travel around the world and experience various cultures; and (5) returnees—those returning to their country of origin to compete professionally.[9] Colonial language aside, most of the athletes interviewed in this chapter fall into the "mercenary" category, one primarily motivated by financial gain.[10] However, as Jonathan Magee and John Sugden articulate in their research, motivations for sporting mobilities do not fit neatly into singular categories.[11] Some athletes, for example, may primarily translate their labor for financial reasons (mercenaries) but ultimately sign with a team located in a country or region most appealing to them in terms of travel (nomadic cosmopolitans). Athletes from other countries may compete stateside for their collegiate careers and return to their home nations to compete professionally following their NCAA eligibility (returnees).

Following interviews with professional soccer players, Magee and Sugden build upon previous models of global sporting labor, adding four categories: (1) ambitionists—those who have a strong desire to pursue a professional career anywhere but can aim to achieve an ideal country or team, based on living conditions or level of talent; (2) exiles—athletes motivated to maneuver their labor due to threats to their personal safety or career in their country of origin, often due to their own racial, ethnic, or national identity; (3) expelled—those forced to continue their careers elsewhere based upon their own behavior and/or issues with a league or team; and (4) celebrity superstars—those who command major headlines and contracts and find themselves part of the global popular culture landscape.[12] Magee and Sugden recognize that these categories are not fixed, that athletes' motivations to migrate their sporting labor are subject to change. Rebecca Harris, who began her professional career in Prague, described her career trajectory as one aligned with the ambitionist category:

> When you understand the way some of these things work, then you should be able to see the climb and know which countries are more competitive, which countries pay more, which countries are better for your career. . . . I was on a team that was near the bottom of the league, and it was my first opportunity. . . . I was in a pretty decent league that had a top-tier team that was in first place and also in my same city. . . . How do I get to that point? And I would take notes, I would set goals, see where their superstars landed in certain areas. . . . And so every year after that, taking those same notes, I would make the climb.

The perks and privileges that NCAA athletes received during their collegiate careers can surpass what they experience as professionals. In a *30 for 30* podcast on their experiences playing professionally in Russia, Sue Bird and Diana Taurasi described the abrupt transition from their time at the University of Connecticut to the WNBA. "Charters, best hotels, best gear, and then alright, my next stop is the pro game; it's only gonna get better," Taurasi said.[13] She was surprised to discover not only her pay in the WNBA ("$45,000 . . . that's what I'm going to make?!?!") but also the sharp difference in what overseas markets offered. "I think I was in the $200,000 range . . . for like four or five months [of work]," Bird said. In Moscow, Bird and Taurasi played together for Dynamo Kursk during a season Taurasi described as "the worst experience ever of playing basketball in my life." She vowed to never go back again but later returned to Russia when she received an offer too lucrative to turn down, one brimming with not only a massive salary but also life-changing fringe benefits. "The only reason you go there is for money," Taurasi said in the podcast. "That is the only reason you leave your country to go to a different country to play basketball."[14]

Pronouncing Putin

Before I arrived in Kazan, Cierra posted a video to her Instagram story in which she realizes, in attempting to discuss Russian president Vladimir Putin with her teammates, that "Putin" is pronounced differently in a Russian context; her attempt to engage in a political discussion with them was lost in translation from the beginning. The timing of her travel and her attempt to engage in political dialogue with her teammates are important: news headlines were circulating daily detailing Russia's involvement in the 2016 US presidential election, with constant updates and evidence suggesting that the Trump administration is a by-product of foreign tampering. Within sport, Russia's role in administering performance-enhancing drugs to its athletes had recently been documented in detail through the Oscar Award–winning documentary *Icarus* (2017) and punished through the exclusion of athletes competing under the Russian flag during the Olympic Games.

Throughout its history, the Soviet Union and later Russia utilized sport as a nation-building mechanism. Key Soviet sporting concepts included (1) "the harmonious development of body and mind"; (2) "Russian physical culture and sport from Russian soil"; (3) "faith in the common people"; and (4) "physical effort as the source of dignity, morality and happiness."[15] As they have in other nation-states, sporting infrastructure and participation aligned with the ebbs and flows of the country's political strife, unification, and in-dustrialization. For example, following the Russo-Japanese War in 1904–5, sport was used in Russia to quell dissent and redirect young citizens away from revolutionary activity.[16] Even though Russia was a founding member of the modern Olympics, competing in the 1900, 1908, and 1912 games, as the political landscape shifted, Russia began hosting its own national Olym-piads in 1913 and withdrew from the Olympics from 1920 to 1948.[17] At that time, sport operated as a means of disciplining the mind and body through physical activity to form the optimal Communist citizen, and Soviet leaders shunned the notion of competitive sport until the 1930s. Then, organized sport societies formed around trades, and the industrialization of nation and sport grew simultaneously.

Basketball teams formed in Russia in the early 1900s, with Mayak, a St. Petersburg sports club, competing against other Russian teams and eventu-ally touring across the United States beginning in 1906.[18] However, the sport, like others, became entrenched in a broader Cold War battle between the two countries in the second half of the twentieth century.

Weeks before I departed for Russia, I ran into an interviewee from a previ-ous research project on Black basketball players competing internationally. He told me that he had recently starred in his first film, which required him to spend a significant amount of time in Russia during shooting. The film, a sports drama titled *Going Vertical* (2017), recounts the men's gold medal basketball game at the 1972 Summer Olympics between the Soviet Union and the United States. Cast as a member of Team USA, he described the surreal feeling of re-creating what is considered Russia's version of the "Miracle on Ice." Whereas the phrase references the 1980 medal-round hockey victory of the United States over the Soviet Union in that year's Winter Olympics as a cultural win over a Cold War foe, Russia's own "miracle" occurred on the hardwood in 1972. The United States, on a sixty-three-win streak in interna-tional play, lost to the Soviet Union in the last three seconds on a controver-sial clock reset that remains one of the most contested moments in Olympic history. The game has been called "sport's Cold War" but can perhaps only be considered a singular battle in a much larger, longer sporting warfare be-tween the two countries, with clashes taking place across the women's game as well.[19] Within a month of its release, *Going Vertical* became the highest-grossing domestic film of all time in Russia. When I arrived, Lera, one of the managers for Kazanochka, told me she had already seen the film twice. The popularity of *Going Vertical* could perhaps reflect what Adele Marie Barker articulates as a sense of nostalgia surrounding the Soviet Union, where the current Russian consumer remains engaged with artifacts and stereotypes of the past as a connection to the lost Soviet subject.[20] In the winter of 2018, as the country prepared to host the Fédération Internationale de Football Association (FIFA) Men's World Cup, Cierra's time in Russia offered her an unparalleled perspective located at the intersection of sport and politics, but not always with the correct pronunciation.

About Kazan

Kazan, the capital of the Republic of Tatarstan, is the sixth most populous city in Russia, with over 1.2 million inhabitants. Located about five hundred miles from Moscow, it is considered the sports capital of Russia, given its role as host city to a variety of global sports tournaments (eight world championships over the past eight years). Kazanochka, the city's professional women's basketball team, was founded in 1946 and competed during the 2017–18 season in Russia's Professional Basketball League (PBL). While located in the most competitive league in the country, Kazanochka is considered an underdog to the aforementioned Dynamo Kursk and UMMC Ekaterinburg, two teams whose owners offer some of the highest salaries in the world to attract top foreign talent, especially from the United States. Kazanochka, on the other hand, has struggled to maintain its status both financially and athletically within this league.

The Basket-Hall serves as the home arena for both Kazanochka and a men's professional team, the Unics. "Mama" Vika, one of the best Russian players on the team, comments sarcastically one day while we are driving to the arena for practice, "We practice more, [but the men's team] play[s] more games." Cierra agrees, noting the constant two-a-day practices and sparse game schedule that often involves away games with long commutes. "The men's team has nicer stuff and more money," Cierra tells me. We walk to the practice facilities across the hall; she's right. Later, in the women's weight room, I'm told that all of the equipment consists of hand-me-downs from the Unics. Sexism is seemingly one of the most consistent translations throughout my time with Kazanochka and in my interviews with athletes competing around the world.

Translating the Game

It's a strange feeling to have déjà vu in a new place. Walking into Kazanochka's locker room, I am immediately transported to a scene in Gina Prince-Bythewood's cult classic *Love and Basketball* (2000), where the main character, Monica (Sanaa Lathan), competes abroad in Spain, thousands of miles away from her friends and family. In one scene, Monica sits alone in the locker room, taping her own ankle as the head coach delivers an emphatic pregame speech in Spanish. At one point, his voice lowers as he points at Monica, and he smiles as he gestures with pride. Following his impassioned pep talk, she approaches a teammate and asks, "Luisa, what did he say?" Luisa simply responds, "He said to give the ball to you."[21] Monica processes this and with a singular expression seems to realize her responsibility as the star of the team. Foreign players, especially Americans, are expected to outperform their homegrown counterparts, bearing the bulk of the burden of ensuring a winning record. At my first practice, I meet Merritt Hempe, nicknamed "Lil Mama" by Cierra, who is the only other American on the team. At six feet four, she hardly lives up to her nickname. She ties her long, blonde hair into a high ponytail and ties her shoes as Cierra explains to me that this is their second time as teammates. The first time, almost a decade before, was on an Amateur Athletic Union (AAU) team when they were both in high school. Since then, they've often played with or against each other in varying capacities. Many Americans competing internationally find camaraderie with other US players not only because of their status as outsiders but also because many competed with or against one another over the course of their careers.

Despite differences in their outward appearances, Cierra's and Merritt's responsibilities on the court are both read and judged by the team's coaches and management in similar terms. As American athletes, both players are expected to outperform their Russian teammates and bear the bulk of responsibility of securing team victories each game. Merritt explained:

> Before every game here, they're like pulling me aside and telling me it's such an important game and we have to make playoffs this year. . . . You'll see them say it to Cierra, too, and like nobody else. Definitely last year [in Germany], if we lost, it was my fault that we lost even if I had twenty points, sixteen rebounds, did everything I could, and my person didn't score. It was my fault we lost. . . . Basketball has always been a crazy passion, and now I really have to look at it as just a job.

She seems disappointed in seeing the game as "just a job" but acknowledges the difference in the expectations she faced as a college athlete in the States and her labor here as one of the highest-paid athletes on the court. While Merritt and Cierra negotiate substantial contracts, their teammates make significantly less, which also correlates to the expectations levied toward them in practice and during games.

This is not unique to Kazanochka or even Russian basketball. Chelsea Davis, a player who previously competed in Ecuador, Spain, and Romania, runs a YouTube channel chronicling her life abroad. In one video, she echoes this notion: "As Americans, we get held up to a certain level of playing, and it has to be full on, score twenty-plus buckets per game no matter how many minutes you play. That's all good and dandy, but if they don't like your playing style, you're not going to be playing many minutes."[22] Here, Davis signals the expectation that Americans should thrive in any system, and should they fail to succeed, their minutes (and potentially their careers) will be cut short. Multiple players I interviewed agreed, noting the requirement to outperform domestic players and prove themselves each game. This reflects what Joseph Maguire describes as the "Americanization" of sport around the world, in the hopes that the "'entertainment' they would provide would produce several benefits, but above all more sponsorship and media coverage, increased attendance figures, greater participation rates and improved playing standards."[23] Elizabeth Williams, the lone American on her team in China, described the situation this way in an interview: "You're expected to do everything, so the pressure is a lot higher for you to perform well. When you're playing in China, they honestly just care about points, because even if you lose games but score forty, like the managers and owners are pretty happy." Seungbum Lee argues that sporting labor is outsourced for several reasons, including cost minimization, quality improvement, and resource access: "More than the possible intangible contributions the foreign athletes may bring to the team, such as leadership or big league experience, they are expected to produce immediate quantifiable impact on the team."[24] Rebecca Harris, who competed in the Czech Republic, Greece, Poland, Turkey, Germany, and Ukraine, confirmed this as she shared how her first season shaped her approach to the game: "I was on a team with no English-speaking teammates, no American teammates. . . . You're expected to handle a lot of the burden anyway. Like you're gonna be the main scorer . . . you know, do a lot of things."

Being the only American has ramifications off the court as well. Merritt joined Kazanochka a month before Cierra and maintained a significantly different impression of both Kazan and the team, given that she felt ostracized immediately. As we sit together on the gym floor after practice one day, she tells me, "People wouldn't try to speak with me, people wouldn't invite me anywhere. It was completely, like, me . . . and everybody else. I definitely gave up trying to build friendships. . . . At the beginning, before Cierra and Lena [Jelena Vucetic, a player from Montenegro and the only other non-Russian] were here, I just gave up. I was like, 'I'm just here to do my job, and I'll never see them again.'" She described herself through her Russian teammates' eyes as "an outsider, a foreigner, an alien, basically." This struggle to fit in reflects what Rebecca told me in an interview regarding her ability to adapt to new countries, players, and the game itself:

> You know, if anything, this path in my life playing basketball and bouncing from space to space, country to country, what have you, I've learned to persevere. I've learned to adapt. I've learned to communicate with others, whether we're speaking English or not. You know, someone who's lived in Georgia their entire life, you go to the University of Georgia, and then your opportunity to play professionally takes you to Turkey. And you've never even been out of the country, let alone been out of your own state too often. I've seen it kill so many people's careers 'cause they weren't prepared to adapt to a different life, a different culture.

The relationships foreign players have with locals on their team vary significantly from one country to another. The previous season, Merritt played for a team in Germany: almost all her teammates spoke English, and her coach was an American. Since her family is German and she had relatives living in Munich, the transition to playing overseas was much easier. In Russia, however, she has struggled to navigate this team and has relied on her fellow foreign players, Cierra and Lena, as well as a team manager named Valeria "Lera" Shuvagina, often referred to as "L," in order to survive socially. Cierra, on the other hand, has adjusted to her life in Kazan and is easily one of the most popular players on the team both on and off the court. As we enter practice or the locker room, her Russian teammates light up and greet her warmly; she is seen as the bridge between the Russian nationals and the imported players, and she navigates this role effortlessly. In an interview, Cierra mentioned that there is sometimes animosity when Americans join international leagues because their presence means that a local starter will automatically lose her position. In Italy, she faced one particularly contentious teammate who refused to acknowledge her for a significant portion of the season. Other players, she told me, felt as if the presence of foreign players, especially Americans, increased their chances of winning and advancing to a championship, so they were less possessive about relinquishing their starting role. When I interviewed Rebecca Harris, she echoed this and added, "You know, you have to watch your surroundings at all times, and you'll figure out who's with it and who's not with it. There's always within a team of ten or twelve, there might be two or three that really are pissed off that you are there, and they wanna show . . . 'You're in my country, and they didn't need to go out and get Americans, 'cause we can play, too.' . . . If you're playing the same position, like—you'll feel it. You'll feel it before you hear it." When I asked her what "feeling it" looked like, she said, "If we're playing one-on-one . . . they're gonna do a little extra to try and show who they think is better—'Coach, watch me, I'm better.' I'm very well aware you feel some type of way, but I'm also, you know, okay with letting you know I'm here for a reason, . . . because if you was able to handle it, they wouldn't have got me. It's that simple."

Watching Kazanochka practice, I settle into a seat on the sidelines, taking in the rhythm and fluidity of those on the court. There is a rather simplistic beauty in basketball—so much is unspoken in the repetition of hand slaps after each rotation, offering up a mutual respect. While there may be language barriers between Cierra and her teammates, there is seemingly a communicative power of sport that erodes any verbal miscues that may arise—for the most part. As the coach barks out the next drill, Cierra makes eye contact with me and shrugs; she has no idea what he's saying. By the end of the practice, the coach is visibly upset, as are the players. As he ends practice, he yells at the team in Russian. When I asked about the practice the next day, Merritt told me, "If he's screaming, I don't even ask for the translation. . . . I don't even want to know." Several players described using either broken English or hand signals to communicate with coaches and players who don't speak the same language.

The game itself varies from country to country, requiring an additional act of translation by players engaged in these sporting mobilities whether in the pace of play or officiating. Elizabeth Williams told me, "In EuroLeague in general, you have better coaches; like, a lot of them have coached a national team at some level. I mean, the players are more skilled for sure, but the level drops off dramatically after those players." Both Merritt and Cierra described the difference in playing overseas and how they've had to translate their approach on the court. Merritt told me that the slower tempo of the game in Russia (and in Europe in general) creates a more methodical style of play, with more controlled plays and where improvisation is discouraged.

As they run plays one day in practice, the head coach yells directions in Russian, and teammates take turns translating to Cierra and Merritt, often without enough time to relay the message. Timing feels off the entire session; there is no sense of hustle, no attempt at urgency in retrieving errant balls or resetting for drills. Merritt and Cierra are both visibly frustrated. Several times, Cierra attempts to intervene during horribly executed plays or ask follow-up questions about where she should be, only to be shrugged off or misunderstood completely by her coaches. I can feel the tension in the gym; the lack of cohesion seems concerning, given the game the following day against Dynamo Kursk, one of the best teams in the league. They spend more money, bring in better players, and, in Cierra's opinion, do more to prepare for each game. In the last game against Kursk, Kazanochka may have been outmatched on paper but had a chance on the court. "We could have won that game—we were down by twenty and ended up losing by five. We just didn't prepare," Cierra laments.

In basketball, preparation takes the form of watching film on both the opponent and your own team, critiquing and adapting your own game while strategizing against your opponent by looking for patterns of play. Cierra tells me that for games against powerhouses like Kursk and UMMC, the coach doesn't watch film on those teams or even his own, essentially considering the game an unavoidable loss. This obviously disappoints Cierra, who sees every game as winnable and who is understandably frustrated, since she is expected to dominate regardless of the amount of preparation or resources provided to her and her team. She described to me the moments leading up to the game as the "calm before the storm—or the blowout."

Translating Race

This chapter shares similarities with Munene Mwaniki's work in *The Black Migrant Athlete: Media, Race, and the Diaspora in Sports* in dissecting the role of "the globally contested terrain of sport in the maintenance of white supremacy and simultaneous adoption and contestation of sport by non-whites around the globe."[25] Mwaniki delves into the experiences of Black African immigrant athletes (men and women) across several sports, noting recurring tropes of the "good" foreigner or the "backward" country of origin. However, what is perhaps most instructive in his work is how these athletes are employed as model minorities while also being subject to anti-Blackness through their experience with teams and leagues, as well as their everyday experience in a new country. In taking a diasporic, multisport lens, Mwaniki offers a broad, vivid picture of how Black athletes experience the global sports-media complex and exploit normative frames to their advantage.

Sport sociologist Ben Carrington defines the Black athlete as a "political entity and a *global sporting racial project*."[26] In *Race, Sport and Politics: The Sporting Black Diaspora*, he argues that sport reproduces race in important ways that affect how Blackness is understood off the court and outside the field of play. For athletes traversing global basketball arenas, each national context contains new challenges for how athletes will be perceived in terms of either their utilization during the game or their off-day experiences. Elizabeth Williams noted the shifts she has seen as a Black woman athlete across various countries: "I feel like my Blackness stands out a lot more here [in China] than in Russia. . . . It's like people will try to take a picture of you when you're walking."

The history of Blackness in Russia is complicated by a variety of factions, including Black communists crossing over to Moscow and interacting with various activist groups, the recent rise in neo-Nazism, and the usage of Black hotep logics in Russian bots designed to tamper with the 2016 US presidential election.[27] Lera, the team manager for Kazanochka, shared her perspective as a Russian on Black American players: "Most of the Black people, they're just very lazy." Unsure if there is a language mishap to blame for her blatantly racist statement, I follow up, asking her, "Do you think Black people are lazy in general?" She backtracks, stating that she didn't want to say every Black person is lazy but that when she dated a Black player from the Unics, the men's team that shares the arena with Kazanochka, she felt he never cared about what was happening in Kazan. She complained that he only wanted to watch Netflix all day, which is why she described him (and, by her extension, an entire race) as lazy. I asked her if this was maybe not a symptom of laziness but perhaps a feeling of being removed from and not culturally connected to the city. When I followed up again and questioned his competitive nature on the court as perhaps a reason why "lazy" might be the wrong word, she admitted that his talent and work ethic challenged this notion of lazy and that "lazy people can't play basketball." I found her word choice interesting because she had just rattled off the names of so many Black players she had worked with who offered a variety of crossover experiences.

That Lera would collapse the experiences of so many into a singular term heavy with history and drenched in racist connotations gave me pause. The struggles that Lera described with her ex-boyfriend's preference to stay at home and watch TV are not unique to Russia. In her book *Breaking Through: Beating the Odds Shot after Shot*, Women's Basketball Hall of Famer Chamique Holdsclaw describes her first season competing for Kookmin Bank in Cheonan, South Korea, in the early 2000s as a repetitive cycle: "It felt like I was living the same day over and over. I would wake up, go to practice, eat, and then head back to my room to prepare to do it all over again the next day. I would call home to talk to family or listen to music in my free time. There wasn't much for me to do in the city where I played, and the walls began to close in on me."[28] She describes herself as being in a "dark place" while in Korea, but her following season in Valencia, Spain, felt different. One of her WNBA teammates played on her Spanish team, and she brought her college roommate along for her season abroad: "Valencia had a good social scene, and Murriel, who was fluent in Spanish, showed us around. Zakiah even rented a dance studio and taught hip-hop dance to the locals. We made friends, and it really felt like home."[29] Creating community with other Americans and later bringing a companion allowed Holdsclaw to shift her crossover experience into a positive one, one that eventually became a solace of sorts when her personal problems as a highly visible athlete in the United States became overwhelming.

Elizabeth described to me the rinse and repeat of waking up, eating, and practicing, which created a routinized monotony. As athletes continuously maneuver their labor around the world, I wondered what this whirlwind does to their sense of place and self. Aleš Sekot writes that "sport migrants may mostly have little sense of attachment to a specific space or local community. Their status and market value is derived mostly from the ethos of hard work, differential rewards and a win-at-all-costs approach."[30]

It seems as if Lera read foreign players (especially those who identify as Black Americans) through their interest in experiencing Russian culture;

there is a potential for mistranslation on her behalf (and mine) in this particular moment.

Community Crossovers

Approaching the gym doors for the final night of practice before the game, we realize we will have to wait before entering; Dynamo Kursk, Kazanochka's opponent, is still practicing. When the doors eventually open, we file into the gym as the players of Kursk break out of their final huddle. I see Cierra approach Angel McCoughtry, Epiphanny Prince, and Nneka Ogwumike, three Black Americans playing for Kursk. Cierra has played with each of them as teammates, whether on national teams, in AAU leagues, or in the WNBA. I also see Cierra's Russian teammates embracing several of Kursk's players; it's fascinating to see these warm embraces the night before a game. I greet Nneka, whom I knew previously from my time with the Sparks, and introduce myself to Epiphanny and Angel. Angel immediately asks me about my hair and how I handle wearing it natural in a Russian winter with a questionable water supply. We begin exchanging information about hair products and regimens; in that moment, I forget I'm in Russia.

Through these and other interactions, I notice the ways in which there are support networks among American players, especially Black women, whether in eating dinner together before or after a game, FaceTiming one another, or offering support via Instagram posts. "The best part [of playing internationally] for me is the travel," Rebecca told me. "It's getting to play with and amongst other athletes, sharing stories. . . . There's so many things that you really understand with one another that a lot of people can't relate to on the outside." There is also a sense of familiarity, which also dictates the decorum of the game. During the game the following day, Cierra falls taking a charge, and Nneka is the first one to offer to help her up instead of a Kazanochka teammate, perhaps speaking to their shared identity as Black women over the jerseys they wear.[31]

Community takes several forms for players abroad. It can begin as soon as players know where they are going, with Rebecca telling me, "Before I even sign to a team, I usually try and figure out who the other American is, and I'll just straight ask, 'Who else are we getting?' If I can touch base with them before we've even gotten over there and before we sign, great. I also want to get to know them. Like, this is somebody I'm gonna share a space with for eight months, you know?" The relationship built between players overseas is also dependent upon their previous experience: one person may be more of a veteran and have more insights on overseas life or a particular team or league that they can share with a rookie or otherwise less experienced player. Part of this investment is also about knowing that the behavior or performance of one player will reflect on another because of their shared race and nationality. "Although we didn't sign together as a package deal, we're a package deal," Rebecca said. "You mess up as the Black American here, they put two and two together always."

Translating Health

One day, as Cierra prepares for practice, I notice her taping her own hand and ankles with no medical professionals in sight. In the WNBA, athletic trainers attend every practice and game and along with team doctors utilize state-of-the-art technology to prevent and rehabilitate injuries. "We have a masseuse but no athletic trainer," she tells me. "We have to tape everything ourselves." In the same way the levels of talent vary across teams and leagues, so too do the facilities, medical resources, and training schedules available for players. In Russia, baked beans are sometimes served for breakfast on the road before game day, and players are responsible for their own athletic training before practice and games. When Kazanochka's assistant coach overhears Merritt complaining of insomnia, he suggests she drink beer before bed to ensure a good night's rest. In another moment, Cierra complains to Merritt about walking into the gym and seeing trash in the bleachers and unracked basketballs. She notes that it's not her job to pick up after other people, to which Merritt replies, "Girl, you are overseas—*everything* is your job." In transitioning to playing overseas, these players seemingly must evaluate their standards surrounding the game, as well as the established norms they enjoy stateside.

After one December game during her season in China, Elizabeth tweeted:

> The gym we played in tonight was so cold! I've never experienced that in my life. Both benches had fan heaters. Coaches were in their winter jackets. Remember we are INSIDE. It was so cold, everyone warmed up in jackets. Some even had gloves on. I had hand warmers in my pocket.

It was so cold, I could see the steam rising from my head. Mind you I'm in China, not Russia. And the kicker is that this gym is in the SOUTH of China. AKA closer to the equator. My hands were icicles all game. Unreal.[32]

Beyond the discomfort of playing in the chilly environment of the arena, the colder temperatures constrict blood vessels and tighten muscles, making it difficult for players to stay loose and ready to play off the bench and increasing the risk of injury in the process.

These discrepancies in medical care and training facilities often place these athletes in a precarious position, especially in the case of injury or illness. Earlier in the season, Cierra injured her knee during a game but didn't feel pain until dinner that night with the team. When she told Lera, one of the team managers, Lera responded, "What do you want me to do?" Cierra told me, "She was basically like, 'Shut up; you're fine.'" Lera, who was driving us as Cierra recounted this story, defended her inaction, claiming she was unaware of how dire the situation had become because Cierra finished the game and walked out of the gym seemingly okay. After dinner, Cierra waited until everyone had left the table before trying to get up, not wanting anyone on the team to see her struggle or know she was injured. She tells me:

> I got up and tried to walk. I can't even take a step. I can't put no weight on it. So I'm trying to call Merritt so she could come back and help me, because I wanted everybody else to leave. I didn't want anyone to see me. . . . I've never had pain in my knees like that before, and I'm kind of scared because . . . I'm in a foreign country. I don't just trust these doctors as it is. I have all of these emotions at once, so I only want Merritt to see me like this.

Cierra perceives Merritt as the only person who can "see" Cierra like this because of their long-standing friendship and Merritt's ability to understand what's at stake as a foreign player. Merritt and Lera helped Cierra make it to her apartment, but she ultimately decided to seek treatment in the United States to ensure she could finish out the season. Merritt had also faced a health scare earlier in the season, falling severely ill within her first weeks in Kazan because she had no idea she should not drink the tap water at her apartment. Having played the previous season in Germany, a country with higher water standards, she didn't question the safety of her faucet, nor did her teammates or managers alert her to the risk of drinking water that had not been boiled. Both Cierra's and Merritt's experiences point to the potential risks of playing abroad in terms not only of their physical health but also of their job security. The team's response to their health concerns remained rooted in their value on the court—the decision of whether to cut them from the team depended upon the terms of their contracts and the length of time predicted for their recovery.

At the same time, some teams are willing to financially secure an athlete's health when possible, given the higher injury risk of year-round labor that is demanded of WNBA players supplementing their salaries abroad. This is why perennial All-Star Diana Taurasi's team in Russia, UMMC Ekaterinburg, paid her hundreds of thousands of dollars in 2015 to sit out the WNBA season. Whereas the WNBA league maximum that season was $107,000, Taurasi made $1.5 million in Russia; her decision was prudent not only for her body but also for her wallet.[33] This difference is also made apparent through an injury sustained by WNBA star Breanna Stewart during a EuroLeague championship game; her ruptured Achilles tendon rippled not only across her team on the court in Hungary but also throughout the WNBA.[34] Her summer season stateside ended before it began; she spent the remainder of 2019 rehabilitating her body and preparing not only for another season abroad but also for the upcoming Summer Olympics.

Translating Finances

While substantial pay compared to their stateside options remains the primary reason US athletes transfer their labor overseas, securing a contract and ensuring timely payments are frequent issues. To negotiate their labor, players enlist agents who specialize in international contracts. This connection can occur near the end of a player's collegiate career, as it did with Rebecca. She told me, "I played for some coaches at Illinois who had some heavy hitters under their belt that have gone to play in the WNBA and overseas and high-level basketball. So letting them know that, 'Hey, I wanna continue playing.' They were like, 'Okay, cool, I have connections with a few agents, let's see what we can do.' . . . Just like anything, the network and relationships are everything." The oft-cited adage "it's who you know" is important for the initial entry into overseas basketball for many players. Rebecca also mentioned how important it is to consider the other athletes represented by an agent in order to gauge the priority hierarchy: "There's some agents out there that, under the radar, if you're not top notch and they don't see you up here [she moves her hand up vertically], [they will] talk down on you; they're not gonna help you get no jobs. They're gonna make sure that their cash cows are fed first obviously, and they work ten times harder for them versus . . . the twelfth man on the roster." She also mentioned that agents will turn down potential clients based on their age, the countries where they've previously competed, or their overall athletic résumé.

Another frequent issue for athletes abroad is receiving timely checks. Rebecca described payment problems in Greece and Turkey: "*That* is an urgency that transcends whatever I love about this sport. 'Cause there's an urgency that goes beyond a passion, right?" For other athletes, the irregular payment schedule is based on the team's relationship with other entities, such as sports gambling fixtures. Elizabeth shared, "When we would get our paycheck, if it was late, it was because the betting company was late, because I guess the clubs were paying money to the betting company, and then people bet, and then they get that money back, or however it works." The uncertainty of payment is disarming in any context of labor, but it is exacerbated with the precarity of living in another country thousands of miles away from those able to assist in a bind.

One night, Cierra mentions she is struggling to access her money within her Russian bank account and is concerned about paying important bills, such as her mortgage for her home in North Carolina and her cell phone. In previous countries, all her money had been directly deposited into her US account. However, in Russia, her Kazanochka employers required her to open a bank account in Kazan, significantly impacting her control over her own finances. She mentions all of this casually in passing, but the next day she tells me at breakfast that she fell asleep and woke up thinking about it. While playing overseas for higher salaries than the WNBA offers, Cierra finds herself unable to cover her domestic expenses. She notes that she's cautious about wiring herself money from her Russian bank account to her US account due to a previous incident when she inexplicably lost $700.

After a significant amount of research, she and I discover that this loss occurred as a result of the exchange rate changing drastically between the processing of her initial transfer and its arrival in her bank account; the time difference between the countries affected the translation of the currency when the markets reopened, costing her hundreds of dollars. This moment represents the difficulties of navigating global markets, as an athlete is also required to compete at the highest level, attend multiple practices almost every day, and find time to train for the upcoming season in the States.

In between practices, Cierra stays at the gym, attempting to determine the necessary resources and timing to access and transfer her money. After over an hour attempting this transfer online, she asks Lera if she would be willing to call the bank and translate with the Russian tellers in order to transfer Cierra's money safely. As Lera negotiates the transfer, she is asked to photograph and send sensitive financial information electronically, including Cierra's Social Security number. As Lera conducts all of these transactions on her phone, Cierra reminds Lera of the information's sensitive nature and asks her to delete the photo as soon as everything is sent. However, at dinner that night, Lera hands her phone to Cierra to look at some pictures and then heads to the bathroom. As she scrolls, Cierra sees that Lera did not delete her financial information and seems visibly frustrated. As she deletes the photo, she and Merritt tell me that in addition to being required to open a Russian bank account, they have to allow the team (primarily through Lera) to see all of their transactions. This often results in awkward conversations, during which Lera might approach Cierra and/or Merritt with detailed information of their whereabouts: "I see you ate at this restaurant yesterday—invite me the next time you go!" Both of them are resentful regarding the team's surveillance of their spending but feel they cannot assert themselves in any substantial way. The instability of their positions as players prevents them from taking full control of their finances and privacy.

One day as we prepare to head home after practice, Merritt and Cierra receive word that Lena, their teammate from Montenegro, missed practice due to the sudden death of her father. As the third non-Russian player (the PBL allows three non-Russians per team), Lena is close to both Americans. They find out that Margerita, a member of Kazanochka's front office, has given Lena three days to bury her father and return to the team, or her contract will be terminated immediately. Merritt expressed anger over Lena receiving such a short amount of time to grieve her father's death, especially given that Kazanochka had more than a week before the next game.

Merritt mentioned that many foreign players' contracts include a harsh penalty if the player leaves before the end of the season; Merritt's contract requires her to pay Kazanochka $30,000 if she quits. For players who experience a variety of hardships (such as the injury or death of a loved one) that require their immediate attention, navigating these financial penalties is difficult.

While on Instagram that evening, Merritt notices that the Kazanochka Twitter account created a bereavement post dedicated to Lena and her family. Both she and Cierra discussed the performativity of supporting players publicly while simultaneously requiring them back in Russia in seventy-two hours. Team policies toward foreign players mirror those of other leagues that seek to regulate their roster through financial means that threaten players' livelihoods.

Translating Citizenship

While the majority of women's basketball players operate within Maguire's "mercenary" category, drawn to different locales each season based on the best contract, some athletes compete annually for the same teams or leagues. At times, dual citizenship is dangled as an opportunity for players to earn more money, given they would pay less in taxes than foreign athletes. Dual citizenship also allows a team to become more competitive, because most leagues allow only a few players from outside the country. Freeing up one of those roster positions for another foreigner creates a stronger roster, which is why teams may assist players to acquire dual citizenship and cover the costs related to this process.

The decision to acquire dual citizenship is not without controversy; US players who obtain second passports have received backlash for their decision. In the case of Becky Hammon, her club in Russia, CSKA Moscow, paid her millions and helped her secure a passport and naturalized citizenship, enabling her to compete for the Russian national team in the 2008 and 2012 Summer Olympic Games. At the time, Hammon received criticism for her decision; Anne Donovan, head coach of Team USA, reportedly said, "If you play in this country, live in this country, and you grow up in the heartland and you put on a Russian uniform, you are not a patriotic person."[35] In response to the criticism, Hammon said, "This is basketball, it isn't the Cold War. I think a lot of things are often blurred with patriotism."[36]

Whereas Elizabeth told me that she would never swap her citizenship to make more money, Rebecca shared that she almost obtained a Ukrainian passport but ultimately decided against it:

Sometimes they want you to do something funky, like marry somebody, you know. Other times there are options to get a passport, but it goes through a chain of knowing the president, and it is all a matter of who you know in the relationships. I considered it because as an American, if you got a passport and you have dual citizenship, that is more money in your pocket right away. That's because a team can sign you, and you're not seen as an American, you have a European passport, . . . which allows them another opportunity to bring in another American. So your team could ultimately have three, four, or five Americans if you have a European passport or somebody else has one, too.

Rebecca outlined how the process of obtaining dual citizenship varies from place to place; some teams have deep connections to the state and can expedite otherwise lengthy processes. In the ESPN *30 for 30* podcast "The Spy Who Signed Me," former KGB spy and Russian oligarch Shabtai Kalmanovich was described as "a pioneer with the passports" by Diana Taurasi. "Apparently he gave an American player a passport of someone who was dead," she says in the podcast. Her teammate with Spartak, Sue Bird, said Kalmanovich approached her and asked if she was Jewish. "Well, my dad's Jewish," she replied. "I think I can get you an Israeli passport," he said.[37]

I discovered a similar situation with Arron, a professional basketball player based in Israel in 2018. Arron, a Jewish American from New Jersey, applied for dual citizenship before joining her team in Israel. For her dual citizenship application, Arron had to prove she was raised Jewish and currently religiously active. Her rabbi wrote a letter for her, detailing her involvement in the synagogue and confirming she attended Hebrew school. She then had to interview and detail her intentions for acquiring dual citizenship. Having played in the Maccabiah Games (described by Arron as the "Jewish Olympics"), in the interview she said she had fallen in love during her short time previously in Israel and wanted to return not for basketball but to "experience the culture." However, upon arrival she signed with a team and now operates in this "in-betweenness" as Jewish American, evaluated differently by both Israeli players and non-Jewish Americans. "I always say you're as good as your Israelis, because your Americans kind of cancel each other out," she told me. "But then if you have Jewish Americans who are considered Israelis, you're as good as those players." In making this distinction, she's pointing to a loophole that allows teams to acquire Jewish American players with dual citizenship as a means of signing more American talent (considered the "best" globally). As a Jewish American placed in a hierarchy between foreigners and Israelis, Arron acknowledges that she is most likely to lose playing minutes should she fail to maintain a steady contribution to the team. "If we make any mistakes, the Israelis will play over us . . . and [coaches] know the Israelis. . . . They've seen those girls play since they were young or they've coached them or, you know, they know them previously, so they trust them more." Sporting citizenship takes a variety of forms, and in Arron's case, her religious beliefs coupled with her previous basketball experience and status as an American allow her expedited access to full freedom and belonging in a region where for others, citizenship, voting rights, and the ability to move freely remain far from reach.

Time Out of the Country

There are few aspects of sport that embody the urgency of a timeout. Players rapidly huddle around a coach and a handheld whiteboard, where a play is furiously scribbled, described, and (in the best-case scenario) successfully executed. Lasting mere moments, timeouts require efficient communication, leadership under pressure, and trust. This is made apparent during a Kazanochka timeout, when I watch two American players stand in the middle of a huddle while their incensed coach screams commands in Russian. One teammate attempts to translate the coach's game plan (and complaints) to them. However, while passing this information along, the buzzer sounds, leaving inadequate time for translation.

The timeout, then, to some degree, offers a useful way of thinking and theorizing about how US athletes spend time competing in professional leagues abroad. Basketball players signed to both WNBA teams and international leagues (as well as national teams) engage in a year-round endeavor for their sporting labor. From training camps to playoff series, seasons frequently overlap, requiring athletes within these transnational labor flows to rapidly adapt to new systems, teammates, coaching styles, and contractual obligations.

Olympic gold medalist and four-time WNBA champion Cynthia Cooper-Dyke played abroad in Spain and Italy beginning in the late 1980s. In her book *She Got Game: My Personal Odyssey*, she details the late-night practices in

Spain to accommodate her teammates' work schedules and the communication gaps with her head coach. However, in Italy she fully immersed herself in the environment, becoming fluent in Italian and traveling around the country on her off days. She eventually relocated her niece and nephew to Italy, creating space for them to access an exceptional education system and improved quality of life: "I began to think Italian and act Italian, using my hands to gesture when I spoke. Italy became such a familiar and comfortable environment for me that I'd face a bigger transition returning to Los Angeles at the end of one season than going back to Parma at the beginning of the next. My family and friends were still living in Watts. Over time, it became harder for me to relate to the things they were going through. Spending seven or eight months overseas every year had expanded my horizons immensely."[38] Beyond highlighting Cooper-Dyke's success in acclimating to life in Italy, this excerpt reveals the difficulty in traversing between discordant spaces. Her increasing comfort with her new life in Italy hindered her ability to fully connect with loved ones back home. The cultural transformation she made speaks both to her success navigating the challenges athletes face in competing outside the States and to the collateral effects on relationships stateside. Moreover, Cooper-Dyke's experience is not necessarily the norm; many athletes do not reflect upon their overseas careers with the same fondness. Rebecca told me, "I used to hate with a passion when I'm overseas and I'm going through something, it could be on the backend, like payments coming late, our ownership group is crazy, coach is crazy, whatever. And you're just calling home, and you wanna talk about anything else. And someone's like, 'Well, you're doing what you love, you'll be fine, whatever.' That'll make you not wanna call home for three months." Here, she articulates how translating her life to loved ones is also an added labor, one that can, at times, bring more stress than reprieve.

One day after practice, Cierra settles in to start yet another career, as a graduate student. She's beginning an online master's program in sports leadership. We sit side by side one evening as I go over field notes from the day and she logs on to Blackboard to download readings and interact with her classmates on their discussion board. The online degree program is but one way that modern technology allows Cierra to connect to the United States. Throughout the day, I constantly saw her use several mobile and social media applications to communicate with friends and family or to document her daily life overseas. Cierra primarily used WhatsApp to keep in touch with fellow players competing overseas and to receive workout details from her trainer back home. Almost every day, he sent workouts to be completed outside her Kazanochka schedule. This, Cierra said, was to keep her in shape for the WNBA season due to the elevated expectation of physical conditioning stateside. On FaceTime, Cierra chatted with loved ones around the world, most often her mother and brother in North Carolina or her girlfriend, a fellow professional basketball player competing abroad. Given the close time difference—only an hour apart in time zones—Cierra and her partner spent a significant amount of time "living" together virtually during their nonpractice time. After a couple of days, I found myself involved in these conversations, chiming in on the day's events and getting to know Cierra's family and partner as they dealt with the distance. Watching her go through her daily routines with her iPhone or laptop in tow is a reminder of how the influx of new information communication technologies and improved infrastructure worldwide enhance the ability for time out of the country to remain grounded in the people and the places that players hold dear.[39] Rebecca told me, "My first couple of years playing overseas, finding Wi-Fi everywhere was nonexistent. Now it's everywhere—Wi-Fi, Google Translate on your phone . . . so that helps tremendously." Instagram also served as the primary mode of communication for my own participant outreach, because athletes were more likely to frequently check Instagram than email while abroad.

When I asked other athletes how they balance relationships with their careers around the world, Elizabeth told me, "Relationships are hard. So if you're trying to communicate with someone and they're asleep and vice versa, it's tough, and so that can be draining, too. But then also you're reminded, 'OK, I'm playing basketball, and this is something I enjoy,' and so you really try to take advantage of the time that you do have with your teammates, and it's nice when you hang out with your team and stuff like that." Rebecca shared that earlier in her career, leaving a romantic partner used to be the toughest part of heading overseas, but that changed for her when she realized that the gender dynamics of those relationships fueled the difficulty:

> Like there's something about that type of relationship. I find that being a female athlete when dealing with men, if they're not an athlete, too, they cannot handle a woman . . . going long distance that's created because of her. Now you flip it, mind you. I come from a military family, you know,

men leaving. But when it's a woman going off, it's a problem. . . . What's made it difficult is running into so many guys that have these insecurities that they need to handle themselves. . . . You'll see your girlfriend, your wife, perhaps as a female athlete that is a star, maybe that is adored by others, that has fans, that has people in her DMs, inbox, or whatever. And you take it upon yourself to feel like you need to knock her down a peg.

She contrasts these previous experiences with her current relationship with another women's basketball player, one that still navigates distance, albeit in a different way: "When I tell you it is not hard to leave, it's not hard," Rebecca said. "Why? We understand what it is, and we game plan. . . . 'OK, let's go here, let's meet here, let's fly here. I'll see you for Christmas.' It's not hard. It's not difficult. Men make things difficult." Rebecca dissects some of the nuances of dating while playing overseas and how a shared identity across gender and career path influences the ease of translating a relationship across borders.

Translating Safety

Media discourses surrounding the plight of Brittney Griner in Russia frequently relied on Cold War tropes of the Soviet Other while obscuring the fact that this incident was not even her first publicly precarious moment abroad. In 2014 she was attacked in Shenyang, China, as she left a practice arena and headed to her team bus. A man wielding a knife chased Griner and two of her teammates, yelling at them as he made stabbing motions. He struck Griner, but fortunately her coat protected her from any major wounds.[40]

Unsafe conditions can take many forms. Rebecca told me that she not only had to acclimate to a new environment around her but also had to keep track of those who shared the same nationality. "I've been in situations where I had an American teammate who would almost put you in a danger zone more than you need to be," she told me. "And I'm like, 'I'm not trying to go out if this is how you roll and I gotta watch my back 24/7 'cause you don't know how to act.'"

Other stories reminded me in the same way of how Black American women looked out for one another abroad in moments of peril. One player later told me that years ago she and two other American teammates (all Black women) were stopped by Russian police while standing near their team hotel for no apparent reason besides the rarity of a group of Black women walking in

Russia. Insistent that the women could not possibly be patrons of the hotel, the police demanded the women's passports and proof they were staying at the hotel. When they refused and began walking away, one of the officers grabbed one of the athletes by her backpack and pulled her toward his vehicle. Another player was roughly apprehended by another officer, while the third ran toward the hotel to find help. Eventually, the women fought off the police officers and escaped. For them, the use of excessive force by police officers is unfortunately a familiar crossover, whether at home or abroad.

Where athletes choose to play also shapes their perceptions of safety abroad. Rebecca, who played in Ukraine the season before Russia's latest invasion into the country, told me, "I try to ask as many questions as possible before signing to certain places. I try to gain knowledge through different avenues, reach out to people that I might know that know people in certain countries versus just watching the news, because you can't necessarily trust everything that's in the news." She shared that she had experienced moments when she was concerned for her safety but that her identity as a US citizen gave her a sense of security: "Most countries I've been in, even if they did have some political issues going on, Americans were off limits . . . and if something is going to happen, we're sending them home for their safety." She also shared that she takes certain precautions in a new place, such as looking up where the closest American embassy is located: "Whenever I go to a country, I'll have the address, I'll look it up just to see how far I am, because if something happens, that is my asylum, that is where I should go, and I know that there will be Americans over there." However, she admitted that even with her own research and preparation, "A lot of this is luck in some ways, 'cause you don't know until you know. Anything can happen at any time."

Missed Connections

Cierra is in Kazan with me, but she is always already looking ahead. She has recently signed a contract to play for the WNBA's Las Vegas Aces as soon as she leaves Russia. To play year-round is to be constantly in a state of preparation for the upcoming season, whether physically in disciplining the body, mentally in navigating logistics, or emotionally in communicating the next contract with loved ones.

Cierra's ability to cross over is limited, however, by these global flows. As she traveled back to the United States for training camp with the Las Vegas Aces, she realized that the team's roster would significantly change once star players returned from overseas leagues. Given the unevenness of these international league schedules, Cierra's early arrival to the training camp did not cement her a spot on the final roster even as she competed on the team throughout the first weeks of the regular season. The week before I was scheduled to visit her in Las Vegas, she warned me that I shouldn't come, because she knew she would be cut as soon as the last player returned from abroad. She was right. In traversing multiple countries, overlapping seasons, and diverse playing styles, athletes continuously find themselves recalibrating, constantly preparing for what's next. Elizabeth told me, "Physically, that's draining, just being on your feet for however many hours a day, and then when you extend that over months at a time, it's even more tiring. And so then by the time you get back, I missed all of preseason, and then our coach is like, 'Alright, you just need to be back.' You just have to." After Vegas, choreographing her career once more, Cierra began preparing for her next overseas season in Poland while coaching girls' basketball in her hometown in North Carolina.

Basketball in Bourges

MAY 2022 | BOURGES, FRANCE | PALAIS DES SPORTS DU PRADO

I'm heading to meet Cierra once again—more than four years after our time together in Kazan. The young rookie I met in 2015 is nearly unrecognizable; now she is a seasoned veteran looking to lead her team to a championship. In a 2021 Instagram post leading up to the WNBA season, her caption reads in part: "A month ago, I flew straight from Poland to Phoenix to embark on another WNBA journey. . . . A younger Cierra would have lost sleep to nerves and anxiety. More seasoned Cierra was just focused on having fun and competing."[41] Since we last shared space, she has competed in Poland and is now based in Lyon, France. She has also worked to grow the 3×3 hoops culture in the United States, representing Team USA in FIBA competitions worldwide.

It's game day in Bourges, and I reach Cierra's hotel as the team finishes the pregame meal. Athletes in matching warm-ups reach for a last banana or pour an espresso to go. Cierra and I embrace, and she introduces me to her French teammates, telling me their names and the WNBA teams they're signed to in the States—a reverse translation of sorts. After she fuels up, we head to her hotel room, where I meet Kayla, another foreigner on the team hailing from Toronto, Ontario. "Amazing!" she says as we greet each other. "Another English speaker!" I follow Cierra through her pregame routine, going through treatment with her athletic trainer as the French Open blares on a nearby television. We separate as she boards the team bus to the arena, where the Palais des Sports du Prado fills nearly to the brim with a raucous French crowd. The trophy is in the building. The in-arena DJ plays mostly Top 40 US hip-hop, mixing French Montana's "All the Way Up" with the instrumental of Fat Joe's "Lean Back." During the game, sonic clashing of drums and giveaway noisemakers couple with the massive display of team flags, offering an environment more suited for a European football game compressed into a gym. That night, Cierra's team loses, so the playoffs will continue in Lyon in a few days' time. I wait for her outside the venue, where eventually both teams spill out into the street. The players walk through the crowd, occasionally stopping to take selfies or to sign autographs for fans.

The next day, Cierra and I take the train from the main station in Bourges to the Lyon-Perrache stop, a commute during which we catch up on everything that has happened since our time together in Kazan. There is, of course, all that has happened in our own lives, but there is also the gossip of the league and the fears and anxieties we share surrounding Brittney Griner's imprisonment.

That night, along with other Lyon players, we attend the men's game and witness a blowout in a hot, packed gym. Afterward, we make the long walk through the tunnels to a room where a spread is provided for the partners and families of the players. I meet more of Cierra's teammates, including a Serbian player who lovingly calls Cierra *sestra*, "sister." A noticeable divide emerges in the room, where Lyon's foreign players—Canadian, Serbian, American, and Lithuanian—collect in one corner away from their French counterparts. "This is the English-speaking corner," I'm told.

The next day at practice, Cierra is a vocal, positive presence both on the court and from the sidelines. She's frenetic in the gym—always moving, always working, always hype. She's also the last to leave the gym and weight room. Whereas her extra conditioning in Russia was part of her effort to stay in "WNBA shape," her extra work in Lyon seemingly reflects her own leadership role on the team and the pending moves ahead following her team's playoff run.

Cierra has already signed with a team in Hungary for the upcoming season. But before she heads there, she'll pack up her entire apartment and move her belongings back to her home in North Carolina. She'll then compete for Team USA in the FIBA 3×3 World Cup in Belgium, which includes a training camp that will begin in France. As she rattles down her upcoming schedule, I pull out a map and a calendar, attempting to conceptualize her flight path amid the geopolitical turbulence of women's basketball in that moment.

Sporting (Un)Diplomacy

On December 8, 2022, footage from Russian state media shows a brief exchange between two groups on an airport tarmac in the United Arab Emirates. It's a brief but important moment as Brittney Griner and Viktor Bout pass one another. Griner, a professional basketball player, and Bout, a globally infamous arms dealer, make for a strange gathering as they board their respective planes. Griner is seen in a red coat, her hair shorn of her signature locs as she departs for her home state of Texas nearly ten months after her initial arrest in Moscow's Sheremetyevo International Airport. Upon her release, US president Joe Biden, flanked by vice president Kamala Harris and Griner's wife, Cherelle, heralded Griner as "an incomparable athlete, a two-time Olympic Gold medalist for Team USA. She endured mistreatment at a show trial in Russia with characteristic grit and incredible dignity. She represents the best America—the best about America—just across the board, everything about her."[42] In an essay on the swap, *New York Times* journalist Nicholas Casey considers how this exchange is decidedly different from those that took place in the twentieth century. Griner's identity as a tall, Black, queer woman made her highly visible as both celebrity and target: "As I grew up in the 1980s, my image of a prisoner swap was the old one from the Cold War: Two men, agents caught by the enemy, standing on opposite ends of a bridge in Berlin. . . . Yet what happened yesterday on the tarmac with Brittney Griner and Viktor Bout was no Bridge of Spies. The ritual was the same, but the players weren't."[43] That she can be used by two countries to represent both "the best about America" and a political prisoner succinctly reveals the role of sport in broader geopolitical implications. The Cold War "ritual" Casey articulates here also circulated more rapidly than in decades prior because it was broadcast across major news platforms, social media applications, and smartphone notifications in an instant.

Derek Shearer, a former US ambassador to Finland, describes sport as a "virtuous form of soft power" that aids in the "promotion of global citizenship."[44] In "To Play Ball, Not Make War: Sports, Diplomacy and Soft Power," he writes, "In a globalized world, sport is a vital part of almost every country's soft power. It can increase national pride, spread national influence, and serve as a useful tool of public diplomacy, encouraging communication and international understanding."[45] What is more difficult to ascertain are international *mis*understandings, the sporting *un*diplomacy at play for women's basketball players.

Russia's most recent invasion of Ukraine shifted the sporting landscape in a myriad of ways, whether through Russian athletes denied access to the field of play, the revocation of sponsorships emanating from Russian entities, or the removal of mega sporting events from the country altogether. However, it can be argued that Griner's detainment and resulting nine-year sentence in a penal colony located two hundred miles from Moscow is one of the most visceral cases of a lack of diplomacy within the current sportscape. Griner's agent, Lindsay Colas, told reporters, "Brittney Griner is being held by Russia simply because she is an American."[46]

However, Griner's Americanness is but one identity worth conceptualizing in this case. Whereas Soviet politics (within and outside of sport) previously used tangible examples of global anti-Blackness to perpetuate the moral superiority of socialism, Russia's treatment of Griner signals a shift in how race, gender, sexuality, and nationality intertwine to inform her carceral condition in the country. Kimberly St. Julian-Varnon, an expert on the Black experience in Russia, told NPR, "She's Black. She's gay. And this is a marijuana case. What are the three biggest issues in the United States in terms of domestic politics? Marijuana convictions, LGBTQ issues, anti-Black racism—and the carceral system."[47] Here, she articulates how the current political environment in the United States informs rather than refutes the logics behind Griner's detainment. Media narratives surrounding the severity of Griner's sentence remain rooted not in a semblance of care but in one of nationalism, rebooting and recalibrating tensions between two nation-states entrenched in carcerality.

Figure 4. A view of Campbell's Georgetown mural.

However, the work of the actual athletes who compete overseas in articulating the struggle to survive abroad recognizes the humanity in Griner's plight. A mural installed in Washington, DC's Georgetown neighborhood makes the faces of eighteen Americans held captive around the world larger than life. Many of the images are the last known photographs of each detainee, resulting in a mixture of high-quality images and grainy, pixelated headshots. Comprised of flour, water, sugar, and paper, the mural is, by design, temporary. According to Isaac Campbell, the artist behind the piece, its ephemerality is intended to invoke urgency in order for the state to "use the tools available to bring these Americans home—before their faces fade away and disappear from this wall."[48]

The crossover continues to bring me back to the unique political and mediated engagement within women's basketball, especially in how athletes refused to remain sidelined in this moment. News of the mural, organized by the Bring Our Families Home campaign, reached the WNBPA, and after practice, members of the Washington Mystics went to see it, only to realize they had an opportunity to join other friends and family members of

Figure 5. Social media posts of WNBA players at the mural.

detainees working to install the public art piece. The artist, Campbell, sees it as more than a mural; instead, it is "the act of creating something together collaboratively to bring these families together."[49]

Elizabeth Williams and Natasha Cloud both picked up tools to paste the fifteen-foot rendering of Griner onto the matte black wall. "It was heavy," Williams told *The Next*. "Puts a lot of things in perspective. It makes me grateful that I could even be in a position to talk to these people and to share BG's story and to know BG."[50] Since then, other teams and individual athletes have visited the mural, less invested in Griner as a tool of the state and more invested in her as a friend, teammate, and member of the broader women's basketball family.

Troubled Translations

In the months following her release from a Yavas prison camp, Griner mostly avoided the spotlight but announced that she would return to the WNBA for the 2023 season. In her first press conference, she told members of the media, "I'm never going overseas to play again unless I'm representing my country at the Olympics. If I make that team, that would be the only time I would leave the U.S. soil. The reason a lot of us go over is the pay gap. A lot of us go over there to make an income to support our families, to support ourselves. So I don't knock any player that wants to go overseas."[51] Throughout this chapter, each participant offered key insights on the current landscape of transnational sporting labor. The very act of translation that permeates their experiences reflects the tenacity, intelligence, and collective strategies necessary to survive (and at times thrive) in the global sports-media complex. Notions of identity, allegiance to country, and athletic success seemingly become deeply entrenched in economic potential, whether through teams gauging Black American players as inherently more capable or the opportunity to attain dual citizenship for higher salaries and tax breaks. Raka Shome and Radha Hegde write, "The shifting fault lines of economic and cultural power in our current times, and the scale and speed at which these lines are re/shifting, are producing new forms of articulations and disarticulations, new configurations of power, and new planes of dis/empowerment that cannot be equated with any other period in history."[52]

While the national rhetoric of Russia's harsh drug laws and inhumane prison conditions permeated the news cycle, the carceral realities here in the States are not lost on me. At the same time, the reignited Cold War narratives play well in this case, because Griner can be an American hero subject to a cruel Russian dictator, and the United States can emerge the moral victor. However, this flattened nationalist narrative is troubled at another airport in June 2023. As Griner traveled with her Phoenix Mercury teammates through Dallas–Fort Worth International Airport, a man aggressively approached her, seemingly looking to attack her.[53] While team security quickly intervened and prevented any physical contact between Griner and the assailant, the incident served as a reminder of the airport as a particularly fraught space, given that Griner's detention in Russia originated at Sheremetyevo; that she is hailed as an "American hero" while facing potential violence at home serves as a vivid reminder of how many challenges to the crossover remain. At the same time, this moment also serves as a reminder of the importance of chartered flights for WNBA players.

For those who choose to stay home, what options emerge? In the following chapter, I examine Athletes Unlimited, one potential alternative for players seeking to stay in the United States rather than translate their labor abroad.

Mission Equity

New Sporting Labor Considerations within Athletes Unlimited

DALLAS, TEXAS | FAIR PARK COLISEUM | MARCH 2023

I'm sitting inside an arena on the grounds of the State Fair of Texas, situated in the shadow of the Cotton Bowl in Dallas. The venue, Fair Park Coliseum, has previously hosted an array of sporting events; hockey, rodeo, soccer, and even roller derby utilized this space in the past. Today it's home to basketball, with a new league and scoreboard setup that starkly contrast with its more historic trappings. After opening lineups, the game announcer asks fans to direct their attention to the video board. In a clip comprised of several athletes' voices and key moments across a variety of sports, the voice-over outlines the mission of Athletes Unlimited (AU): "This, this is what we always dreamed of—a place to compete, a place to be seen and heard. A platform to be unapologetically ourselves and celebrated for it. A space to be loud or resilient, ruthless, radiant. Athletes Unlimited defies all expectations. And only we know the determination it takes to get here. This is where champions are forged. No asking, explaining, or justifying what we do. Get ready because this is—Athletes Unlimited."

In lieu of the standardized ritual of "The Star-Spangled Banner" before US sporting events, spectators see this clip before every game, with AU forgoing the nationalistic performance to reinscribe its mission for this basketball season and, more broadly, the league. With the recent reengagement of the national anthem as a site of protest through kneeling or perhaps a raised fist, many leagues' attempt to address the role of the anthem remained limited to supporting resistance through bowed praying heads or allowing athletes to remain in the locker room until the song's final notes. Other organizations toughened their stance on how players should respond to the pregame anthem, utilizing it as a disciplinary mechanism where full attention and even a hand over the heart remained mandatory. For this league, members of the player executive committee decided for themselves whether the anthem would be played.[1] This is particularly important to note given that the state of Texas passed a law in June 2021 requiring "The Star-Spangled Banner" to be played before professional sporting events. Teams who refuse risk the revocation of government funding.[2]

The absence of the anthem is but one shift in how AU Basketball operates in comparison to other professional sports leagues. There are the points scored on the court, of course, but there is also a specialized individual and team point system that rewards sound basketball strategy. On the individual level, players earn points for assists, steals, blocks, rebounds, and making shots (free throws, two-pointers, and three-pointers). They can also lose points for committing fouls, turning the ball over, or missing shots. At the end of each game, the players (and fans that subscribe to a membership, the Unlimited Club) vote on the top three performers, who also receive points. Teams gain points collectively by winning quarters and/or the entire game.

This all takes place over a short season lasting less than two months in one city, where players constantly swap squads each week via a draft captained by the four highest point earners that week. Beyond their leadership in creating teams and calling plays, AU athletes receive a 50 percent revenue split and are actively involved in the day-to-day decisions of the league. They are also able choose a nonprofit organization to support, amplifying their cause across AU media, programs, and theme nights as well as through financial contributions. (Their on-court performance also translates to funding for their charity of choice.)

In this chapter, I examine the 2023 and 2024 AU Basketball seasons as an alternative and/or supplement for players who previously competed at the collegiate, international, and/or WNBA level. Using participant observation conducted over two weeks of the five-week 2023 season and one week of the four-week 2024 season alongside interviews and a content analysis, I argue that the structure of new leagues such as AU offers new crossover possibilities for the players who comprise its rosters while serving as a reminder of the limits bound up in corporate sport.

About Athletes Unlimited

The story goes that on one Christmas Eve, two friends met for breakfast and over the course of the meal considered the current sporting landscape and imagined something different: a league uninterested in place-based affinity or static stars signed to rosters and instead invested in growing women's sports across the board.[3] The friends, Jon Patricof and Jonathan Soros, are fairly important here. Patricof, the former president of Major League Soccer's New York City FC and president and chief operating officer of Tribeca Enterprises (Tribeca Film Festival, Tribeca Film, Tribeca Cinemas), brought the sport management acumen. Soros, the founder and chief executive officer of private investment firm JS Capital Management and formerly of Soros Fund Management (founded by his father, famed billionaire philanthropist George Soros), brought the capital and the connection to nonprofit organizations. In a 2021 interview with the *Harvard Business Review*, Soros described himself as "an owner of capital who wants to use it to improve the world. . . . On the one hand, I seek to smartly grow that capital through investments. On the other hand, I seek to use capital for the public benefit through charitable and other giving."[4] He also brings a key political lens to Athletes Unlimited. In 2012 he started Friends of Democracy PAC, a political action committee focused on campaign finance reform. Together, Patricof and Soros's partnership offers a deep knowledge of the sports-media complex with an imperative to build something bigger than sport.[5]

AU initially launched on March 3, 2020, with an eighteen-game softball season and eventually expanded to volleyball, lacrosse, and basketball (beginning in 2022). While women's basketball offers a stateside option in the WNBA, the pull of the basketball arm of AU is in the dual opportunity to compete at home (whether one makes a WNBA roster or not) and have a voice both politically and within the league's daily operations. Rebecca Harris, who competed in AU Basketball in each of its first three seasons, told me that in 2022 she initially signed a contract to play overseas in Iraq, but when she found out about AU, she decided to opt out of that deal to play in the States. "I just knew that my parents probably wouldn't be able to sleep," she told me, "just because there's so much going on in the world."

Athletes Unlimited, in creating a league specifically focused on women's sports and located at one site per season, seemingly goes against the very

fabric of professional sport in three key areas: geographical fixity, static rosters, and gendered hierarchies. The concept of home and, in turn, of the
home team continues to be troubled by the effects of late capitalism, creating diasporic fanbases in disparate locales where spectators root for their
home teams from afar as a means of making home in new places.[6] As Tegan
Alexandra Baker writes, sports fandom "construct[s] and troubl[es] feelings
of home and belonging across distance."[7] AU Basketball's inaugural season
in 2022 operated out of the Sports Center of Las Vegas, while the 2023 and
2024 seasons were based in Fair Park Coliseum in Dallas, Texas. Because of
AU's singular location for the duration of the season and constantly shifting
rosters each week, there's an interesting sonic experience that diverges from
standardized professional sport spaces and the expectations of arena aes-
thetics. Without the feel of a home court advantage, the perpetually neutral
site lacks the chants of "Charge!" and "DE-FENSE!" Instead, the crowd is
consistently loud in yelling for calls, hyping individual athletes, and collectively reacting to the highs and lows of the game. There is no jeering from the
crowd or coordinated action during free throw attempts; instead, a mostly
respectful, silent crowd allows for full concentration.

Because AU is freed from the travel woes that plague so many other leagues,
its single site allows it to claim to be the first US-based, carbon-neutral set
of pro sports leagues.[8] Portions of each ticket price go toward carbon cred-
its that offset emissions generated from goods and services, vehicles, fuel,
electricity, waste, and even fan travel. AU also partnered with Aspiration,
a climate action company, to develop a reforestation program that plants a
tree for every three-pointer scored.[9] Beyond the greenwashing that so often
plagues sports, AU seemingly attempts to acknowledge its role in climate
change and work to mitigate the effects.[10]

While the location is fixed, the players themselves are constantly in flux.
Each week, the top-four point earners become captains and draft teams,
reshuffling rosters and creating new lineups. Throughout the week, these
captains run practices and design game plans as they also compete in games.
Rebecca told me, "I've had captains who are pretty proactive in sending out
messages and be like, 'We're gonna have practice at this time, make sure
you're ready to go.' Or 'Hey, we're not gonna have practice, but here are the
game notes. I want you to look at this, pay attention to the scout, and be
ready to go.'"

Without the grounding of a home team or a consistent roster for the duration of the season, rooting interest is primarily driven by fans' preferred collegiate or WNBA teams; during games, fans don jerseys connected to players' other squads. In the online live chats for the AU Basketball drafts, those in attendance declare their fandoms, whether through shouting out individual players or identifying themselves as fans of a particular WNBA franchise.

To consider women's sports fans as "underserved" (not to be confused with "undeserved") is to acknowledge that a market exists and that women's sports are a valuable product worthy of serious investment. In combining these two elements—centering women's sports and basing an entire season at one site—the league avoids the frequent displacement of women's sports for their male counterparts at the collegiate and professional levels. In confronting the very essence of sport and disrupting the hierarchy of decision-making processes, AU emerges as a curious new venture bound up in unconventional approaches to media, labor, and politics in women's sports. "We founded this organization to start a revolution," the cofounders declared in their 2023 annual letter.[11]

A League of Their Own

As a player-led league, AU Basketball operates without coaches. Instead, there are four facilitators, one for each team, who operate in varying capacities based on how captains utilize the facilitators' expertise. Captains can request their facilitators to call plays and timeouts, make substitutions, and otherwise take the standardized coaching role. They can also ask facilitators to serve as assistants, providing feedback and support as captains make key team decisions. Rebecca told me, "Some captains really want to take on a bigger load and kinda show what they could bring to the table. Some captains would rather just play and let the facilitator be the coach. Some captains want to do half and half, break it up and will be like, 'I want to run these three plays, and these are what I'm bringing as a captain.'" These leadership opportunities possess the potential for much-needed experience to propel athletes' future careers as members of front offices or coaching staffs, two areas within the sport slowly experiencing demographic shifts and new offerings for former players.

While each of the facilitators brings valuable coaching experience, a certain amount of additional respect is given to Pokey Chatman, a decorated coach at the collegiate and professional levels and a facilitator during the 2022 and 2023 AU Basketball seasons. "Pokey is Pokey, she's a legend. She demands respect. I don't care who you are," Rebecca said, "you're gonna see Pokey as coach." Her knowledge as a legend in the game coupled with her willingness to give captains room to flourish made her not only popular with players but also a dynamic force even when seated in the crowd during other teams' games.

In an online segment, Sydney Colson described how being on an AU team feels a lot like previous WNBA rosters where everyone felt as if they were on the same page: "I feel like Athletes Unlimited provides an opportunity for you to create teams like that. Like, you know who people are, you've played with some of them, you've played against them. You kind of know what makes them tick, or you've experienced things, so you're like, 'I can create this team with people who are like-minded, and we can go get this.'" Once teams are solidified, captains can choose how and when to conduct practice and other prep sessions with their new teams. In 2023 the first game of the week happened on Wednesdays, and if a team won, they were likely to take the next day off from practice. However, a midweek loss calls for a necessary Thursday practice before the Friday and Saturday double headers.

Entering at the midway point of the season, I walk into an intimate crowd and settle into my seat at the media table as players move through familiar warm-up routines, finding rhythm in both getting shots up and the music blaring from the in-arena DJ's mix. As I survey the stands and seats closest to the court, I realize that the athletes and facilitators scheduled for the second game of the night are mingling with spectators; some are dressed in street clothes, while others fuel with granola bars and sports drinks as they take in the game seated next to fans. Frequent captain Kierstan Bell is rocking a grill, an array of jewelry, and fluffy slippers as she holds court in one section of the arena after her game. Throughout the seasons, she seems to revel in the casual closeness of AU. She pulls out her phone to record the jumbo-tron announcement of her game MVP award, and when a ball goes out of bounds during a game, she daps someone nearby in the crowd before game play resumes. Other athletes move throughout the arena, checking in with friends and family in attendance. Given this unique access, many super fans of the sport make the trek to Dallas, bringing binders full of trading cards, basketballs, and other merchandise for athletes to autograph when they're not on the court.

Watching the first game, I described the style of play to Arie Graham, an AU beat reporter sitting next to me at the media table, as "smart, athletic, pickup basketball." Graham described it to me as "basketball with playoff intensity," since every possession matters for the point system. Rebecca Harris agreed with the pickup analogy, telling me in an interview, "I adapt real easy, and I think that's a credit to how much pickup ball I play. Like if I go to the gym and I'm playing pickup with my guys and there's fifteen of us on a regular basis, every day we're going." AU officiating is far more lax than in the college or WNBA game, and teams are allowed to challenge referee calls (many of them successfully), resulting in a different sort of athlete agency on the court. It frequently felt reminiscent of Drew League games I previously attended in Los Angeles, where the combination of lenient officiating and skilled athletes creates a fast-paced, aggressive style of play; each possession seemed to captivate the crowd. Sydney Colson told me that in AU Basketball's first season in Vegas there were more true bigs; with smaller lineups in the seasons that followed, the game is faster, more frenetic. Because athletes are compensated in part by their individual performances and penalized for shoddy decision making, no one seems to take a single play or minute off.

Throughout each quarter, the athletes sitting in the crowd are seemingly just as invested in the entertainment value of the game; the novelty of the proximity of professional athletes who are up next is a unique aspect of this league. When things got particularly chippy between two players on the court, DiJonai Carrington, an AU player in the crowd inexplicably holding a puppy, could be heard yelling, "Let's not make this personal!" It's a difficult ask, given how much time these athletes spend playing with and against one another while being subject to their peers' drafting approach (not unlike being chosen to play on a blacktop playground team) and coaching strategies. Rebecca notes this when she tells me, "I mean a big piece to this is—it's not just basketball, there is a social element to it as well . . . because it is who you know. People wanna win with people they can see themselves winning with."

The adaptation to the style of play seems to be both athletically driven and culturally specific. Rebecca also told me, "Some people do not play pickup enough; they don't decipher between enemy and, you know, friendly. If you came as a competitor, whatever team you're on, that's who you rocking with until you're not on their team no more. You know, doesn't mean you gotta be mean-spirited or anything, 'cause I want everybody to win. I want everybody to be safe, have a good game, play well. But if you're on the opposite end of me, I wanna win those quarters, and I wanna win that game." The intimacy of the league's rosters and spectators' closeness to the court continued throughout the season, sometimes resulting in verbal confrontations between players and other athletes' family members or the ability to hear the details of a player-on-player altercation. "For the ones that really get it and understand it, I know they are having such a blast, and for the ones that haven't adapted to it just yet, you're probably not having the best time," Rebecca said. During one game I watched, a frustrated player screamed an expletive as she headed out of bounds with the ball. Sitting next to me, journalist Arie Graham said, "That would have been a technical in the WNBA."

Like other leagues previously described in this book, Athletes Unlimited maintains its own pace, style of play, and expectations of each player. All of the forty-four athletes who played in AU Basketball's 2023 season competed at the collegiate level. Twenty-three had previously played in the WNBA, and of those, seventeen were currently signed to team rosters. Many of these athletes also competed internationally, representing either a national team or a privately-owned overseas squad. Given these factors, there is a range of experience and talent represented across each team. Rebecca described these different levels, whether athletes have just left college, played overseas, or secured a roster spot in the WNBA: "It comes out, you know. A group of people could be talking about certain things and dynamics within the game of basketball, but if you've never experienced it based on where you played, then you're kinda outta sync."

AU can allow on-the-job training for rookie players that prepares them for the next level, whether that materializes as an overseas opportunity or as a roster spot on a WNBA team. For veteran players possibly overlooked by other leagues, rejuvenating their stat line and relevance in a five-week season could have long-term ramifications for their career prospects. As Clare Brennan writes of the league, "Despite AU not being the cash cow international play is, the condensed competition does allow players to stay closer to their W markets and introduce—or reintroduce—themselves to a distinct fan base."[12] This is important not only for endorsement opportunities but also for future employment in other leagues. At one point, Sydney Colson comes over to talk to me after her game and shares that the 2022 season at AU formed the foundation of her current contract with the WNBA's Las Vegas Aces. She's not alone.

Journalist Arie Graham told me that several players shared with her that AU offered them new looks in other leagues, sometimes beginning with short-term contracts that expand as they prove themselves on the court and other roster shifts occur. Multiple fans I interacted with, including a college coach, expressed how impressed they were with Air Hearn, an incredibly dynamic player on both sides of the floor. When asked to name an AU player who deserves a WNBA contract, several players sang Hearn's praises. In an interview, Tasha Cloud said, "Air Hearn needs a job in the W, and I'm gonna keep advocating. I'm trying to get Phoenix to bring her into the camp too. . . . This girl has continued to prove herself over and over and over again against the most elite-level players in the WNBA."[13] Allisha Gray told W. G. Ramirez in the same piece, "I've been on the Air Hearn train since last season, so it's not new to me."[14]

For other players coming back from injury, AU offers a chance to get reps at game speed and prove one's readiness for the upcoming WNBA season. Isabelle "Izzy" Harrison, who tore her left meniscus in 2023, had a forty-one-point game during the 2024 AU Basketball season, an outstanding performance that left her understandably emotional during a postgame interview on the court as she described her journey back from surgery and rehab.

When I asked what made AU unique from overseas leagues, Rebecca first mentioned the lack of financial precarity: "I don't have to question when I'll get paid or anything like that. Also, the pay scale for five weeks is pretty great." She also mentioned resources, including meals and snacks readily available for players constantly looking to refuel before or after practices or games. Another player, Lexie Brown, took a holistic approach to joining AU after a tumultuous WNBA season and a disappointing setup overseas. In an AU video titled *All on the Table*, she says, "I was on a [WNBA] team, then I wasn't on a team, [and] then I had to prepare for my future. . . . I did end up going overseas, I went to France, and I just realized that it wasn't giving what I thought it was going to give."[15] Part of her decision to come back to the States and compete for AU was due to the compressed schedule. In the segment, she told Ari Chambers, "You know, being overseas for seven months, you play once a week. They released the schedule for AU, and you're playing three times a week in six weeks. I'm going to be playing the same amount of games in a shorter amount of time. I get to be home, I get to do things off the court that I care about and be with people that I know."[16]

Another key element that varies from other leagues (including, until recently, the WNBA) is a separate living space. "You know, I've got my own hotel room, and what I find when it comes to women's sports and the women's game, a lot of people like to take shortcuts and certain things that we feel like you shouldn't treat us like you would treat the guys or treat us like we should be as professional athletes," Rebecca said. "Automatically they wanna put two, three women in a room no matter what the budget is. 'Oh, you guys are women, y'all can stay in the same bed' type stuff. And I'm like, I'm grown."

Rebecca credited AU not only for accommodating the privacy of individual athletes in their lodgings but also for considering athletes in relationships or as parents: "You know, they're very accommodating in a lot of ways. . . . If you have a child and you want them to be here with you the entire time? Done. No questions asked. If you're married and you want, or you are not even married but you want your partner with you the entire time? Done, OK."

Being too "grown" for the overseas offerings came up in a segment produced by Athletes Unlimited in which Essence Carson, who last played abroad in the 2016–17 season, told Ari Chambers,

> [Teams] demand so much of you, and they don't reciprocate that. Look, we know what we're signing up for when we go over there. . . . Alright, they want you to be the leading scorer, they want you to help the team win. So if I'm helping this team win, what are you doing for me? This is a business, right? It's supposed to be a tradeoff. . . . You shouldn't have to ask for the bare essentials. *Like, we're grown.* Why are you putting someone in a studio? Why are you doing that? Why when you show up the internet don't work?[17]

Carson mentioned that she'd been fortunate to not experience some of the hardships other athletes describe with late payments, but she discussed how her previous attempts to articulate her expectations as a professional athlete resulted in team management "getting pissed because I'm advocating for myself." Many of the built-in accommodations for AU players are battles that other leagues have struggled to win for years, both domestically and around the world.

Many of these athletes have competed with or against one another either in their youth leagues in the Amateur Athletic Union (AAU) or in the AU, allowing for a lot of shared community (or trauma). Rebecca told me, "Last night, I went out to eat with a few of us, and we're sharing stories about our worst overseas experiences. And it's like, 'Oh yeah, I've been through that before. Oh yeah, I know that team. I was over there.' And there's so many things that you really understand about one another that a lot of people can't relate to on the outside."

Understanding Unlimited

Given the continued struggles embedded in women's basketball around the world, it felt difficult to walk into Fair Park Coliseum without a significant amount of cynicism. On its website, AU appears to say all the right things: "Athletes Unlimited was founded on the belief that athletes are what make the sport—and that athletes are more than the sport they play. Our model challenges the conventions of traditional leagues by eliminating team own-ers, giving a bigger voice to athletes, and providing athletes opportunities to engage meaningfully in their communities."[18] In their executive summary, cofounders Patricof and Soros declare an intent to promote players' ability to engage in management opportunities and other long-term financial pos-sibilities, including profit sharing and a formalized space for athlete voice in AU governance. This includes at least one athlete seat on the board of directors and a player executive committee for each sport. For a league that runs for such a short amount of time, what the season lacks in longevity (or even the salary offerings of some WNBA contracts), it arguably makes up for in a more intentional commitment to athlete agency. Following the well-documented challenges athletes faced battling owners in the WNBA or waiting for overdue payments abroad, the league seemed too good to be true.

Players continuously reassured me that AU actually backed up the savvy branding presented online. Rebecca told me, "For the most part, they've re-ally taken the player-led approach to listening to what is needed or wanted, what we need to feel as professional athletes. . . . A lot of organizations don't wanna do that. But you'd be surprised if the athletes and players themselves feel valued. Because there's a difference between just paying a player to play.

Do they feel valued showing up to work today? Like it's a different vibe." Across the AU website, much of the language of "celebrating diversity" seemingly replicates prominent diversity, equity, and inclusion (DEI) corporate language. However, I began to notice smaller shifts across AU's media offerings from my earlier encounter with the league. For example, its Racial Equity Working Group is now named the Intersectional Equity Working Group, seemingly considering how various markers of identity simultaneously shape how athletes experience sport.[19]

As I enter the concourse, I see a massive display, *Celebrating Black Women's History*, that features images and quotes from prominent Black women authors, athletes, and politicians. A statement posted with the images reads, "In honor of Black History Month and Women's History Month, these icons were selected by AU Basketball athletes *to celebrate the crossover* and showcase a few of the many Black women in history who have paved the way for our athletes" (emphasis added).

In placing Brittney Griner and other current and former professional athletes alongside Toni Morrison, Angela Davis, and Barbara Jordan, AU players articulate a lineage that connects them across industry and time. That

Figure 6. A section of the AU Basketball concourse in Fair Park.

they can see themselves in conversation with contemporaries such as Naomi Osaka as well as historical figures such as Althea Gibson in tennis speaks to a broader conceptualization of what it means to be a Black female athlete. This timeline is also animated by the thinkers, writers, and political figures pictured, with the Angela Davis quote reading, "Our histories never unfold in isolation. We cannot truly tell what we consider to be our own histories without knowing the other stories. And often we discover that those other stories are actually our own stories." Here, the notion of crossover, invoked in the AU concourse, is about the convergence of intellectual and athletic figures, those whose "stories" and "histories" have more in common than often meets the eye and too often operate outside the purview of mainstream discourses.

Chair Chats and Hot Seats

In its public benefit corporation (PBC) report, Athletes Unlimited specifically addressed its approach to media: "When we set out to reimagine professional sports, we also wanted to reimagine the ways we watch, support, and learn about our favorite leagues and athletes."[20] Before heading to Dallas for the 2023 AU Basketball season, I reached out and requested credentials, alerting AU officials of my intention to conduct field observations and interviews for research. Both through their media representatives and across their website, I accessed more in-depth, engaging information about the league and its players than anywhere else I've worked as a former employee in sport or as a researcher. Before, during, and after games, I found a wealth of information, dynamically presented and ideally situated for anyone who may need it, whether a journalist on deadline or a passionate fan looking for more postgame coverage. This may feel trivial, but for a new league emerging in an oversaturated sports media market, these details are more important than ever.

During the 2024 season, I interviewed Arie Graham, AU beat reporter for *The Next*, an online publication devoted to women's basketball. When I asked her to describe the difference between covering the WNBA and AU (Graham also covers the Dallas Wings for *The Next*), she told me, "Athletes Unlimited is definitely more laid back. You have greater access to the players. . . . [AU Media Relations] are really good. You hit them up, say, 'I need to talk to such and such,' it could be done within the next couple of days. It's the same with the players. Like, they're more relaxed. It's not as much pressure. They're not really in a box to say, 'Oh, I can't say this, I can't say that' with the fear of getting fined." She described AU as a space free of the WNBA's gatekeeping, where access to players takes the familiar form of press conferences or long waits to get one-on-one interviews for feature-length articles. This willingness to work with media members to expand the reach of Athletes Unlimited can also be seen in its ad campaigns to promote the season. Arie told me that even though AU is a new league, its presence across broadcast media is a sharp contrast to its WNBA counterpart in the city: "I've heard more Athletes Unlimited commercials since they've been here than Dallas Wings on the radio. Every day they're saying, 'Hey, you know, we got tickets for AU.' The first time I ever heard a Dallas Wings commercial on [local hip-hop radio station] 97.9 was last year, and that was just for the playoffs. After we lost, they were still playing the same thing. Like, we're not going to the championship. Why is this commercial on?" Beyond this, being seen and heard across broadcast media operates in myriad ways for AU. Fans interested in watching from home could view twenty-five of the 2023 season's thirty games on WNBA League Pass; the other five were broadcast on the CBS Sports Network.[21] During the 2024 season, games aired on the WNBA app, ESPN+, the Bally Sports regional sports networks, and locally in Dallas on CBS-owned KTXA.[22] Imani McGee-Stafford, who played during the 2022 season, noted the importance of this access in an AU segment posted online: "Women's basketball fans are always on a scavenger hunt. . . . It's the fact that it's hard to find WNBA games. I don't own channel 1127. I can't watch it. So that's one of the biggest things I love about this league is that every game is streamed. Because I think it isn't about not having the fanbase so much, that it's about everybody ain't trying to fight to do something. I think we've always struggled with the casual fans."[23]

In thinking through the experiences of both women's basketball fans and casual viewers, McGee-Stafford succinctly articulated the continuous struggle for momentum and growth within women's sport. Rebecca shared this sentiment: "So many programs and organizations, you're like begging them for information—'Who had a good game? What was the score? Why can't we see nothing?' You know, when you should just be posting it, promoting your players. . . . [At AU] some of that wealth could be spread, and [they could post] other people, whatever, sure. But for the most part, it's something that I'm proud to be a part of and want to continue to help and push the needle." She lauded AU's work with social media and marketing, given its constant presence across Instagram, Twitter, and TikTok. With the continuous content creation occurring at AU, there's also a deep investment in making sure athletes have access to quality material that can allow them to build their own brands. An AU employee told me that the media team posts all the content to SmugMug and GreenFly, two digital content distribution sites that allow players to use anything that is helpful for them. They also host regular "Athletes Plus" sessions that teach athletes various skills, such as editing Instagram Reels or TikToks, that demystify aspects of social media for players who may be less savvy on their socials. They also explain how each platform has different formatting practices and the role of algorithms in getting seen online. "They're so helpful in that regard because they know that personal branding, especially for women's sports, like, content creation, is so important because, like, we're underpaid, so we have to, like, find those brand deals, and they're there to help us," an AU employee told me.

It's seemingly not just the quantity but also the quality of the media offerings that makes Athletes Unlimited a bit different. Throughout the 2023 season, much of the arena's setup and game production remained geared toward the broadcast rather than the in-person crowd. During games, the league employs a "chair chat," where athletes not currently playing hop on a headset and give their perspectives on the game in real time. The segments invite fans to experience a bit of players' personalities and basketball IQ. Following the first AU season, elements of the league's media presence rippled across other leagues. Rebecca told me, "As soon as we popped off last season, you started seeing something added in the All-Star Game for the NBA. Looking at our leaderboard, they can certainly take away our digital marketing and how we just pump out stuff. They've taken the chair chat a little, having that chair at the end, people to talk in game. I hope they try to take as many things as they can while acknowledging what we're doing and, you know, giving props where they should." Here, Rebecca sees AU as an innovative model not just for women's sports but also for the current sports-media complex as a whole.

For fans in the arena and on YouTube, a recurring series, the "hot seat," also serves as a space where athletes are asked random, sometimes messy questions about other players, such as "Who is most likely to shoot an air ball?" and "Who could you see making an appearance on a reality TV show?" The segment showcases the camaraderie of AU players while also providing entertaining content that translates across social media. Another segment that ran inside of the arena during a timeout asked players to talk about what it meant for them to be able to play stateside; players described how important it was to play in front of their family members, some for the first time since their college career. Others articulated how crucial it was for their families to see them on a network and readily access their games and highlights. For two athletes, this went even deeper: sisters Dorie and Isabelle Harrison both competed during the 2024 season and eventually played on the same team, an opportunity nearly impossible at the pro level elsewhere. Across the games each season, players used these short segments to entertain and enlighten crowds at Fair Park and fans watching around the world.

Cindy Brunson and Sheryl Swoopes worked throughout the seasons as play-by-play announcer and color commentator, respectively, a broadcasting duo that speaks to AU's investment in the professional pedigree and dedication necessary for the sport's growth. Brunson, a former ESPN SportsCenter anchor who currently calls games at both the college and WNBA levels, offers a wealth of experience within the world of women's basketball. She is paired with Hall of Famer, three-time Olympic gold medalist, and four-time WNBA champion Swoopes. The duo's investment in the sport and the league is palpable as they run through each play. Rebecca told me, "[Swoopes is] a WNBA legend, and the WNBA hasn't highlighted her as well as they should have over the years. You know, she's someone, if we're being honest, . . . that should always have a job within the W. I feel like no matter what, [she's someone] you make sure you take care of, the pioneers." Here, Rebecca speaks to how other leagues failed to properly elevate their former athletes, especially someone like Swoopes, the very first player signed to the WNBA. Frequently, when Sheryl Swoopes is discussed in popular media or sport studies literature, she is framed within her status as a pioneer of the sport, especially as it relates to her branding endorsements and, relatedly, her coming-out narrative.[24] However, what I would like to consider here is how the voices of the AU broadcast assist in a continued move away from what Michela Musto, Cheryl Cooky, and Michael A. Messner describe as "gender-bland sexism," a move away from the blatantly disrespectful language hurled at female athletes over highlights and broadcasts to the delivery of sporting action "in a lackluster and uninspired manner."[25] Gender-bland sexism, working in perhaps the same way as color-blind racism, runs the risk of being seen as "progress" even as it obscures how it continues to shape a sporting hierarchy that suggests women's sports are less interesting or valuable than their male counterparts. We see this in game calls where announcers mispronounce star athletes' names, exude more energy toward male athletes in attendance than the women competing on the floor, or fail to provide key context shaping the matchup's storylines. That Brunson and Swoopes intimately know the women's game, actively advocate for the sport beyond their broadcasting duties, and enthusiastically articulate the game for those watching at home is evident in every game call and segment they contribute to Athletes Unlimited.

AU also incorporates key influencers and younger journalists who represent the future of women's basketball. During the first season, the league enlisted Ari Chambers of HighlightHER as a moderator of a roundtable discussion called *All on the Table*, episodes that allow three or four athletes to discuss their journeys in basketball together and debate the latest issues in the sport. Chambers also attended games during the second season and rejoined the media crew for season 3. Khristina Williams (Girls Talk Sports TV) and Savanna Collins previously hosted weekly Instagram lives during the first season of AU and in the second season led a weekly preview show discussing the upcoming slate of games. Their guests included journalists like Terrika Foster-Brasby (ESPN) and Myles Ehrlich (Winsidr), two key voices across women's basketball media. Mariluz Cook, a rising sports journalist, joined the broadcast team for the second season as a sideline reporter. This expansion in the second season also included local basketball figures in Ivy Winfrey, previously the official DJ for the NBA's Dallas Mavericks, who joined AU as the in-arena host, bringing both the energy and the spatial specificity of Dallas hoops culture. This integration of journalists and influencers at the cutting edge of women's basketball is fascinating and, as Forbes.com contributor Erica L. Ayala writes, "one of the largest signs that AU is integrating the suggestions of its athletes in real time. Women's basketball players and fans know who has their finger on the pulse and I for one am elated to see what I would call the All-Stars of women's basketball coverage working with the league."[26]

During the 2024 season, AU seemingly expanded its arena production as more fans attended in person, even selling out available tickets online for at least one of the games I attended. When I walked into the arena, I saw a massive LED monitor projecting the names and images of each of the AU champions, a vivid, larger-than-life tribute to the league's winners across each sport. Before each game, in-arena host Olivia West addressed fans from one corner of the arena, giving them an AU 101 class, which included coaching the crowd through the point system, explaining the game ritual of standing up until the first bucket of the game, and leading them in the emphatic "A-U!" chant. She quickly became a crowd favorite; I watched one day as fans approached her, with one proclaiming, "You're doing an excellent job, by the way!" West also serves as the in-game host for the NBA's Indiana Pacers, a role she continued to perform throughout the AU season, traveling back and forth between Indianapolis and Dallas as both seasons operated simultaneously, a seemingly exhausting travel schedule that mirrors the continued labor translation of the players on the court. Also joining AU in 2024 was content creator Janae Sims, a women's basketball fan who brought her social media savvy (and following) to the media team, representing what the future of women's sports content could look like for the next generation. Given how difficult it is for young journalists and creatives (especially women of color) to break into the sports industry, Cook, Sims, and West seemingly represent the opportunities AU offers to those both on and off the court.

Just as important in the media coverage is what is not covered within Athletes Unlimited. Throughout the 2023 AU season, I noticed one player who was consistently dressed in street clothes. In media reports, pregame coverage, and even the drafts, there was no clear reason provided as to why DiJonai Carrington wasn't playing. She attended each game (with her puppy in tow) and supported her team throughout the season, but I frequently heard murmurs throughout the concourse or in the crowd, with spectators unsure of why she wasn't on the court. AU sideline reporter Mariluz Cook shared with me the intentionality behind this—keeping medical updates of athletes in-house. I realized the potential impact of disclosing injuries for athletes seeking (or in the midst of) contracts in other leagues. Historically, as James Blake Hike argues, protecting players' personal health information (PHI) is weighed against the interests of teams, media, and fans.[27] While debates swirl surrounding what types of injuries or illnesses are fair game to disclose, the semblance of community and the financial investment formed around professional sport, including taxpayer-funded stadiums and the ever-expanding reach of gambling, add to the entitlement many feel regarding athletes' bodies.[28] Other unionized US professional leagues collectively bargain for how players' PHI is shared, so AU's policy within a nonunionized league is an important one. Too often, as Hike writes, "the athlete's interest in keeping [their] PHI private arguably succumbs to the interests of athletic organizations, the media, and the public . . . [given] the athlete's choice to thrust themselves into the lime-light by playing a collegiate or professional sport."[29] The fact that this league normalized the privacy of athletes' health data without compromising the design and execution of the league requires further examination that could offer new insights for other teams and leagues in the future.

Activating Agency

Like other aspects of women's basketball, the networked relationships be-tween players allow them to share opportunities with one another, especially with an up-and-coming league like AU. Multiple athletes shared that they learned about AU from a fellow athlete or reached out to someone they knew who planned to play. Rebecca told me that her AU career started with a direct message to Sydney Colson. In a segment on how the first season came to be, Lexie Brown said, "Nobody was chosen at random. . . . They're good players, but they're better people."[30] This approach seemingly guided not only the players who took the court but also the staff and media that worked behind the scenes to promote the sport. When I chatted with one player after a game, she shared that she loved the folks selected by AU to cover the sport in game and across social media; for her, it wasn't just about prior media experience but about how those covering the teams each week treated athletes and staff members.

In between games one day, I met Molly McCage, an AU Volleyball player who worked during the 2023 basketball season as manager of player care and coordination. She described her position as operational in regard to travel as well as serving as a liaison between staff and athletes. When I asked her to give a rundown of her day-to-day routine, she told me, "I'm talking to the athletes the most for game days. . . . I'm the one, you know, getting them miked up, encouraging them to get in the chair chats and share their stories. But I'm re-ally there to help be the voice of the athletes so that the staff hears them and listens to them." She originally got started with the league when a former USA teammate, Jordan Larson, reached out to her after she retired from playing overseas in 2019 and asked if she was interested in playing stateside.

Playing in the United States was a major draw for AU athletes across all sports. Molly's international career as a volleyball player required her to leave in early August and return to the States around May: "It's a wonderful opportunity to even play this sport professionally because we had to go over-seas. There was not an option whenever I graduated. And so [it was like], 'You should be grateful for the opportunity, right?'" While she told me that she felt she had "lucked out" and had a good experience playing in Germany—she lived in a safe city and was paid on time—she also mentioned how her experience as a professional athlete varied significantly from her collegiate career. "The word 'professional' is a broad term," she told me.

At The University of Texas at Austin, medical staff used bloodwork to find the specific vitamins to optimize Molly's performance. There were nutrition-ists to assist with meal planning, and workout and practice schedules were clearly defined. "All of a sudden you go overseas, and you have to do those things yourself. They're like, 'Go lift on your own. I am assuming you know how to take care of your body.' And I truly didn't." At Athletes Unlimited, she sees the dedication to players' experience differently:

> There's an entire athletic experience team . . . and they have meetings with you: "What would you like your game day meals to be, and what time would you like them to be? How many athletic trainers would you like on site? Do you need Theraguns [massage guns]? Do you need NormaTech [compression therapy equipment]?" Even down to the uniforms, I was like, "I really hate wearing spandex, like short spandex. I think they're very uncomfortable for me. Is it possible to wear leggings for our games?" And they were like, "Sure, yeah." Wow. That had never happened in profes-sional volleyball ever. . . . They ask and they listen. Like, it's just that we're always a part of the conversation.

Being "part of the conversation" and being able to advocate for attire and accommodations that make the athlete experience better were recurring themes across sports. "I just feel like there's such a team within staff in AU, and somebody's always gonna advocate for me, and that is not something I felt overseas," Molly said.

In her position within AU Basketball, Molly not only ensures that athletes have everything they need to compete on the court but also serves as a voice for them off it. "I know that these athletes wanna make an impact outside of their sport, and they've expressed that, but this is their job," Molly told me. "I'm trying to make sure that they feel well taken care of and that they're rest-ing in between games and able to take care of their bodies." In considering the role of wellness from this holistic framework, Molly becomes an important connection between AU employees and athletes so that the role of advocacy does not solely fall on players actively working to compete at the highest level: "If our partnership team is like, 'You know, it'd be super great to have five of them come to this event and hang out with [league] partners,' and it all sounds awesome, we try to make those events happen. But sometimes the athletes can get overloaded with people trying to pull them in different directions . . . and I'm there to kind of monitor what exactly are we giving the athletes." In her role, Molly assists in outlining the difference between mandatory and optional events and gauging athlete interest in participating in each. "Sometimes it's just not appealing to a certain player, and that's totally fine," she said. "I'll be like, 'This is exactly what you're doing, this is what's expected of you, this is what you'll get out of it. Are you interested?' And if you're interested, great. If not, that's okay."

During one game, I sat for a while with WNBPA president Nneka Ogwumike, who attended her first AU game during my time there. I learned a lot from a union president taking in another league, gleaning the similarities and differences between the W and AU. She first learned about the league from a softball player and came to see the game firsthand. Like Nneka, several players expressed doubts surrounding how "real" this league actually was; for many, the promise of stateside salaries, quality opponents, and a long-term investment in the sport felt like fantasy. In an AU-produced segment on the first basketball season, Sydney Colson says, "It was difficult because this sounds like a pipe dream to a lot of people, because once again, the WNBA is what's existed. So people have heard about other things happening in previous years, like maybe even decades ago, but it never happened. So when you hear something like this, and you hear you're going to be paid, it's going to be in one location, there's going to be great competition, people are like, 'Yeah, sure' [scoffs in disbelief]."[31] In the same segment, Lexie Brown says, "I feel like we're pioneers of this. Nobody thought that we'd be able to gather this many players and come play in a league that's competitive, that's fun, that's going to be enjoyable, that's going to be exciting." Athletes Unlimited seemingly offers a game-changing approach to the sport. However, new questions have emerged as to how a league invested in player agency might sustain itself in a white, heteropatriarchal sports-media complex deeply entrenched in late-stage capitalism.

Beyond Corporate Social Responsibility

In their 2022 report, AU's cofounders describe establishing the league "because investing in female athletes is good business."[32] Much has been made recently of the profitability of women's sports, with recent business reports declaring the "immense potential value, not just in monetary terms, but also in terms of what it signals for gender parity."[33] In an article for Forbes.com, Liz Elting wrote, "Sports are a business, after all. And while that is of course true, the facts don't support the claim that women's sports aren't good business. Just the opposite in fact."[34]

In blending a business imperative with an attempt to do right by women's sports, Athletes Unlimited delineates itself not as a nonprofit organization or in line with other corporate leagues in existence but as a PBC. In the United States, this designation began in 2013 and defines a for-profit corporation that offers a public benefit and conducts operations in a responsible, sustainable way.[35] Companies certified as PBCs must navigate a difficult balance in ensuring that investors are satisfied with profit margins while also meeting preestablished standards of progress in delivering public benefits.[36] AU argues that "in a world in which female athletes receive less than 5% of sports media coverage, distributing high-quality productions of women's sports becomes a public benefit in itself."[37]

The concept of "public benefit" seems to move beyond the now rehearsed ritual of corporate social responsibility (CSR) in sport; breast cancer awareness merchandise, initiatives aimed at increasing youth sport participation, and athletes serving food to those in need become shorthand visuals for attempts at care by corporate entities. As Aaron C. T. Smith and Hans M. Westerbeek argue, "Sport, more than any other potential vehicle, contains qualities that make it a powerful force in effecting positive social contributions."[38] Whether through private philanthropy, strategic development projects, or even social justice partnerships, the current CSR in a sport framework poses several questions: What are the tangible benefits and social impacts? Who are corporate entities ultimately accountable to? What are their politics? And what are the potential risks to organizational reputation when CSR is considered merely a PR maneuver to cover previous bad press?[39]

That the "public benefit" from a top-down standpoint addresses gender disparities in sport makes room for an intervention from below by athletes.

Perhaps due to a cofounder heavily entrenched in political action and philanthropy, AU is situated miles from discourses that ponder whether sports and politics should mix.[40] Instead, AU is directly located at that intersection, given that each athlete chooses their own organization to amplify and financially support through their play on the court. Leading into the season, Cause Reveal Night allowed each athlete to share how they chose the organization they represent and support. One AU employee told me, "I was bawling. . . . It was so moving and so powerful. I think that's something I've seen across all [of the AU leagues] is that element of 'we're really here to make a change.' . . . Everybody has this fight of, like, 'We're really pushing the needle here.'"

While these decisions may not feel particularly revolutionary, given the fraught landscape of nonprofit organizations and the neoliberal politics of corporate social responsibility, it is important to note that within sport, professional athletes seldom have the opportunity within their teams or leagues to individually advocate for causes. That athletes' causes are incorporated into opening lineups, halftime engagement, and media outreach speaks to the centralization of their voice in the decision making and programming of the league itself.

We need only consider how other pro sports organizations previously penalized players for individual forms of advocacy, even when the cause itself is pushed by the top brass of the league. Take, for example, the National Football League's Crucial Catch program, a partnership with the American Cancer Society (ACS) that aims to raise awareness for early detection and to honor those currently battling cancer. This partnership includes a significant amount of National Football League (NFL) merchandise, with Crucial Catch emblazoned across the hats and hoodies designed to raise awareness and funds for ACS. A Google search for Crucial Catch is more likely to direct you to a link to purchase from the NFL Shop than to resources to assist in understanding cancer risk and detection.

The NFL's advocacy for cancer detection and treatment is amplified perhaps the most in October, when players, cheerleaders, and fans are decked out in pink for Breast Cancer Awareness Month. The league's partnership has been criticized for massive disparities in the amount of money generated by the merchandise versus the amount that reaches the ACS. In 2015 sports journalist Julie DiCaro wrote, "The NFL's gift to ACS is the couch change teams find after cleaning out their stadium suites."[41] That year the NFL also fined running back DeAngelo Williams $5,787 for wearing eye black that read "Find the Cure." Williams, who lost his mother and four aunts to breast cancer, has continually advocated for breast cancer awareness off the field, connecting with hospitals and funding mammograms.[42] Given this preestablished relationship with breast cancer advocacy, he previously requested to wear pink shoes and/or wristbands for the duration of the season, a full commitment that extends beyond the league's one-month pink extravaganza; the NFL told him no. Williams is not the only player to face fines for eye black advocacy. His then Steelers teammate, defensive end Cam Heyward, also faced fines for eye black honoring his father, Craig "Ironhead" Heyward, a former NFL player who passed away at age thirty-nine from bone cancer. "It was the 'wrong' kind of cancer in the 'wrong' month, with [NFL commissioner] Roger Goodell & Co. having nothing to show for it," DiCaro wrote.[43]

Athletes Unlimited, on the other hand, emphasizes the individual investments players have in various organizations. Their causes range from massive national nonprofit organizations (Special Olympics, Ronald McDonald House Charities) to local grassroots foundations (Latino Network, Heart N Hands). What I found particularly important in examining all of the causes by athletes is the number of organizations started by or in memory of a fellow athlete. During the 2023 season, athlete causes included Katie's Save, the Shaquille O'Neal Foundation, Mamba & Mambacita Sports Foundation, Morgan's Message, the Virago Project, Kay Yow Cancer Fund, Ron Burton Training Village, One Love Foundation, and the Layshia Clarendon Foundation. The Layshia Clarendon Foundation is perhaps the closest to the AU's rosters. Clarendon, the WNBA's first out trans and nonbinary player, started the foundation to provide health care and advocate for the trans community; AU's setup allowed them in 2023 to simultaneously compete as an athlete on the court while raising awareness and funding for their foundation. Another AU player, Kierstan Bell, also chose the Layshia Clarendon Foundation for her cause.

Playing against Politicians

As the 2023 AU Basketball season tipped off at Fair Park Coliseum, the political landscape in the United States reflected the realities of continued economic precarity, distrust of government figures, and a sharp rollback of key liberal victories of the twentieth century. In June 2022 the reversal of *Roe v. Wade*, the landmark Supreme Court case legalizing abortion in the United States, resulted in individual states now possessing the right to determine whether to ban the procedure and, furthermore, whether those who have an abortion (or aid someone else) could be subject to prosecution.[44] In the months following that decision, fourteen states made abortion illegal.[45]

At the same time, new debates emerged concerning the rights of the LGBTQ+ community. Don't Say Gay educational policies, legislation passed to ban drag shows, and the ongoing threat to same-sex marriage point to a wholesale homophobic turn. "I think we're actually in an exceptionally ugly moment in terms of some figures deciding that there's utility, political utility, in targeting trans people and LGBTQ people more generally," Pete Buttigieg, US transportation secretary and the highest-ranking out government official, told *Time Magazine*.[46] "The situation of an upper-middle-class, married white gay dude is not the same as a trans kid in Texas, or any number of LGBTQ people of color trying to survive right now," he said.[47] In the interview, he pointed to how homophobic Republican leaders see political clout in these attacks, whereas he sees distraction and true harm.

Speaking of Texas, at the state level, lawmakers passed bills banning gender-affirming medical care for transgender children and restricting athletic opportunities for trans athletes at the collegiate level.[48] Meanwhile, in a plotline straight from a dystopian novel, book banning also proliferated across the state, with a report finding that Texas banned more books from school libraries than any other state in the country. The ban stems from Matt Krause, a Republican state representative based in Fort Worth who created a list of 850 books with themes related to race or sexuality and sought information on how many of the books were available in school libraries.[49]

While some called for other women's basketball events, such as the 2023 Final Four (also scheduled for Dallas) to be moved out of the state, the AU response, driven by players, reflected a different strategy.[50] Below the scoreboard station, a recurring sign cycled through the electronic billboard that read, "We Support the Transgender Community," emblazoned with the blue, pink, and white hues of the trans flag. Rosters and media materials include player pronouns. The venue has been retrofitted with all-gender restrooms. A play area for kids is set up next to the AU merchandise area.

In addition to these physical designations of inclusivity, the league and its players have also addressed the political climate through their promotions. A Bookshop collaboration allowed players to select books that fans can enter a drawing to win. Not only do athletes pick titles that are important to them, but in segments aired on the jumbotron, they explain their choices.

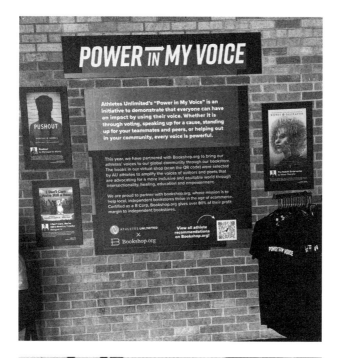

Figure 7. Promotional materials for AU Basketball's Bookshop collaboration.

Clarendon, when explaining why they picked Nnedi Okorafor's *Akata Witch*, described how historically science fiction had excluded Black characters, creating period pieces that didn't imagine Black folks in the future. Another player, DiJonai Carrington, chose Monique W. Morris's *Pushout: The Criminalization of Black Girls in Schools*, and explained how the book articulates racialized and gendered disparities faced by Black girls in the US educational system. In a promotional element placed in the entry to the arena beneath the QR code to enter the drawing, Carrington is quoted as saying that the book reminded her why, "one, representation is so important and, two, one of the reasons that sport has always been like an outlet for myself and many Black girls growing up." The book promotion was part of AU's Power in My Voice initiative and was designed to "[advocate] for a more inclusive and equitable world through intersectionality, healing, education, and empowerment."

In a moment when online discourses often discarded the South as "backward" or beyond repair, the AU players seemingly chose to make an intervention within it. The 2023 AU Basketball season was a reminder of how the "magic" of the crossover often lies in exposing the weaknesses of a defender, one seeking to prevent forward momentum; the crossover must be initiated from close range. While the league is static in its location each season, the political mobilization of the athletes who comprise its rosters is adaptable and aware of the spatial specificity required to execute each maneuver. There is perhaps a question of how this league can "afford" to be so outspoken. Are its politics the result of how it is funded? Is it able to leverage its political stance because of the impermanence of its location? Or is the absence of team ownership in lieu of a more equitable business model a key driver in this mobility? As I constantly considered the relationship between the league, its athletes, and their strategic choices throughout the season, I returned to a quote from historian Amira Rose Davis, who, in charting the activism of Black athletes past and present, has written, "Black women athletes have, and continue to take great risk in advocating for social and political change inside and outside of sports, even as they garner less visibility for their actions."[51]

Clashing Causes

The 2024 AU Basketball season saw an increase in sponsorship presence, including Madam Paleta, an infused tequila brand, and the US Air Force. AU also continued previous partnerships with other entities, including Nike, the

US Air National Guard, and Gatorade. New elements also emphasized the local, with the Dallas County Commissioners Court tabling in the concourse; a recurring video ad for Reunion Tower, a local attraction; and a theme night partnership with Girls Empowered by Mavericks, an organization connected to the NBA's Dallas Mavericks that fuses wellness initiatives with elements such as financial literacy and education.

Upon first glance, the 2024 season felt a bit more politically muted than its previous iteration. The upfront support of the trans community in 2023 was replaced by a visual with the blue, pink, and white trans flag in the background with the words "We believe in the power of sport to tear down barriers, inspire individuals, and unite people" obscuring the continued threat to trans life and instead offering a generic sporting empowerment statement. A recurring in-game element on the jumbotron connected the league to former First Lady Michelle Obama's When We All Vote initiative, one centered around voter registration. The 2024 Bookshop Power in My Voice collaboration featured self-help books such as James Clear's *Atomic Habits*, Jon Gordon's *The Energy Bus*, and Don Miguel Ruiz and Janet Mills's *The Four Agreements*. Player voice and agency felt ever present, but one theme night in particular revealed key shifts in the league's investments.

On March 17, 2024, I entered Fair Park Coliseum and, following the usual bag check and ticket scan, was handed a black bucket hat with the words "Supporting Black Women in the Military," flanked by the Athletes Unlimited and US Air Force logos. Behind me, a military officer in uniform stood behind an Air Force Reserve table, handing out giveaways to a young boy walking through the concourse. It was a Special Impact Day for Athletes Unlimited, one of several theme game days chosen by AU athletes and amplified by league partners. That day, which was centered on Black women in the armed forces, included the overwhelming presence of camo, the bucket hat giveaway, and focused in-game production that signaled a shift in how this league might grapple with clashing causes.

The LED board beneath the scorer's table featured many of the same elements from other games, including the revolving "Serve Your State | Serve Your Nation | Serve Your Way" Air National Guard ad. However, it also included "Supporting Black Women in the Military" warmup shirts worn by some players pregame, game ball delivery by Black women veterans working for various military-oriented organizations, and two video segments that aired during each game in which players stated why this particular impact theme was important to them. In one video, Rebecca Harris shared her own identity as a "military brat," while Whitney Knight honored her veteran father. Angel McCoughtry discussed her desire to highlight the contributions of women in the armed forces. Settling into my seat as I took in the militarization of this space, an arena where soldiers in head-to-toe camo took to the court during timeouts to assist in the T-shirt toss, I considered how much felt like it had changed in just one year within this league. During the second AU game that afternoon, dozens of young air force trainees filled the court and took their oath of enlistment, our halftime entertainment before the second half of game play. Watching this, I couldn't help but think of Michael Butterworth's work at the intersection of sport and militarism that succinctly captures the powerful combination of consumption, entertainment, and patriotism within the field of play, especially in moments of rupture.[52] That sport can conjoin with militarism somewhat seamlessly and, in turn, sell this ideal of a unified nation is at the heart of his work.

However, leaving the arena that evening, I considered how this theme game did not commemorate the US military-industrial complex in quite the same way as previous iterations across sports, such as Major League Baseball (MLB) and the NFL, for three primary reasons. First, AU Basketball's player executive committee chose this Special Impact Day rather than the front-office decisions leveraged in other leagues. Across both games, players shared their relationship to the US armed forces through their friends and family members and chose to honor them through the programming and partnerships of the day. This stands in sharp contrast to mandated camo uniforms, required participation, and penalties for opting out. Players who did not want to wear the merchandise or record videos had the option to refuse. Second, the concept of centering Black women's experiences within the US military-industrial complex felt a bit different from the familiar tropes of law enforcement or the military that often center a white able-bodied heterosexual male soldier as the face of the nation; it instead employed a racialized empowerment feminism logic for the event, with a hyperfocus on how Black women specifically encounter this space as a means of combatting overly rehearsed rituals of allegiance to the nation-state. During an interview at half court with one of the invited representatives from the Veteran Women's Enterprise Center, she compared the experience of women in the military to those within sport: "They're not putting their life on the line but putting their livelihood on the line." Even in a league that begins its games sans anthem, this connection signals the sportswashing that can still occur by the US armed forces and their representatives. The familiar connection of teamwork, discipline, and work ethic to both military engagement and sporting practice was employed here not only through the role of the body as weapon, as barrier (military defense vs. sporting defense), but also as a shared experience of discrimination and the sexist systems in place for both uniformed officers and uniformed athletes. This is a shift from how Michael Silk describes the post-9/11 discourses and performances of nation within sporting spaces. He describes this landscape as "characterized by a mostly unquestioned masculinized, racialized, patriarchal, and militarized body politic," one that he argues is manifested through fear, patriarchy, and the celebration of white masculinity.[53] To flip the focus to the experiences of Black women offers a different encounter, one similarly rooted in the same forms of empire but updated for the #LeanIn and #girlboss aesthetic.

Finally, I want to consider what it means to understand this theme game as not representative of every Athletes Unlimited player. I considered, for example, how athletes who protested the militarization of law enforcement through the Movement for Black Lives might understand the shirts, hats, and pageantry of the day. I also contemplated how an athlete's chosen cause might operate in direct conflict with the impact game. For example, Natasha "Tasha" Cloud's 2024 athlete cause is Palestinian Youth Movement (PYM), a transnational grassroots organization dedicated to collective organizing, educational training, and cultural events for Palestinian youth around the world. Given the US imperial collaboration with Israeli occupation and the direct military weapon support offered by the federal government, Cloud's collaboration with PYM brought necessary tension, what Butterworth might call "engaged citizenship," one that shares a "recognition that there are times when, as athletes, it is important to acknowledge, or even resist, the political associations that are commonly featured in sport."[54] In October 2023 Cloud tweeted, "As a pro athlete, I will lose deals because of my support of Palestine. I won't get certain endorsement sponsorships because of my stance moving forward. I knowingly take food out of my families' mouths in hopes that another can eat. I choose my moral compass over money."[55] Natasha Cloud's cause and her investment through her online advocacy and her official cause throughout the season (the designation one "plays for" throughout AU) serve as a key reminder that the league is called Athletes Unlimited, not Athletes Unified. I found myself struggling to understand how there might be space for both Cloud's cause and this athlete-driven theme game, slipping into the same trap that Butterworth warns against in pursuit of "unity" or an easy understanding. He instead considers what it might mean to balance "sport's unifying potential with its inherent comfort with conflict," a position he admits is particularly difficult for members of marginalized groups.[56]

Pushing the Game Forward

"Do you know how hard it is to maintain a job for ten years with zero stats?"[57] It's a question Theresa Plaisance asks during a pitch meeting for her show with Sydney Colson. *The Syd + TP Show*, produced by Togethxr, focuses on the intangibles of two athletes known more for their larger-than-life personalities than their on-the-court prowess. Their popularity during the AU season and their continued relationship as teammates with the Las Vegas Aces translated to their own online series as well as several WNBA commercials for accounting firm Deloitte. These media openings are but one example of the potential of Athletes Unlimited as a player-forward league. In considering how the athletes within this compressed season create space for one another and breathing room in a congested year-round schedule, I draw upon Gaye Theresa Johnson's concept of "spatial entitlement," where new collectivities can emerge that are based not solely on being excluded from the mainstream but on creative uses of technology, space, and resistance.[58] Spatial entitlement allows us to understand not only how power shifts over time but also how we might perceive "everyday acts of resistance and survival demonstrative of more than just the courage of freedom seekers."[59] In her work, Johnson considers how music, and popular culture more broadly, offers strategies to create new political possibilities.[60] In the same way she thinks about how, for example, a DJ might use turntables to beat juggle, to conjure new ways of knowing through an intimate understanding of the structure of songs and where they might conjoin in order to find balance, new complexities, new ways of hearing, so too do the players of Athletes Unlimited navigate a new opportunity, a new league that requires them to tap into the knowledge they have acquired from collegiate, WNBA, and/or overseas careers in order to create something different.[61]

In an episode of *All on the Table*, Imani McGee-Stafford calls AU a "beautiful opportunity."[62] Molly McCage shared with me the general sentiment she has experienced during her time as a volleyball player and basketball employee for AU: "Women's sports just need this. Like we have deserved it tenfold. You know what I mean? ... We've, like, skipped generations of legends, and I think we're so ready." AU cofounder Jon Patricof told *Forbes*, "When you combine the financial opportunity but also what this might mean from a personal family perspective ... and also from an overall wear and tear on players' bodies, a more condensed experience may be better than it would if they were overseas through a grueling seven-month season."[63] For those who may not have the opportunity to compete for the WNBA or thrive in overseas markets, Athletes Unlimited offers an accessible, inclusive opportunity stateside that seems to sidestep so many of the previous perils of new women's basketball leagues. Ayala writes, "Athletes Unlimited is doing what even the WNBA has been slow to do—it is starting with Black women at the forefront."[64]

Several questions lingered for me at the end of the 2024 Athletes Unlimited Basketball season. Is this a sustainable model? Would potential pressure from politicians or sponsors shift the mission of AU? And as the sporting calendar continues to build, how will AU compete with other sports seasons for spectators and viewers? In designing what it calls an "innovative player-centric model," the league seems to offer new insights on player labor, the potential of athlete activism, and sports media practices.[65] However, I constantly returned to what the "limits" of Athletes Unlimited might truly mean. I watched Odyssey Sims share a touching moment with a loved one who brought her flowers, only to be interrupted by a fan who wanted to take a picture with her. She kindly told them she would come find them after her postgame routine and eventually emerged, following through on her promise. After another game, I sat with another player who suffered an injury during the game and needed to go home to ice and elevate but stayed behind to do an interview with a journalist. Watching her limp toward the camera setup and stand for the duration of the conversation, I wondered what the long-term costs of this amount of access to athletes could mean for their mental and physical health. And in considering how AU's "Supporting Black Women in the Military" game invoked familiar tropes of uniting sport with the (militarized) nation, I wondered how the growth of the league might also cause it to conform to the standardized US professional sport partnerships and programming.

When I asked how other leagues could learn from AU, Molly told me, "Ask questions—have an athlete in every single room where you're making decisions." That being said, AU is still fairly new, and participants identified spaces for improvement within the league. Some of these aspects cut across sports. "There are pain points, right? Like the changing every week isn't fun. . . . Team chemistry, that's hard to work through," Molly told me. "I really miss being on a traditional team with, like, a home team and a fan base. I know that is the opposite of AU, right? Like the model is individual centric—the fans wanna cheer on this specific athlete, and I'm all for that. But as a team player, I miss a team, you know?"

Rebecca had thoughts on the point system and shared, "I think maybe one day we might add some things to it. Or change some things. But it makes you think differently. It makes you do things differently. You wanna be more aware of the shots you take. You wanna be more aware of the passes you make." She also conceptualized shifts in how minutes operated in the league: "If I could change anything, it might be the amount of time allotted for people to play. Because I think that would change a lot of things. . . . I think something should be made where the minimum—and this is really just something that I'm thinking about right now for real—but like the minimum everyone should play is ten minutes. So everyone gets an opportunity to do something."

Finally, the growth potential of AU looks different from various vantage points. "Sometimes I wonder if we could add more players, but if you add more players, that changes how many people you can have on a team," Rebecca told me. "Do we need to add more teams? Which means we need to add more jerseys, which means we need to change the color scheme of everything. So there's that. . . . But, you know, with time . . . I'd love to see more people get an opportunity to be in this mix."

As the 2023 season came to an end in late March, the city of Dallas prepared to host another major women's basketball event: the NCAA Final Four. In the next chapter, I consider how the conclusions of the collegiate women's basketball season in 2023 and 2024 offer key insights into the future of the sport.

You Can't See Me

Moving Past Misogynoir during March Madness

MARCH 31, 2023 | DALLAS, TEXAS | VICTORY PARK

Pulling up to the American Airlines Center (AAC), I'm barely out of my Uber when scalpers begin to approach me constantly, not to sell me entry into the arena but to ask whether I have extra tickets that they could buy from me. It's a strange role reversal for a set of semifinals games that will determine the two teams that advance to the 2023 NCAA Women's Final Four title game. Ultimately unable to secure tickets to the semifinal games that Friday, I watched the game at Hero Bar, mere steps from the entrance to the AAC. It felt good to be in a sports bar blasting the audio of a women's sporting event in a massive standing-room-only space where the raucous crowd lived and died with every possession. Commercial breaks served as key moments when chants rained down. In a sea of fandom—University of Iowa, University of South Carolina, Louisiana State University (LSU), and Virginia Tech—it seemed that beyond the numbers, the energy behind the women's game felt more dynamic than ever before. One fan near me wore a shirt boasting "Iowa: The Women's Basketball State," acknowledging the storied state history of the sport at all levels. Another passed me wearing a shirt that read "WBB vs. Everybody." That day, it felt like the game could take on anyone.

In this chapter I consider discourses of growth and futurity of women's basketball at the conclusion of the 2023 NCAA season. Here, the hypervisibility of the sport ran concurrent with a yearlong celebration of the fiftieth anniversary of the passage of Title IX, signaling how far the game has come and, perhaps more vividly, the work that remains.

For me, Final Four represented a homecoming of sorts. Returning to my own hometown, Dallas, for the tournament's conclusion felt serendipitous after eight years of fieldwork for a book that focuses on labor as it circulates around the world. Whereas frigid Russian nights felt so far from what I knew as a researcher or a sport fan, the coziness of the familiar in my home state washed over me both spatially and intellectually. As I attended various events around the city, I found myself constantly running into the participants and concepts that frame this project. At breakfast one morning, I found myself seated next to Mark Campbell and Xavier Lopez, two previous assistant coaches at the University of Oregon who recruited Satou and Nyara Sabally to the Ducks. Before the pandemic, I met both coaches for coffee as I began to consider how the Sabally sisters' experience as German athletes migrating their labor to the United States for a collegiate career differed from the mobilities I experienced for professional US players competing overseas. However, a global pandemic and the resulting end of the 2020 NCAA season shuttered the potential for in-person interviews and field observations. Campbell, the newly-appointed head coach of Texas Christian University women's basketball, not only brought Coach Lopez along but also hired his former players—Minyon Moore, the Sabally sisters, and Ruthy Hebard—onto his staff. As we greeted one another, a wave of déjà vu washed over me, reminding me not only of the journey of completing this book but also of the research possibilities that remain.

At a pop-up event hosted by Playa Society, a clothing brand dedicated to women's sports, I found myself running into participants from Athletes Unlimited and hoops fans I had met at Sparks games years ago. My next stop, a book signing for *Hoop Muses*—a basketball book cocurated in part by WNBA champion, coach, and Athletes Unlimited facilitator Seimone Augustus—featured a panel that included Augustus and Nneka Ogwumike discussing the WNBA's growth and the work that remains to ensure athletes' safety and financial security.[1] Outside, the Sneaker Politics storefront exterior featured a massive Nike campaign centering Sydney Colson.

The night before the championship game, at a party hosted by the WNBA's Dallas Wings, I found myself surrounded by the athletes and journalists who informed so much of this work. The following day, while I was standing outside the arena, a security guard from Athletes Unlimited who remembered my face from my time there approached me. Sports journalist Natalie Weiner wrote of the weekend, "Even more than on the men's side, the Women's Final Four acts as a hub for all tiers of the sport, with pros cheerfully mingling with fans—the kind of fans actually equipped to recognize them out of uniform."[2] In research, we would perhaps call this a point of saturation in the work, proof that all bases were sufficiently covered to ascertain thorough findings. However, it also speaks to the constant reminder that the women's hoops world is so small, an interconnected place even as it spans continents.

The Value of the Game

On April 2, 2023, 19,482 fans packed into the AAC for the championship game, the finale of a tournament run that brought in a total of 357,542 spectators, the highest in women's college hoops history.[3] Outside the arena, fans desperate to get into the game haggled with ticket scalpers, paying upward of $600 each for nosebleed tickets just to get into the building. It was soon reported that ticket prices for the NCAA Division I championship game surged beyond the other hot ticket in town: recording artist Taylor Swift's three-day stand in the Dallas–Fort Worth metroplex occurring the same weekend. The 9.9 million viewers watching from home made the game the most viewed women's college basketball game ever. As I entered the venue, an AAC employee told me, "Hold on to those tickets. They're going to be worth something later." I smiled at him. "I'm serious," he replied.

This concept of value or worth is an important one. Two years prior, during the 2021 NCAA tournament, a group chat between team performance coaches of several women's basketball programs expressed shock and anger at disparities between their workout facilities in San Antonio, Texas, and what was offered to men's teams in Indianapolis, Indiana. Due to the ongoing COVID-19 pandemic, both tournaments operated out of fewer, localized venues rather than the usual regional setup of the college basketball postseason. When some of the women's team coaches posted side-by-side comparisons of the expansive weight room of the men's tournament and their singular dumbbell tree and yoga mat offerings on their social media accounts, they were told by university officials to delete the posts. Ali Kershner, a performance coach at Stanford University, told *Yahoo! Sports*, "Their school administrators wanted to exude an air of positivity, and gratitude for being at the tournament."[4] This notion of being "grateful" often operates as a means to silence demands for what athletes and the sport deserve. Some coaches also received thinly veiled threats to their employment should they continue to speak out against the NCAA.[5] As Kershner's post gained traction, a TikTok posted by University of Oregon women's basketball player Sedona Prince became the smoking gun of sexism. "I got something to show y'all," Prince begins. "This is our weight room." They point at a lonely rack of low-weight dumbbells. "Let me show you the men's weight room." The viewer sees a panoramic view of a spacious array of benches, free weights, and plates. Prince then articulates the NCAA's reasoning behind the disparity: not money but space. Prince then pans out from the single dumbbell station to an expansive amount of practice space free of any lifting materials. The clip ends with a challenge to the viewer: "If you aren't upset about this problem, then you're a part of it."[6] The TikTok instantly went viral, compelling fans and journalists to press the NCAA for answers.

In a letter posted to Twitter the following day, South Carolina head coach Dawn Staley outlined several grievances related to gender inequality at the tournament level, such as the NCAA's social media coverage and the disparity in amenities provided to athletes based on gender, including the sponsored "swag bags" given to each player. In her letter, she chides the NCAA and its leadership for its shallow commitment to equity less than a year after the association claimed a renewed obligation following the racial reckoning of 2020. Staley saw these understandings of justice and equality as connected and concluded her letter: "Women's basketball is a popular sport whose stock and presence continues to rise on a global level. . . . It is also time for the NCAA leadership to re-evaluate how they value women."[7]

These were not the only disparities. Everything from food to outdoor space revealed the lack of resources planned and produced for women's basketball. COVID protocols also significantly varied; men's teams received PCR tests, while women's teams received the less accurate antigen tests, causing rampant false positives throughout the tournament. Signage, photography, media coverage—all provided vivid examples of the lack of investment by the NCAA when the sport doesn't involve men. While the NCAA scrambled to respond to the outcry by fans, athletes, and coaches across social media, it constantly opted for makeshift fixes rather than holistic solutions to an evergreen problem. After being caught (literally) on camera, later evidence revealed that much of the planning surrounding the tournament that year in San Antonio operated as an afterthought to the men's controlled environment

I cannot be quiet.

In a season that has been focused on justice and equality it's disheartening that we are addressing the glaring deficiencies and inequities in the WOMEN'S and men's NCAA Tournament experiences for the student-athletes, but here we are. First, I believe that LynnHolzman and her team have done a tremendous job with the resources they were "given." It is not lost that a great deal of preparation and planning went into getting 64 teams to San Antonio. We all need to acknowledge and thank them for their efforts.

The issue here looms larger. Let's start with the NCAA @marchmadness official verified Twitter account. The tag line leaves no run for misinterpretation – "The Official NCAA March Madness destination for all things Division I/NCAA Men's Basketball." Those words mean one thing – March Madness is ONLY about men's basketball.

How do we explain that to our players? How can an organization that claims to care about ALL member institutions' student-athlete experiences have a copyrighted term that only "represents" one gender?

Next, the inequities that are circulating on social media. There is no answer that the NCAA executive leadership led by Mark Emmert can give to explain the disparities. Mark Emmert and his team point blank chose to create them! The real issue is not the weights or the "swag" bags; it's that they did not think or do not think that the women's players "deserve" the same amenities of the men.

What we now know is the NCAA's season long messaging about "togetherness" and "equality" was about convenience and a soundbite for the moment created after the murder of George Floyd.

We cannot as leaders of young women allow Mark Emmert and his team to use us and our student-athletes at their convenience. Every team here in San Antonio has earned and deserves at a minimum the same level of respect as the men. All the teams here dealt with the same issues as the men's teams this season; yet their "reward" is different.

It is sad, but not unusual, that the headlines for the women's tournament have turned to disparities and nightly meetings about how to try to fix what should not need to be fixed. We need Mark Emmert and his team to own this mistake and address these issues and the overarching issues that exist in our sport.

Women's basketball is a popular sport whose stock and presence continues to rise on a global level. It is sad that the NCAA is not willing to recognize and invest in our growth despite its claims of togetherness and equality. We all came to San Antonio with one goal; it's time for us to turn our attention to preparing our teams for that. But, it is also time for the NCAA leadership to reevaluate the value they place on women.

Dawn Staley

Figure 8. A letter posted to social media by South Carolina head coach Dawn Staley.

in Indianapolis. This included the NCAA's chief medical officer stating that he "was not under the impression that female athletes would even want a full weight room."[8] When asked why the women's tournament could not use the trademarked March Madness moniker, NCAA brass reportedly suggested that the women's game "chose to pursue their own brand identity," a statement later proven false.[9] The weight room, it seems, was merely the canary in a misogyny mine.

Following this, an independent investigation by law firm Kaplan Hecker & Fink resulted in the first phase of the "NCAA External Gender Equity Review."[10] Colloquially referred to as the Kaplan Report, the 118-page document detailed how sexism continues to seep into the decision-making process at the NCAA level, trickling down to corporate partnerships, resources, and, ultimately, the sport's ability to generate revenue. While the document focuses on "NCAA policies, practices, and culture" that directly impacted athletes' experiences, the authors acknowledge other gendered disparities within officiating, coaching salaries, and more. Even within this frame, the firm found that "the results have been cumulative, not only fostering skepticism and distrust about the sincerity of the NCAA's commitment to gender equity, but also limiting the growth of women's basketball and perpetuating a mistaken narrative that women's basketball is destined to be a 'money loser' year after year. Nothing could be further from the truth."[11]

Of the many frustrating findings offered by the Kaplan Report, the continued undervaluation of the sport is perhaps the most damning. According to Ed Desser, an independent media consultant brought in by the firm, the estimated 2025 valuation of NCAA women's basketball broadcast rights agreements is between $81 million and $112 million—a significantly higher amount than what ESPN currently pays for the rights to women's Division I basketball as well as twenty-eight other NCAA championships combined.[12]

It is important to note that these disparities came to light for two key reasons: (1) the pandemic's impact on the sport, consolidating sporting sites and making disparities more readily visible in a concentrated space, and (2) the social media posts of athletes and coaches, despite attempts by college administrators and NCAA leadership to silence them. As the Kaplan Report illuminates, "The pandemic gave rise to a view on the part of tournament organizers that, after the NCAA was forced to cancel the 2020 tournament, a failure to hold the 2021 men's championship would have had a disastrous financial impact on the NCAA going forward. That attitude resulted in prioritization of men's basketball that shaped every facet of the 2021 championships, starting with the public announcement of the host cities and continuing through the planning process and into the tournaments themselves."[13]

I resurrect the 2021 tournament and the resulting changes in the sport as a means of understanding the stunted growth of women's basketball and the significant shift that occurred within two years' time. That year's debacle is merely an entry point to interrogate the NCAA's double standards for men's and women's basketball rather than a singular moment of sexism. In 2022, unsatisfied with the NCAA's stalled progress in rectifying the issues uncovered the year prior, congressional lawmakers got involved, writing a letter to NCAA president Mark Emmert accusing him and the NCAA of "violating the spirit of gender equity as codified in Title IX."[14] Since then, the new commitments have already paid dividends. All weekend in Dallas in 2023, the record-breaking attendance and viewership numbers testified not only to the sport's growth but also to the possibilities when they are no longer bound to the long-held patterns of scarcity attached to the sport. Given that 2023 marked only the second year that the women's tournament could claim the March Madness moniker, which is worth millions of dollars in advertising revenue, the swift turnaround signals new possibilities for women's basketball.

The years 2021 and 2022 also signaled key shifts in college athlete labor more broadly, with the growth in athlete transfers due to the NCAA no longer requiring athletes to lose years of eligibility to compete for a new team. This, along with a transfer portal designed to facilitate this new market, offered new forms of agency previously unheard-of for college athletes. Athletes also received an extension of eligibility due to the impact of the COVID-19 pandemic, resulting in an additional year for many players to compete.

Perhaps most importantly, 2021 also signaled an important shift in how athletes could financially capitalize on their college careers. Given that college athletes are bound to the NCAA's definition of amateurism, barring them from earning money from their labor on campus, two political developments offered new possibilities for their unpaid status. The first, *NCAA v. Alston,* a 2021 Supreme Court case, found that the governing body violated antitrust law when limiting the number and dollar amount of education-related benefits so-called student-athletes could receive from a college or university. The unanimous ruling offered resounding support for college athlete labor from the country's highest court. The first paragraph in the Supreme Court's ruling of *NCAA v. Alston* reads, "Colleges and universities across the country have leveraged sports to bring in revenue, attract attention, boost enrollment, and raise money from alumni. That profitable enterprise relies on 'amateur' student-athletes who compete under horizontal restraints that restrict how the schools may compensate them for their play. The National Collegiate Athletic Association (NCAA) issues and enforces these rules, which restrict compensation for student-athletes in various ways."[15]

While the court did not make any judgment concerning whether athletes should receive additional compensation, a response to the ruling published by the *Harvard Law Review* argues that "although the student athletes did not challenge the remaining rules in the Supreme Court, the *Alston* decision, combined with background principles of antitrust law that the Court did not consider, lays the groundwork for a successful future challenge to the NCAA's restrictions on compensation unrelated to education."[16] This is especially promising given the language of the Supreme Court ruling: "These rules depress compensation for at least some student-athletes below what a competitive market would yield."[17]

The second key shift involved individual states determining that athletes should be able to profit from their name, image, and likeness (NIL). I currently live in Oregon, where state Senate Bill 5 of 2021 proposed giving athletes control and the ability to profit off their own image but also would have required royalties paid out to current athletes from merchandise and apparel deals.[18] As politicians deliberated across the country at the state level, Emmert took umbrage with their involvement, even resorting to threatening state senators. Oregon senator Peter Courtney told *The Oregonian* that in a private meeting "Mark [Emmert] told me that if I keep [the royalties portion of NIL] in the bill, they will disqualify Oregon athletes. They will ban them. And I went crazy because he says it'll make them employees. I basically at this stage of the game just want to get a bill passed, but I can tell you to me it's symbolic. The UO has fought this thing from Day 1, Oregon State has fought this thing, Portland State is now on board, I hear. I can tell you that I'm not happy . . . I'm too mad."[19] After an amendment that removed the royalties addition, the Oregon bill mirrored other state laws scheduled to go into effect on July 1, 2021, in Alabama, Florida, Georgia, Mississippi, and

New Mexico; these laws joined those of eleven other states that previously passed NIL legislation. With this momentum and the potentially lopsided nature of college sport resulting from one-third of states allowing NIL, the NCAA eventually relented and adopted its own interim NIL policy for all member institutions in the summer of 2021 (on the same day as the newest state laws), with Emmert responding to "the variety of state laws adopted across the country" and vowing to pursue congressional clarity on a national level going forward.[20]

While discourses surrounding NIL often hail it as a significant victory for athletes' rights and financial agency, new equity issues emerged for the more than twenty thousand international college athletes on rosters around the country. General counsel at my home university describes the immigration laws and regulations these athletes face as "silent regarding NIL but loud when it comes to penalties."[21] While it can be argued that the game of basketball is more popular and international than it has ever been, the NIL reality for collegiate athletes born outside the United States requires further examination. The F-1 visa, most commonly used by international college athletes, does not allow students to pursue employment on or off campus that exceeds twenty hours per week. If, for example, representing a brand is designated as "off-campus work," then the athlete enters precarity in terms of their visa. If they choose to argue that the use of their likeness is considered compensation for "work not performed," they can then face sanctions by the NCAA. These policies reflect holdovers from 9/11, according to Ryan Allen and Krishna Bista: "The United States has had a paradoxical relationship with international students, viewing them as both important talents but also as suspicious threats."[22] Each of these developments—the enforcement and invocation of Title IX, Supreme Court rulings on college athlete benefits, state NIL laws, and immigration policies affecting college athletes' ability to profit off their own popularity—reveals the continued intertwined nature of collegiate sport with US politics, whether urging change or seeking to maintain the status quo.[23]

More of the Same

With all the changes to the college game, there are so many things that haven't changed at all. In the 2023 Final Four weekend's first set of games, the Iowa

Hawkeyes, led by an emphatic forty-one-point performance by AP Women's College Basketball Player of the Year and Naismith Trophy recipient Caitlin Clark, persevered over the University of South Carolina Gamecocks 77–73, a team helmed by Naismith Defensive Player of the Year Aliyah Boston and, until this loss, on a dominant forty-two-game winning streak.

In the postgame press conference following the loss, a reporter posed the following question to South Carolina head coach Staley: "Other coaches and colleagues that are sitting in that spot talked about you all being bullies. What's the truth about your team?" Staley took a beat, a brief hesitation, before responding, "The truth about our team, 'kay. It's a good question. We're not bar fighters. We're not thugs. We're not monkeys. We're not streetfighters. This team exemplifies how you need to approach basketball—on the court and off the court. And I do think that's sometimes brought into the game. And it hurts, 'kay."[24] She then pivoted:

> And I do think that some of . . . I'mma say it because I said I was gonna say it whether we lost or whether we won. Some of the people in the media, when you're gathering in public, you're saying things about our team, and you're being heard, and it's being brought back to me. And these are the people that write nationally for our sport. So you can not like our team. You can not like me. But when you say things that you probably should be saying in your home, on the phone, or texting, out in public, and you're being heard. And you are a national writer for our sport. It just confirms . . . what we already know. So watch what you say when you're in public and you're talking about my team in particular. Just watch what you say about our team. Because it's wrong. You have young lives that . . . if you really knew them like you really want to know *other players that represent this game,* you would think differently. So don't judge us by the color of our skin. Judge us by how we approach the game. You may not like how we play the game. . . . That's the way I coach. I'm not changing. I'm not changing, but I hear you. I *hear you.*[25]

The press conference was posted to YouTube, where several comments below the video specifically addressed this part of the interview, with many noting how Staley "stood up" for her team. One user wrote, "Preach Coach!! Yesss reiterate the assignment of character, accountability and responsibility to these media reporters and others that have racist issues."[26] Another wrote, "Good job Coach, stand up for your team and girls of color. People love to pass judgement and don't know the path that has been taken. #TipsHat."[27]

Feminist communication scholar Moya Bailey coined the term "misogy-noir" to describe the intersecting relationship between racism, sexism, and mediated representation of Black folks. In her book *Misogynoir Transformed: Black Women's Digital Resistance,* she continues the work of Black feminist scholars who interrogate the role of media in distorting the lived experiences of Black women in the United States. I am thinking here of Patricia Hill Collins's concept of "controlling images," various caricatures and stereotypes "designed to make racism, sexism, poverty, and other forms of social injustice appear to be natural, normal, and inevitable parts of everyday life."[28] That Staley is even asked to justify the accusation of "bully" on behalf of herself and her team following a crushing loss is exactly what Bailey is getting at when she writes, "Black women's bodies are never their own, resulting in a subtle pressure to not only be useful but explain oneself to others."[29] Staley's reference to how "other players that represent this game" are covered is also important to note. Many have previously written about the racial biases within women's sports, affecting both the quality and quantity of coverage in an already undercovered space such as basketball.[30] That she would have to tell media members to avoid judging her team "by the color of our skin" and instead report on "how we approach the game" mimics the rhetoric of Martin Luther King Jr.'s "I Have a Dream" speech, delivered with a quiet force that feels both intentional and absolute.

What is perhaps particularly concerning is the racialized language surrounding Staley and the South Carolina team. The invocation of "thug" and "monkeys" moves behind veiled connotations, award snubs, and absent coverage. Staley defending her athletes against national media members is a reminder of head coach C. Vivian Stringer's defense of a Rutgers women's basketball team that faced misogynoir following their loss to the University of Tennessee in the 2007 Women's Final Four title game. The now-infamous "nappy-headed hos" commentary by conservative radio host Don Imus rapidly circulated across mainstream media, dissected by those pointing fingers at the cause of Imus's inflammatory language, blaming hip hop, his age, or his political leanings. While many understood the racialized misogynoir as yet another example of how female athletes continue to face disrespect in media coverage, less time has been dedicated to the impact of these moments on the players and coaches required to sit in press conferences and address hate speech, whether spoken to them directly, overheard in public spaces, or emphatically declared in front of radio microphones.[31] The key difference between these two cases is one of proximity. While the racist, sexist antics of Imus feel predictable, the invocation of "thug" and "monkey" by beat reporters focused on women's basketball is particularly troubling but not surprising. As Bailey writes, "Whether in film, television, or . . . digital media, misogynoir has found a home in each of the communication advancements of the last two centuries."[32] Both Stringer and Staley have spoken to the effects of misogynoir in the media; in the press conference, Staley notes how it "hurts," while Stringer, asked to comment once more on Imus following his death in 2019, reiterated the same: "To say that it didn't hurt isn't true. But if you allow those hurtful things to consume you, they own you."[33] Stringer is still linked to the harm caused by Imus, even after his death, a fact she acknowledged as she sent his family her condolences. "I'm tied to that now. No getting around that. It is what it is," she told the *New York Post*. "Proud of the way the team responded. Proud of the support we got from so many fans and people. Proud of the fact we stood up for what's right. All our players learned a really good lesson."[34]

Bigger Than Basketball

With that valuable ticket acquired for the title game on Final Four Sunday, I entered an AAC sharply divided between LSU and Iowa fans, marked not only by their team colors but also by their regional aesthetic and demographics. In a sold-out arena, I sat in a section populated by white, middle-aged Iowa fans and Black, millennial LSU ones. The electric crowd ramped up to a new peak with every bucket, but in the fourth quarter, it reached unspeakably high levels as LSU's Angel Reese mimicked the famous "you can't see me" gesture toward Iowa's Caitlin Clark, a move first popularized by rapper Tony Yayo, amplified by wrestler John Cena, and previously used by Clark herself. Coupled with the waving motion, Reese then pointed toward her ring finger on her opposite hand, signaling the championship ring she soon expected to wear.

The championship confetti hadn't even cleared the hardwood floors before the unsurprising misogynoir began to take form. Reactions rapidly circulated across social media. Previously, when Clark employed the move during the Elite Eight, she received a range of praise and positive press. John Cena tweeted, "Even if they could see you . . . they couldn't guard you," congratulating Clark and her Iowa team on their advancement to the Final Four.

Figure 9. LSU's Angel Reese replicates Iowa player Caitlin Clark's famed gesture.

However, when used by Reese, viewers and pundits alike reacted sharply, accusing her of unsportsmanlike behavior and denoting her actions on the court as completely unacceptable. The word "classless" circulated across Twitter.[35]

Perhaps less discussed is why Reese decided to use the move in the first place. After the game, she told ESPN, "I don't take disrespect lightly." She accused Clark of disrespecting LSU and South Carolina players. Her teammate Alexis Morris had spoken out previously against Iowa's defense, saying that she "[took] it personally" when watching them play South Carolina.[36] That the same motion, employed in the passion of play on the court, could be read completely differently depending on whose hand is waving is important. Moya Bailey writes, "The media that circulate misogynoir help maintain white supremacy by offering tacit approval of the disparate treatment that Black women negotiate in society."[37]

In the postgame press conference, LSU's Angel Reese took to the mic and said, "All year, I was critiqued about who I was. I'm too hood, I'm too ghetto, y'all told me that all year. But when other people do it, y'all don't say nothing. This was for the girls that look like me. . . . It was bigger than me tonight."[38] Here, like Staley, Reese offers a clinic in maneuvering through a hostile sports-media complex not designed with her in mind. Instead of shying away from her actions on the court, she pivots the conversation to the uneven media coverage of her and LSU as a team. She also said, "I want to take on that role of being the Black woman that's going to stand up for the girls that may not have a voice. . . . I don't care what anybody has to say about me. I love who I am. . . . I'm authentically me."[39] Reese's words echoed across social media, with many Black women quoting her words and relating to her experience. Actress Gabrielle Union posted a photo of Reese on the court with the caption, "Black women deserve to be celebrated, applauded, encouraged, and uplifted. For far too long we've carried the weight of others on our backs, shoulders, bosoms, and heads. Now is our time to be seen in every form of the human experience, whether in loss, grief, or celebration. . . . To every Black woman who has felt misunderstood, under-appreciated, or unseen this is your permission to be unapologetically you."[40]

While many rightly critiqued the racial double standard of the fallout following the Final Four, there was also an undercurrent of how female athletes are expected to comport themselves on the court. Dating back to the Victorian era ideals of "womanly conduct" in sport, these notions sought to regulate the attire and actions of athletes, restricting not only how they could compete but also who could even suit up to play in the first place. To her credit, Clark responded that she felt it was wrong for anyone to criticize Reese when the very reason fans tune in to sport is the emotion and passion that drives the game itself. "I think the biggest thing is we're all competitive. We all show our emotions in a different way. Angel's a tremendous, tremendous player. I have nothing but respect for her. I love her game. . . . I'm a big fan of her."[41] That these two athletes at the top of their game can relish their ruthless approach to an expanding, thriving sport despite those seeking to minimize their resources and range as athletes, as people, signals the true potentiality of women's basketball. As Angel told *Sports Illustrated,* "It's just being able to force people to accept that women can talk trash. The women's side gets penalized for it or we're considered as not being ladylike and that we're not playing by the rules. We work just as hard as the men. Women can be who we are; women can be competitive."[42]

That competitive spirit between these two teams was also dampened by politics when US First Lady Jill Biden, who attended the championship game, later remarked, "I know we'll have the champions come to the White House; we always do. So, we hope LSU will come. But, you know, I'm going to tell [President] Joe [Biden] I think Iowa should come too, because they played such a good game."[43] Champions from US-based collegiate, Olympic, and professional teams are invited to visit the White House, a tradition dating back to the Civil War era that, as Brett Siegel argues, has now evolved into a "vital site for rearticulating and reconstituting a vision of the ideal American citizenship and patriot."[44] Given this, how might we read Biden's nontraditional offering in terms of her own preferred champion or perceived "ideal" representation of the citizen or the nation? In what way does Biden's conciliatory invitation, an exception of sorts, alert us to her hesitant acceptance of the actual champions (LSU) while simultaneously seeking to defuse the competitive nature of these two women and their respective squads? While Jill Biden's press secretary responded shortly after, clarifying that the First Lady's comments were intended only to show how much she "admires how far women have advanced in sports since the passing of Title IX," they also illuminate for some just how far the game still must go for true equity.[45]

Don't Let the Money Make You

In the summer of 2023, Amazon debuted a new commercial, "Dormz," featuring Angel Reese and Flau'jae Johnson. In the ad, the two LSU stars take the viewer on an *MTV Cribs*–style tour of their dorm rooms; Reese flaunts her Bayou Barbie style—"Light pink. Hot pink. Dark pink. Off pink."—while Johnson shows us how her room doubles as a recording studio and houses her roommate—a bearded dragon. When Angel says she has never seen Flau'jae studying in her room and asks her to tell her the first rule of accounting, Flau'jae immediately responds, "Make the money, don't let the money make you."[46]

The commercial is only one of the new opportunities for the team's two most recognized stars following the championship. Flau'jae Johnson, whose freestyles frequently go viral, secured a record deal with Jay-Z's Roc Nation and appeared on *Red Bull Rap IQ* alongside Bay Area rapper Kamaiyah. Meanwhile, Angel Reese appeared in a spread for *Sports Illustrated*'s annual swimsuit issue and made a cameo in Cardi B and Latto's "Put It On Da Floor Again" video. In the song, Cardi B raps that she's "ballin' so damn hard / coulda went to LSU." Balling indeed—Reese and Johnson both currently claim millions of dollars in endorsement deals from the likes of Amazon, Puma, JBL, Coach, and McDonald's.

In this new landscape, the crossover emerges as a strategy of survival, of expression, and of endorsement potential. It also carries with it the responsibility of "growing the game." This becomes particularly important in moments of amplified visibility when naysayers and detractors seek to push the women's game out of the spotlight. The persistence of misogynoir in the sport—through awards, media coverage, and even the time-honored tradition of a champion's White House visit—is unsurprising, but what remains key in terms of the crossover is the response by the coaches and athletes most vulnerable to these attacks. That other high-profile Black women could see themselves in Dawn Staley or Angel Reese is telling; it alerts us to the resonance of having to cultivate a public persona while bearing the pressure of "representing" those less likely to be seen.

For those who felt the 2023 season was but a blip on the college basketball radar, the sport's continued success shows the continuity of the previous season and the possibilities moving forward. One need only look at the University of Iowa's (and, more broadly, women's college basketball's) debut opener, a home exhibition game against DePaul University played in front of 55,646 fans.[47] Two weeks after the Final Four, Iowa head coach Lisa Bluder began considering how to maintain the momentum of the previous season: "The wheels started to turn, like, what can this team accomplish? . . . Fifteen thousand—we can sell it out for every game. Maybe we can do even more."[48] She took the idea of a basketball game at Kinnick Stadium, the home field of Iowa's football team, to the athletic director, who began the process of planning the highest-attended women's basketball game in NCAA history. Dubbed the Crossover at Kinnick, the game sought not only to capitalize on the previous season's success but also to further build the university's relationship with the children's hospital that overlooks the stadium. It's not a one-and-done situation; Jess Rickertsen, Iowa's assistant athletic director for ticketing and premium seating, announced that season tickets for every home game had sold out before the start of the season: "To my knowledge, it hasn't happened for any women's sport here at Iowa."[49] Less astonished by this "growth" is Caitlin Clark, the team's star player: "I wasn't surprised just because of the year we had [during the 2022–23 season] but also the exciting style of basketball we play."[50]

For another Final Four team, the University of South Carolina, their season kicked off thousands of miles from their home arena in Columbia, South Carolina, as the Gamecocks faced the University of Notre Dame Fighting Irish in Paris, France. That two Black women head coaches, Dawn Staley and Niele Ivey, might lead the first NCAA game played in Paris is not lost on me. As Ivey told media members, "It's always been my mission to break barriers and provide opportunities for my players to have life-changing experiences. Women's basketball is on the rise, and having this exposure will help to grow the game on an international level."[51] For Staley, who played professionally in France in addition to her legendary career across the American Basketball League and WNBA, told the Associated Press, "We're the first, but we won't be the last."[52]

Growth Opportunities

I began this book with a defiant Cheryl Miller speaking in front of Congress, urging politicians to preserve the progress of Title IX of the Education Amendments of 1972, legislation that has continuously required a battle to maintain its lasting legacy of equality. In the more than fifty years since its original passage, Title IX's visibility through prominent sporting sites continues to reverberate across the basketball landscape. In a series documenting the Crossover at Kinnick game, Iowa head coach Lisa Bluder dedicated the game to "the women that didn't have the chance to participate in sports— those pre–Title IX women that would have loved to have been a part of . . . women's sports and didn't have the opportunity. I really believe that they're living through our dreams, too, and they're dreaming them right along with us." As she geared up her team to march into Kinnick, she told them, "I was lucky to play in front of fifty people, let alone fifty thousand. That's how far this game has come. That's how far *you* have taken it. Without what you did last year, this would not be happening."[53]

With the incredible growth from the outset of the 2024 college basketball season, the new stars, new numbers, and new records across the top programs point to a new era for women's hoops. By the time the conference championship tournaments began that season, there were early signs that the viewership and attendance records set the previous year could be easily broken. In perhaps one of the most anticipated rematches of the season, Dawn Staley's South Carolina team faced off against Kim Mulkey's reigning champion LSU Tigers in the Southeastern Conference (SEC) championship, a chippy, thrilling game that hauled in a crowd of 13,163 at Bon Secours Wellness Arena in Greenville, South Carolina, as well as 2 million viewers tuning in from afar.[54] In the final minutes of the game, an intentional foul by LSU's Flau'jae Johnson on South Carolina Milaysia Fulwiley led to Johnson bumping opposing player Ashlyn Watkins on the way to the bench, a move that quickly escalated as South Carolina's Kamilla "Kam" Cardoso shoved Johnson to the ground. Players rushed over from both benches, and a man later identified as Johnson's brother leaped over the scorer's table, attempting to reach Cardoso before being escorted away by police. After players were ejected for leaving the bench (or engaging in the altercation), play eventually resumed, with South Carolina taking the SEC title on the road to the NCAA tournament.

Following the game, media reports framed the altercation as a "tussle," a "fight," and even a "brawl." South Carolina head coach Staley approached Johnson after the game, checking in with her as well as apologizing in the postgame interview to both LSU and the fans watching for her team's behavior. "For us playing a part in that, that's not who we are. That's not what we're about," she said.[55] Staley showed poise while being very aware of how she and her team might be perceived, especially given that her player executed the shove.

Mulkey, on the other hand, when asked about the altercation during the postgame press conference, told reporters, "It's ugly, it's not good, no one wants to be a part of that. But I'll tell you this," she then said coyly. "I wish [Cardoso] would've pushed Angel Reese. If you're 6'8", don't push somebody that little. That was uncalled for in my opinion. Let those two girls who were jawing, let them go at it."[56] Her call to "let them go at it" does not lament players physically engaging; instead, it merely points out the size difference, where she frames Cardoso as a bully ("pushing somebody that little") and insinuates that Reese would have responded in kind.

Given the previous season's misognoir surrounding LSU and South Carolina, I expected that discourses following the game might mirror the NBA's
2004 Pacers/Pistons brawl, affectionately dubbed the "Malice at the Palace."
That fight, involving NBA players and fans alike, changed the league as we
know it (including a dress code policy and the implementation of a minimum one-year postsecondary school to enter the draft) and along the way
blamed hip hop, single-parent homes, and multi-million-dollar contracts
for the resulting violence.[57] However, the SEC Championship's media afterlives (mostly) avoided a Blackness as pathology narrative, instead honing
in on Mulkey's "wish she would've" comments as an example of the double
standard between the two head coaches. Across networks and op-eds, some
considered whether the optics of Staley escalating the situation would have
been perceived far differently from that of her white coaching counterpart.

This would not be the only moment during the postseason when Mulkey
would make headlines. Ahead of her team's matchup against Middle Tennessee State University in the second round of the tournament, Mulkey unleashed a four-minute tirade during a press conference, accusing a *Washington Post* journalist of writing a forthcoming "hit piece" on her and threatening
legal action. "This is exactly why people don't trust journalists and the media
anymore," she told a room full of journalists and media members.[58] And
while the eventual *Washington Post* feature by Kent Babb did indeed drop
during March Madness, it lacked the severity her rant seemed to suggest,
reading less like a hardcore critique and more like a regurgitated rundown
of her past with very little new information.

However, Mulkey's indignation toward the media took a righteous turn
following a *Los Angeles Times* op-ed that described UCLA as "America's
sweethearts" and LSU as "its basketball villains."[59] In the original version
of the commentary piece, author Ben Bolch asked, "Do you prefer America's sweethearts or its dirty debutantes? Milk and cookies or Louisiana hot
sauce?"[60] Fitting two of the top basketball programs in the country into a
binary of objectification rightfully earned Mulkey's ire. In the press conference following her team's win over UCLA, she told media members, "The
one thing I'm not going to let you do, I'm not going to let you attack young
people, and there were some things in this commentary, guys, that you should
be offended by as women. It was so sexist, and they don't even know it."[61] The

article was soon edited, eventually losing the "dirty debutantes" paragraph. In each of the instances outlined above, the media's uneven coverage, framing, and promotion of women's basketball point to challenges that still remain for the sport.

MARCH 31, 2024 | PORTLAND, OR | MODA CENTER

It's exactly one year to the day since my Final Four experience in Dallas, and I'm now heading into the Moda Center in Portland, Oregon, where across the weekend's slate of Sweet Sixteen and Elite Eight games, fans packed in to witness a new set of hoopers continuing the sport's promising upward trend, including Madison Booker, JuJu Watkins, and Paige Bueckers. Settling in for Sunday's Elite Eight matchup between North Carolina State University and The University of Texas, a friend pointed to the court and asked, "What is it they're measuring?" After teams competed on both Friday and Saturday inside this venue, it was revealed before the first Elite Eight game that one of the three-point lines was nine inches shorter than regulation. Tasked with deciding between delaying the start of a nationally televised game (and potentially losing the ABC slot) to address the discrepancy or playing on the same incorrect court both teams had played on previously, NC State and Texas ultimately decided to tip-off on time and deal with the uneven line. Texas coach Vic Schaefer, when asked about the line following his team's loss, responded, "I hate to say this, but I have a lot of colleagues that would say, *only in women's basketball.* It's a shame, really, that it even happened. But it is what it is."[62] Schaefer's dejected response reflects the difficulty not only of making the right decision on behalf of his team (with neither choice being ideal) but also of holding space to consider how this dilemma seems to be symptomatic of the women's basketball experience.[63]

Narratives around "growing the game" constantly hovered around the 2023 and 2024 seasons, whether in Caitlin Clark's historic individual accomplishments, the sport's viewership records, or NIL deals. But are these the only ways to measure growth? What does it mean to measure the growth of the game through shortened three-point lines? What do we lose in solely gauging growth through quantitative means? What I would like to consider is what the current turn in women's basketball illuminates in terms of the sport's growing pains and potential.

Some of these pains are societal. Take, for example, how Utah's basketball team experienced drivers yelling the N-word at them as they walked both to and from dinner in Coeur d'Alene, Idaho, before their first tournament game. Utah was one of three teams staying in the area due to a lack of hotels near the host venue in Spokane, Washington. The dearth of lodging options and large-scale planning remains disappointing, but it's also difficult to see how support systems of care can also exist in this space. "Racism is real and it happens and it's awful," Utah head coach Lynne Roberts told reporters. "It was really upsetting . . . for our players and staff to not feel safe in an NCAA tournament environment, it's messed up."[64] How do you begin to measure growth when it feels as if there's so far to go?

Another example: Before the championship game against the Iowa Hawkeyes, Dawn Staley sits in yet another press conference, where someone asks her whether trans women belong in sport. "Damn, you got deep on me, didn't you?" She pauses and says, "I'm of the opinion—if you're a woman, you should play. If you consider yourself a woman and you want to play sports or vice versa, you should be able to play. That's my opinion. You want me to go deeper?" The interviewer does. She doubles down on her response and notes, "Now the barnstormer people are going to flood my timeline and be a distraction to me on one of the biggest days of our game, and I'm OK with that. I really am."[65] The "barnstormers," the predictably transphobic commenters sure to flood her inbox and mentions, represent the barriers to growth when we consider how governing bodies of sport govern athletic bodies. That Staley is both aware of those who might try her and resolute in the response to the question represents the crossover potential of coaches advocating for athletes. As institutions such as the National Association of Intercollegiate Athletics rule on trans participation, I ask, How can you define growth without an inclusive, expansive perspective?

Finally, as some of the stars of the 2023 and 2024 seasons pursue careers in the WNBA, I am reminded of the growth needs at the next level. After becoming the first overall pick in the 2024 WNBA Draft, Caitlin Clark takes a seat for her first presser as a member of the Indiana Fever. During the press conference, a local sports columnist addresses her: "Real quick, look, I'm going to do this" and makes her iconic heart symbol with his hands. She smirks a bit quizzically before saying to him, "You like that? . . . I do that at my family after every game so it's pretty cool." He responds, "OK, well, start doing it to me and we'll get along just fine." Uncomfortable laughter rains down across the room in the clip. She leans forward but doesn't laugh, continuing to make eye contact. I've returned to the clip often, each time both a bit more uncomfortable with the journalist's choice to disrupt an important tone-setting moment in a rookie's season and increasingly disenchanted with the echoing giggles and guffaws of those in attendance. Famed sports journalist Jemele Hill tweeted that what happened to Clark during that press conference is "obviously something that never would have been said to a male athlete." She continues, "I said this some time ago, but another upside of Caitlin Clark's popularity is that it is going to finally force the sports media to grow up."[66] Outside of the stuffy media tables and rows of seating, I've also witnessed both online and offline spaces that pick up where the microphones turn off. Bars that exclusively show women's sports. Websites, blogs, and social media accounts dedicated to individual teams or leagues. Influencers and designers who create specifically around women's hoops. How can you measure when the growth spills out into the streets, lives inside sports bars, and thrives in online communities? The game itself is grown; it only needs the sports-media complex to catch up.

The Game Is Grown

"One of the main challenges is that women are still not respected as athletes, so it's a really hard sell. People don't respect it." It's 2015, and I'm sitting in the conference room of the Los Angeles Sparks' headquarters, where an account executive is describing the challenges of selling tickets to WNBA games. Back then, I unknowingly began this project while I worked as a Sparks intern on #WeAreWomen, a season-long initiative designed to sell out a game and break the league attendance record. Following my season with the Sparks, I interviewed front office employees, including the one quoted above, about their experiences working in the sport. Almost everyone I interviewed or interacted with that year pointed out how the Sparks are perceived differently from their male counterparts within the Clippers and Lakers organizations. A member relations specialist who was less than six months into her time with the Sparks had already experienced the marginalization of the team in Los Angeles: "We're a huge basketball and baseball city with two professional men's basketball teams, so I feel like people just kind of push us under the rug."[1] Another sales employee spoke of being "taken seriously": "I guess I would like people to take us more seriously as a women's sports team. I think it would be great if people would give it a chance and see what it's all about. I think that the way women play basketball—why couldn't it be the same as a Lakers game or a Clippers game? It would be nice to see that happen. . . . I want people to be more serious about the whole league itself." These employees, in voicing their desire for the WNBA and, more broadly, women's basketball to gain the respect and the "serious" following they knew it deserved, felt ambitious in that moment.

That year I worked a minimum of three days a week in the Sparks office, primarily in the sales department, reporting to the vice president. I also attended and worked each home game, primarily at a sales table located on the arena's concourse advertising the #WeAreWomen game. I also represented the team at community events and assisted in marketing #WeAreWomen at business meetings. Throughout this campaign, whether making phone calls, talking to casual patrons at games, or wearing Sparks apparel in public at the grocery store, I experienced firsthand how difficult it is to sell the WNBA when so many people didn't acknowledge or respect that it existed. There were many times when I spent a considerable amount of time explaining to lifelong Angelenos who the Sparks were and where (and when) they played. In other moments, it became difficult to communicate the main talking points of the #WeAreWomen campaign itself, given there was such a lack of understanding when it came to the WNBA and its athletes. In the interviews that followed the season, several employees used the term "education" to describe the additional labor of selling the Sparks in Los Angeles. An account executive told me, "My challenge a lot with our other reps is educating people out there that just don't understand what we're about. Once we talk to them about the empowerment of women, looking at our players not just as women players but as role models in our city, in our town, in our country . . . they have a better appreciation." The Sparks' play on the court was seemingly not a sufficient reason to support the team for many in Los Angeles, so the creation of a campaign such as #WeAreWomen served to fill this gap. "Selling" the Sparks often included selling everything but basketball, including meet-and-greets with players, tours of STAPLES Center, and group packages. One Sparks employee who primarily worked in group sales told me, "We have the STAPLES Center, so a lot of times you sell experience instead of the team. . . . Sometimes I sell a lot of groups that come out, and they don't even care about the team." When I asked her about the challenges she faced in selling Sparks tickets, she responded, "Because I focus so much on group sales, I [don't] really have a lot of challenges just because I was providing them with an experience. So the game was a little plus thing that they got. But we do have challenges where people are like, 'Well, we don't wanna come watch women play basketball.' But once they come and see how fun it is, you know, that goes kind of away. But they have to experience it."

In returning to these transcripts recently, I reflected upon how much has changed in the world of women's basketball now that new audiences, those who finally "experienced it," have realized what was there all along. Whereas our 2015 goal of selling out a single game required months-long planning and coordinated collaboration with sponsors and community partners, attendance and viewership of the women's game continue to reach new heights at both the collegiate and professional levels. Since beginning this project, new leagues have emerged and with them new opportunities frequently described as "growing the game."

Across each of the previous chapters, I considered how athletes and advocates of women's basketball encounter a global sporting landscape across various markers of identity, circulating their image and labor more rapidly than ever before. While I identified the role of racism, sexism, and homophobia in athletes' experience, this project aimed to center their response to and refusal of normative scripts. Through dozens of interviews, hundreds of hours of observation, and even more time analyzing media artifacts to scratch the surface of a woefully undercovered world, I offer the crossover as a conceptual framework that binds together the places and people that informed this project. It is my hope that this framework proves useful for future research, especially as it relates to understanding how Black athletes experience the sports-media complex.

In this book, I have been aware of the difficulty of the double crossover asked of the athletes I study. They are required to overcome rigid notions of race and gender, to perform at the highest levels at home and abroad, and to thrive across both physical and digital spaces. The choreography of the crossover is bound up in a set of practices with structures, conventions, and styles that separate them from other social interactions of daily life, even as they affect them. It becomes a sharing of codes rehearsed, repeated, and incorporated.

Considering the Crossover in Containment

In a conversation with cultural critic Greg Tate, visual artist Arthur Jafa explained how the current sporting structures render Black athletes simultaneously "on display" while competing on a "playing field [that] is a containment field." When describing how Black performance and creativity can survive within this system of containment, Jafa described it this way:

I think there are these modes of Black expressivity which are familiar; one is this whole idea of rhythm. Most people would acknowledge Black people have an acute sensitivity to rhythm. Most people would say that . . . but there's all this other stuff that is much harder to get a grasp on. For example, there is an acute sensitivity to spatial arrays, to how figures operate in space. There's no name for it, we don't have a name like rhythm for it. . . . Maybe it comes from being in a slave ship chained next to people . . . your acute awareness of . . . how you occupy in a fixed space.[2]

Here, Jafa perfectly encapsulates the crossover and begins to interrogate its origins. The fixed space that the participants of this book occupy within basketball is gendered, rooted in labor, highly mediated, and always political. On the court, teams can employ a range of defensive strategies to keep the opposing team from scoring; contain defense is one such approach. Contain defense requires you to keep an offensive player in front of you in an attempt to keep the ball handler under control. When I hear Jafa speaking on Black innovation in containment, I see the crossover as a means of maneuvering past without losing speed or balance, maintaining despite all strategies to control or deter.

Over the past nine years, I attempted to document the maneuvers and awareness required to sustain a life in sport. In following athletes across digital platforms, national borders, and the rupture of the COVID-19 pandemic, I hope that this project contributes to sporting mobilities literature and offers an expansive approach to athletic sites of study. In the same way, I also hope the crossover proves useful as an intersectional lens to consider how Black women and nonbinary athletes maneuver their lives and labor across time and space. Acknowledging the barriers that exist alongside the technique and execution (successful or not) is key to the crossover, a metaphoric framework that borrows from performance studies, feminist theory, and communication literature.

In practice, what would putting respect on women's basketball truly look like? Is it limited to economic metrics—"selling" the sport—through ticket sales, endorsement deals, or impressive max salary figures? Or can we better assess respect through equitable, quality media coverage that gives the game to the masses on a regular basis? With more eyes on the game than ever before, what does this heightened visibility reveal about how far the game has come and where it needs to go next?

What I offer here is merely a start to answering these questions. I do not claim this book to be a comprehensive examination of the sport by any stretch of the imagination. There is an array of athletes absent from this book who have so much to offer journalists and scholars and a range of vibrant sites left unexplored. For example, the growth of 3×3 hoops, which I briefly mention in the first chapter via Cierra's role with Team USA, is one area I believe is worthy of further investigation, given the proliferation of this genre of the game, from the Big 3 league operating stateside to the Olympic level.

As more current and former women's basketball players enter the coaching and front office ranks on the men's side of the sport, there is important work to be done on this type of crossover. The success of former WNBA players such as Lindsey Harding and Swin Cash in this domain requires further exploration as to how their leadership positions contribute to our current knowledge of the coaching landscape and how athletes envision their relationship to sport after their playing career is over. Off the court, fan communities challenge dominant narratives of women's basketball and confront the shortcomings of sports media coverage and the WNBA itself through bars exclusively showing women's sports or online spaces such as The Committee that incorporate trash talk, humor, and player engagement on social media. Advocates of the women's game also fill the gap in merchandise, creating gear that attends to the athletic needs of fans and athletes in tandem with the politics of the sport itself. Playa Society, a brand started by Esther Wallace, features shirts that declare, "80% of WNBA players are Black womxn influencing basketball, culture, and society."[3] The company also creates clothing that spans other leagues (such as the NCAA) and sports (such as soccer's USWNT). On its website, Playa Society describes the brand—and Wallace's vision—as "elevating the culture to a point in society where women athletes are treated as athletes; and women's sports are treated as sports."[4]

There is also much to be written about athletes disrupting the gender binary one dribble or choice of dress at a time. The fashion forward athletes of today transform the tunnel into pregame runways that deserve our attention. When asked about how she approaches getting dressed, WNBA star Chelsea Gray told *Women's Wear Daily*, "My style is so fluid. All of the women's styles won't fit me right, and men's, too, but I'm able to mix and match. . . . My wife helps me a lot, but my everyday tunnel look is me creating something."[5] How athletes "create something" in a world (fashion or otherwise) that too often refuses to accommodate them is the essence of the crossover.

In a moment when sport operates as a key battleground for trans rights, future research must continue to engage with how trans athletes disrupt the gender binary; it is my hope that the crossover might serve as a useful starting point here, given that, as C. Riley Snorton writes, "Trans is more about a movement with no clear origin and no point of arrival."[6] As a descriptor for gender, he intends "trans" as both unfixed and "fungible," "which is to say, revisable within blackness, as a condition of possibility."[7] In the introduction to his book *Black on Both Sides: A Racial History of Trans Identity*, he proposes an expansive characterization of "trans" unhinged from the normative categories of gender, sex, and species. Instead, he centers the terms "transitive" (ever changing), "transitory" (impermanent), and "transversal" (crossing yet never linking) in relation to both Blackness and gender.[8] Given this, how might the transversal inform how the crossover traverses the sporting boundaries of gender?

Mobilizing Future Crossovers

Sporting citizenship remains a key aspect of how we understand sporting (im)mobilities today. The controversy surrounding the IOC's refusal to allow Nneka Ogwumike and Elizabeth Williams, two of the world's most talented basketball players, to compete for Team Nigeria during the Tokyo Olympics in 2021 reveals the contentious, liminal space afforded to second-generation immigrant athletes and opens new inquiries into the role of governing bodies in determining who can play and under what flag. At the same time, the French government's ban on religious headwear for its Olympic athletes ahead of the 2024 Summer Olympics in Paris requires renewed attention to how Islamophobic sporting policies continue to affect hijabi hoopers around the world.[9] In 2023 French sports minister Amelie Oudea-Castera announced that French athletes wearing hijab could not compete for the country, citing "the absolute neutrality of the public service."[10] Whereas Islam has been depicted as a symbol of female oppression in Western culture, recent Islamophobic policies within Europe and North America seemingly restrict Muslim women more than any religious text or leader.[11]

France's ban on the hijab in the name of maintaining a secular state echoes previous bans by FIBA (the global governing body of basketball) and FIFA (the global governing body of soccer). In 2007 FIFA published Law 4 of the laws of the game, stating that "the basic compulsory equipment must not contain any political, religious or personal statements. . . . The team of a player whose basic compulsory equipment contains political, religious or personal slogans or statements will be sanctioned by the competition organizer or by FIFA."[12] The federation's policy on the hijab would later change to one of safety, arguing that the hijab posed a strangulation risk to athletes should they take the pitch to play while covered. Eventually, following a two-year provisional period, FIFA was forced to acknowledge that no medical research exists confirming any risk or incident of injury for athletes wearing headscarves. However, the influence of FIFA instituting the ban impacted other sports that had originally followed suit, including FIBA, which maintained the ban until 2017. The implementation of FIBA's discriminatory policy not only affected international play but also seeped into sporting regulations at every level of the game, including elementary and secondary school levels.[13] This ban affected leagues and teams not only in majority-Muslim countries but also in the United States. Part of this failure to prioritize the rights of these players is due to the lack of diversity at the hoops headquarters. In an interview I conducted with journalist Shireen Ahmed, she told me, "My critique of FIBA is that they had nobody on the inside, and they made this policy, and it was ridiculous and had no basis, but they also didn't feel moved to change it. FIBA have all men on their executive committee; they don't give a shit if Muslim women in hijab play. They also sadly didn't give a shit if men in turbans didn't play. . . . So for me, this is not only rooted in misogyny, it's rooted in xenophobia, because heads of federations are all in Switzerland." Sporting regulations surrounding the attire and covering of Muslim women mirror larger societal and political shifts across North America and Europe. Since 2003 the West's obsession with legislation controlling the attire of Muslim women has expanded, with Germany banning teachers from wearing headscarves, to France and Belgium banning the burqa and niqab in 2011. Austria and Germany followed suit, albeit with partial bans. And in 2017 Quebec adopted new legislation, Bill 62, which forbids anyone from giving or receiving public services while wearing a face covering.[14] Around the world, from the individual to the institutional, discourses surrounding Muslim women's attire continue to frame policies that constrict their movements within public spaces.

The various forms of meaning attached to Muslim women's decision to cover (or not) results in what Manal Hamzeh defines as a "dual hijabophobia"—a gendered form of Islamophobia directed toward Muslim women—by both Islamic and non-Islamic factions. The racist, colonialist discourses of the West are defined as Islamophobic hijabophobia, while Hamzeh defines Islamist hijabophobia within the constraints of nationalist and religious groups that use hijabophobia to blatantly police women's bodies in specific countries and contexts.[15] "These two hijabophobias," Hamzeh writes, "construct the body of the Muslim woman as a threat to the nation's unity and the purity of Islam, as well as a threat to the secular notion of freedom, the security of the West, and playing sports or 'the game.'"[16]

Hijabi athletes are caught between not only the federations and lower organizations that dictate if they can take the court but also their own communities, which seek to contain them. In an interview, when I defined dual hijabophobia to Ahmed, she became animated as she described a question she received from a fellow Muslim in the crowd during a conference panel session. He asked, "What do you think of Muslim women not being covered modestly because you can see the shape of their legs when they wear tights?" The question was obviously directed toward athletes like Ahmed (a former soccer player) and Bilqis Abdul-Qaadir (a basketball player), who wears tights underneath her shorts for modesty. Ahmed described her emotions in the moment:

> I was so frustrated. I was like, after all this shit. My face is legitimately like—I'm not good at poker face—I was like scowling at the man. . . . So then I get to him and I'm like, "Wait a minute, who do you mean by people, do you mean Muslim men? Who is asking these questions about what Muslim women are wearing? First thing, stop asking these questions. What Muslim women wear is not your business." I was so pissed off. But that is a perfect example of what happens in our community, and I'm not going to lie about it. . . . They're not off the hook.

In this case, "after all this shit" refers to the struggles against regulations such as the FIFA and FIBA bans, where Islamophobic hijabophobia dominated.

After all the structural oppression the panel had just discussed, Ahmed had to also contend with the misogyny of the man's question. She expressed hesitancy in addressing Islamist hijabophobia in front of a primarily white, Western audience because of the way that the religion is vilified as misogynistic within a Western context, but she felt she had to speak up:

> Every community suffers from misogyny. . . . Issues in Nigeria of women not getting paid there—the national team after Nigeria won the African Cup, they hadn't played in one year. The women had to do a sit-in to get the money they were owed. Let's fast forward to Denmark—the women went on strike and almost missed a World Cup qualifying match. OK, let's go to Ireland and talk about how the women had to wear tracksuits and take them off in the airport to hand them back to the federation. Let's talk about Pakistan, how the federation there was blocking women from trying out overseas because they didn't want them to. . . . So my point is that there's issues and instances of misogyny all across the world, but the way that it's written up it's easy for white people to point at folks and say, "Look at the Global South. They're a mess." No, look at all of y'all; the US women's team just sued US Soccer. You're not immune to these systems. It's literally misogyny everywhere.

As she rattled off the variety of sexist practices across geography and sport, she also invoked how women of color are perceived as "disadvantaged" through this lens, illustrating the various intersections within Muslim women's identities.

Bilqis Abdul-Qaadir, a decorated collegiate basketball player and the most visible casualty of FIBA's ban, eventually met with FIBA officials following the lifting of the ban in 2017. During her presentation at Muslim Women in Sport Network's inaugural online summit in 2018, she described the meeting as "terrible":

> I was in a room full of men—no other women in this meeting. And after coming out of the meeting, I know exactly why it took so long [to end the FIBA ban]. These two representatives they had were very insensitive. They didn't care about a Muslim girl trying to play basketball, it was evident. You know, when I shared my story with them and, you know, what the goal was to try to get them in the future to maybe use a different process or different protocols to help these rules get removed faster if they ever came upon something similar to this situation. And they were like, "Why

are we going backwards? What's the point? The rule is gone, now get out of our face," basically. And I was just like I actually broke down in tears, not because I was sad but because I was so angry I wanted to really slap all of them in the room.

Her attempts to remedy the exclusionary policy-making protocols of FIBA failed to resonate with leadership within the basketball federation and rendered her helpless in her efforts to prevent future marginalization by the governing body. During the Q&A portion of Bilqis Abdul-Qaadir's keynote address, a viewer asked, "What would you say were the key lessons of this journey?" She replied:

> I learned that we cannot measure our success or our identity in the eyes of society because through that journey there were three things that I began to question about myself that I couldn't change. Number one, that I was a woman. Number two, that I'm a Black woman, and number three, that I'm a Black Muslim woman. And in society's eyes, I'm looked at as the bottom. We're looked at as if we are not going to succeed at anything. It was a time where, you know, I didn't want to be those three things. It's really a disadvantage, you know, but I learned very fast to not measure my success or who I am in the world's eyes.

In her response, Abdul-Qaadir acknowledged the racialized, gendered, and religious hierarchies that render her at "the bottom." In order to defend herself against the perceptions placed on her as a person read through these three identities simultaneously, she self-identified how success appears for her as an athlete pushed to the periphery.

I resurrect the battle of hijabi hoopers against FIBA to consider how Bilqis Abdul-Qaadir, a Black, Muslim woman from Springfield, Massachusetts, the birthplace of basketball, is denied the ability to be seen, heard, or represented at the highest levels of the sport. The struggle represents Gayatri Chakravorty Spivak's articulation of the subaltern, how marginalized subjects might speak and know their conditions.[17] I also point to this particular case because it illuminates the importance of considering sporting immobilities alongside sweeping narratives about the accelerating momentum of people, products, and ideas around the world.

France's current hijabophobic policy affects athletes like Diaba Konaté, a point guard from Paris who played in the 2024 NCAA tournament for the

University of California, Irvine. Her hopes of enjoying home court advantage as a member of the French national team in the upcoming Summer Olympics were first dashed in 2022, when the French Senate instituted a hijab ban in sports competition and specified the policy within national sports regulations in basketball. The Big West Best Defensive Player of the Year learned of this policy hours before she was set to compete in a 2022 3×3 tournament in France. "My first reaction? I was not understanding. And then I felt ashamed. I cried," she said in an interview with the *Orange County Register*. "'Is it going to be my whole life now, because I wear the hijab? Am I, like, done playing basketball in France?' . . . [L]ots of questions came up in my mind, and it was very humiliating. And I couldn't say anything, I couldn't do anything."[18] Konaté's experience—having to advocate for something bigger than basketball, migrating to play basketball in the United States, and being unable to tap into NIL opportunities because of post-9/11 politics—speaks to many of the key themes across the previous chapters. I do not see these issues as disparate but rather as an interconnected system that structures an athlete's access and ability to thrive in sport. In the same way, I consistently observe how athletes theorize the jointed nature of injustice. WNBA player Layshia Clarendon articulated this when they said, "No one should have to choose between honoring their faith and playing the sport they love, and it's heartbreaking and unacceptable that Muslim women in France are being forced to make that choice."[19]

Konaté's case also serves as a reminder of what Chandra Talpade Mohanty was speaking to when she wrote, "Feminism without borders is not the same as 'border-less' feminism. It acknowledges the fault lines, conflicts, differences, fears, and containment that borders represent. It acknowledges that there is no one sense of a border, that the lines between and through nations, races, classes, sexualities, religions, and disabilities, are real—and that a feminism without borders must envision change and social justice work across these lines of demarcation and division."[20] Research focused on the global flows of sporting cultures and economies must remain attuned to how athletes experience this space across multiple identities simultaneously. Raka Shome and Radha Hegde write, "The subaltern produced by such maneuvers of nation-states with global capital is not always caught between the 'west' and the 'rest,' or between nation and colonialism. Rather, the condition of subalternity in such situations is often constituted through, and located within, the contradictions produced by alliances (partial or otherwise) or collisions, or both, between sections of the national and the global."[21] Whereas Spivak asks, "Can the subaltern speak?" Shome and Hegde question, "Can the subaltern move?"[22] In this book, I continuously interrogate, Can the subaltern hoop? And if so, under what conditions?

APRIL 13, 2024 | PORTLAND, OR | MODA CENTER

Less than a week after the 2024 NCAA championship game, I'm sitting inside of Portland's Moda Center taking in the Nike Hoop Summit, one of several corporate-sponsored events (e.g., Jordan, McDonald's, and Chipotle) that showcase the future of basketball. For only the second time in its twenty-five-season tenure, the Nike Hoop Summit has included a women's game, where U-19 (under nineteen years old) players populating the next rosters of the NCAA, WNBA, and Olympic national teams converge on one court. Players hail from all over the world; on the floor at any given time are athletes from the United States, Slovenia, Luxembourg, Canada, Nigeria, Ukraine, Germany, and Croatia. The structure—"U.S. vs. World"—features classic American exceptionalism baked into the "us versus them" design of the game, even as the game operates under international rules. The score is close on the court the entire time, with the US team barely eking out the 83–80 victory in the final minute. The crowd seems to feel an indescribable giddiness not only inspired by the excitement they're experiencing in person but also feeding off the incredible conclusion to the 2024 college hoops season and on the cusp of the 2024 WNBA Draft.

Most of the Nike Hoop Summit players have already committed to a college program, including the top recruit in the nation, Sarah Strong, who recently announced she would be taking her talents to the University of Connecticut in the fall. In many ways, Strong represents the next generation of a global game depicted across each chapter of this book. She spent the first ten years of her life in Spain, since both of her parents played basketball overseas. She grew up watching her mother, Allison Feaster, compete for teams such as CB Alcobendas after her tenure in the WNBA. An ESPN feature on Strong describes her in this way: "The accolades and commitment are just the most recent steps in a basketball story that has spanned multiple continents. . . . Her rise as the top recruit in the country is uniquely her own—a distinction well-earned after understanding who she is and where she comes from."[23] Strong's journey is but one in a much broader one that disrupts an easy "US vs. World" binary—she has already straddled both and seems poised to step into this next phase. This current moment holds the residue of so many of the themes of this book. With more viewers tuning in, there are more questions concerning how the game works, why gendered disparities still exist, and why certain players are promoted over others. The recurring call to support the WNBA through ticket sales or buying merch obscures broader battles within the collective bargaining agreement, the racial logics that continue to shape league marketing, and the lingering reluctance by media organizations to cover women's sports. It is my hope that this book opens space for more questions and, I hope, a few more answers.

Watching all of this play out across television and social media, I see a new State Farm commercial featuring WNBA player Jewell Loyd. The insurance company's signature representative, Jake, stands beside her, calmly looking directly into the camera as he introduces her to the viewer: "This is two-time WNBA champion. WNBA scoring leader. Five-time All Star . . . All-around record breaker, Jewell Loyd." She's poised until he says, "And this is you getting crossed up." Loyd suddenly steps into action, dribbling side to side, weaving the ball between her legs, pushing past the camera, dribbling out of the frame, boundless. "Ouuu!" Jake responds with delight: "Don't do it to 'em!"[24] The camera turns on its side as if the camera operator's ankles were wiped out. The crossover, alive and well, on full display.

Note on Sources

Given the structure of this book and its combination of a variety of sources, I submit this note as a bit of an explanation of how everything came together. My primary goal throughout this project was to seek out and center athlete voices when possible by using participant observation in several settings, conducting interviews virtually and/or in person, and analyzing the content of athlete-created media, including social media pages, YouTube accounts, and memoirs. I also utilized quotes from media interviews (features, press conferences, etc.), documentaries, and reality television to inform this project. All of these sources are cited in the endnotes.

I also actively participated in the media creation process, producing media for several outlets, serving as an expert voice for several articles, and even finding myself on a local NBC affiliate offering my thoughts on an incorrect three-point line. These experiences also shaped how I wrote about the sports-media complex across each chapter.

For any information not cited, I provide additional details about my methodology for each chapter. I recorded my field observations by hand, by using my phone's Notes app, or via my laptop. I directly transcribed all quotations, while I derived some generalizations ("Athletes shared that . . . ") from what I heard during observations, or I combined them from multiple interviews. I am indebted to several athletes and advocates of women's basketball whom I did not directly cite in this book but who shared their time and insights with me. Their knowledge informed much of the thematic organization of this book even if their direct words are not included in the text.

For me, being "in the field" from 2015 included the observations listed below in each chapter. In addition, I attended two USA Basketball Women in the Game events, Los Angeles Sparks games and affiliated events (2015–22), University of Oregon women's basketball games (2019–24), and University of Illinois women's basketball games (2021–22). I also made a trip to one of the Paris Hoops Factory locations (2018).

Pregame

Research anecdotes and quotations in the Pregame chapter are derived from field observations in Lyon, France, in May and June 2022, when I followed Cierra Burdick during her postseason run with Lyon ASVEL Féminin. This portion of my time in France with her occurred in an otherwise empty locker room as she maneuvered through an off day. We began in Bourges that morning, took the train to Lyon, and headed to her team gym, where she eventually shared her thoughts on various styles of play in different countries. I combined the data I collected with Burdick in 2022 with an interview I conducted with Rebecca Harris in Dallas, Texas, in 2023 during her season with Athletes Unlimited. While I attended games in person that season, I conducted this interview during an off day via Zoom. I placed these interviews and observations into conversation with the experiences of athletes competing overseas as portrayed on their YouTube channels (cited in the text).

First Quarter

This chapter primarily focuses on how ESPN Films' documentary *144* depicts players' experiences in the Wubble, but I have included material from an interview I conducted with WNBPA member Sydney Colson in 2021 following her time in the bubble and asked her not only about her experience that season but also how she navigated playing overseas and her own approach to content creation. I also attended one of the WNBPA / Social Justice Council Zoom sessions held in July 2020—I took notes and considered this a virtual ethnographic opportunity to understand how the union created these spaces to engage with media members. I later received a recording of the meeting, which allowed me to fully analyze the meeting and transcribe the direct quotations that appear throughout this chapter.

Second Quarter

In this chapter I analyzed interviews conducted with athletes between 2015 and 2023. I used technological platforms such as Skype, Google Hangout, and Zoom for these interviews in order to reach athletes competing overseas and to record the interviews for transcription. I also conducted in-person interviews (audio recorded with my phone) and field observations in January 2018 in Kazan, Russia, with Cierra, her loved ones, and members of Kazanochka's team and front office. I also conducted participant observation in Lyon and Bourges, France, as well as Geneva, Switzerland, in May and June of 2022 during Cierra Burdick's playoff push with Lyon ASVEL Féminin.

Third Quarter

I attended part of both the 2023 and 2024 Athletes Unlimited Basketball seasons held in Dallas, Texas. I conducted interviews and participant observation in the arena and via Zoom, and I virtually observed live drafts each week held on YouTube. In the first season, I obtained press credentials through AU and primarily recorded observations via laptop from the media table. However, in the second season, during each game I attended, I sat in a different spectator section of the arena in order to better understand the crowd dynamics and how athletes were engaging with the space before, during, and after games as they sat in the stands. I took notes via a small notepad or the Notes application on my phone. I derived direct quotations from recorded interviews or conversations that occurred in the arena that I documented while in the field; paraphrases denote summaries/memos written from field notes.

Fourth Quarter

The NCAA chapter involves a combination of participant observations conducted in April 2023 during the NCAA Divisions I–III Women's Basketball Final Four weekend. I attended sports bars, pop-up events, parties, and other festivities related to March Madness. I also attended the championship games for Divisions I, II, and III in person and conducted participant observation outside the American Airlines Center on each day of the games.

In 2024 I attended the Portland Region of the NCAA Division I Women's Basketball Tournament, attending all of the Sweet Sixteen games hosted at

Moda Center and one of the Elite Eight games held there (NC State v. Texas). I also attended sponsored events surrounding the games, including the official watch parties hosted by AFLAC and two local bars, Spirit of 77 and The Sports Bra. I combined these observations with media coverage surrounding the tournament both years, adding a critical discourse analysis that centered how athletes and coaches described their experiences across mainstream outlets and social media.

Overtime

In the conclusion, I draw upon a range of interviews and participant observations conducted between 2015 and 2024. I begin with interviews conducted following my season with the Los Angeles Sparks in the fall of 2015. After spending a season working for the Sparks, I exited the field and then scheduled interviews across a single day: I camped out in the conference room of the Sparks headquarters and invited employees to participate in a semistructured interview that lasted between thirty minutes and one hour. I recorded and transcribed these interviews, but as part of informed consent, I let employees know that I would not attach their names to their responses. In earlier iterations of this analysis, I use pseudonyms to identify each participant, but for the purpose of this chapter, I avoid this and acknowledge them generally via their position with the Sparks. I do this to avoid any confusion, given that I use the actual names of participants throughout the rest of the book. I also include portions of an interview conducted online with journalist and advocate Shireen Ahmed in 2017 leading up to the first Muslim Women in Sport Network Global Virtual Summit, held in 2018. The summit, streamed live and archived on YouTube, is the source of the Bilqis Abdul-Qaadir quotations featured in the chapter. I conducted a thematic analysis of the event and considered the afterlives of FIBA's hijab ban in a separate chapter published in an edited volume but resurrected some of the poignant anecdotes from Ahmed and Abdul-Qaadir to signal how important these conversations and perspectives are as these hijabophobic policies continue around the world. Finally, I end with the Nike Hoops Summit held on April 13, 2024, which I attended as a spectator. Given that this event involved athletes under eighteen years of age, I did not do any interview outreach in order to adhere to the Institutional Review Board's guidelines that I submitted for this project, but I offer the event as an example of future directions and implications for this work.

Notes

Prologue

1. "Grove City College v. Bell—Facts and Case Summary," United States Courts, n.d., https://www.uscourts.gov/educational-resources/educational-activities/grove-city-college-v-bell-facts-and-case-summary.

2. "S.2568—Civil Rights Act of 1984," April 12, 1984, https://www.congress.gov/bill/98th-congress/senate-bill/2568.

3. *Civil Rights Restoration Act of 1985: Joint Hearings before the Committee on Education and Labor, and the Subcommittee on Civil and Constitutional Rights of the Committee on the Judiciary, House of Representatives*, 99th Cong., 1st sess. (Los Angeles, March 22, 1985), 608.

4. *Civil Rights Restoration Act of 1985*, 608.

5. *Civil Rights Restoration Act of 1985*, 609–10, emphasis mine.

6. In a *Seinfeld* episode titled "The Susie" (season 8, episode 15), Kramer finds himself in the middle of the infamous Spike Lee / Reggie Miller beef and gets kicked out of a New York Knicks game. As he relays the events to Jerry and Elaine, she responds in surprise, "Cheryl Miller's brother?" Kramer finishes his incredible story, and Jerry responds, "Can you believe it?" Elaine, in disbelief, responds, "I didn't know Cheryl Miller's brother played basketball."

7. J. R. Gamble, "Our Game 2: The Incomparable Cheryl Miller, Part II," Shadow League, June 25, 2014, para. 4, https://theshadowleague.com/our-game-2-the-incomparable-cheryl-miller-part-ii/.

8. Darcy C. Plymire and Pamela J. Forman, "Speaking of Cheryl Miller: Interrogating the Lesbian Taboo on a Women's Basketball Newsgroup," *NWSA Journal* 13, no. 1 (Spring 2001): 3.

Pregame. Introducing the Crossover

1. Hanif Abdurraqib, "It Rained in Ohio on the Night Allen Iverson Hit Michael Jordan with a Crossover," in *They Can't Kill Us Until They Kill Us* (Columbus: Two Dollar Radio, 2017), 128–29.

2. *It REALLY Ain't Fo' Errybody / Overseas Women's Basketball Pros and Cons Part 1* (YouTube, 2016), https://www.youtube.com/channel/UC60E8wxSah5sXLWX boseHxQ.

3. "Facts and Figures," FIBA.basketball, accessed August 15, 2018, http://www.fiba .basketball/presentation.

4. In an essay for *Jacobin,* Abdul Malik writes, "The ongoing commodification of Black culture made sneakers into a powerful cultural totem," and "sneaker markets show us the current state of capitalism in microcosm—and give us an excellent idea of where it's headed" ("Luxury Sneaker Markets Are a Preview of Capitalist Dystopia," *Jacobin,* December 6, 2020, https://jacobin.com/2020/12/luxury-sneaker-markets -capitalist-nikes-resale).

5. Todd Boyd and Kenneth L. Shropshire, "Basketball Jones: A New World Order?," in *Basketball Jones: America above the Rim,* ed. Todd Boyd and Kenneth L. Shropshire (New York: New York University Press, 2000), 3.

6. Yago Colás, *Ball Don't Lie! Myth, Genealogy, and Invention in the Cultures of Basketball* (Philadelphia: Temple University Press, 2016), 25; Pamela Grundy and Susan Shackelford, *Shattering the Glass: The Remarkable History of Women's Basketball* (New York: New Press, 2005).

7. Michael A. Messner, *Power at Play: Sports and the Problem of Masculinity* (Boston: Beacon Press, 1992), 16.

8. Colás, *Ball Don't Lie!,* 20.

9. Colás, 23.

10. Colás, 29.

11. Colás, 31.

12. Colás, 32 (emphasis mine).

13. See Eileen Narcotta-Welp, "A Black Fly in White Milk: The 1999 Women's World Cup, Briana Scurry, and the Politics of Inclusion," *Journal of Sport History* 42, no. 3 (2016): 382–93; Cheryl Cooky, Faye L. Wachs, Michael Messner, and Shari L. Dworkin, "It's Not about the Game: Don Imus, Race, Class, Gender and Sexuality in Contemporary Media," *Sociology of Sport Journal* 27, no. 2 (2010): 139–59; Sarah Banet-Weiser, "Hoop Dreams: Professional Basketball and the Politics of Race and Gender," *Journal of Sport & Social Issues* 23, no. 4 (1999): 403–20; Amira Rose Davis, "No League of Their Own: Baseball, Black Women, and the Politics of Representation," *Radical History Review,* no. 125 (May 2016): 74–96; Terese M. Peretto Stratta, "Cultural Expressions of African American Female Athletes in Intercollegiate Sport," in *Athletic Intruders: Ethnographic Research on Women, Culture, and Exercise,* ed. Anne Bolin and Jane Granskog (Albany: SUNY Press, 2003), 79–106.

14. Nirmal Puwar, *Space Invaders: Race, Gender and Bodies out of Place* (New York: Berg, 2004); Letisha Engracia Cardoso Brown, "Sporting Space Invaders: Elite Bodies in Track and Field, a South African Context," *South African Review of Sociology* 46, no. 1 (2015): 10.

15. Historian Deborah Gray White articulates this when she writes that "while white women saw ladyhood as constraining and designed tactics meant to show themselves beyond its confining boundaries, black women had to present themselves as ladies in order to do the political work necessary to uplift the race and the social/psychological work necessary to support black men" ("The Difference That Difference Makes," in *Women's Activist Organizing in US History,* ed. Dawn Durante, [Urbana: University of Illinois Press, 2022], 7).

16. Aimee Meredith Cox, *Shapeshifters: Black Girls and the Choreography of Citizenship* (Durham, NC: Duke University Press, 2015), 28–29.

17. Cox.

18. Cox, 27.

19. Cox.

20. Joanne Lannin, *Finding a Way to Play: The Pioneering Spirit of Women in Basketball* (Portland, OR: Portlandia Press, 2015), 46–47.

21. Lannin, 46–47.

22. LaKesha Whitaker, "Theodora Boyd," Ivy@50, n.d., para. 10, http://ivy50.com/blackhistory/story.aspx?sid=1/5/2009.

23. Rita Liberti, "'We Were Ladies, We Just Played Like Boys': African American Womanhood and Competitive Basketball at Bennett College, 1928–1942," in *Sport and the Color Line: Black Athletes and Race Relations in Twentieth-Century America,* ed. Patrick B. Miller and David K. Wiggins (New York: Routledge, 2004), 108, https://digital.la84.org/digital/collection/p17103coll10/id/1441/.

24. Liberti, 108.

25. Liberti, 100.

26. Fran Harris, *Summer Madness: Inside the Wild, Wacky World of the WNBA* (BadAss Media, 2013), loc. 122–26, Kindle.

27. Harris, loc. 127–30.

28. Stacy Landreth Grau, Georgina Roselli, and Charles R. Taylor, "Where's Tamika Catchings? A Content Analysis of Female Athlete Endorsers in Magazine Advertisements," *Journal of Current Issues and Research in Advertising* 29, no. 1 (Spring 2007): 55–65; Janet S. Fink, Heidi M. Parker, George B. Cunningham, and Jacquelyn Cuneen, "Female Athlete Endorsers: Determinants of Effectiveness," *Sport Management Review* 15, no. 1 (2012): 13–22.

29. Victoria Carty explains the larger issue at hand regarding the difference between Black and white women on the court in this way: "Black female athletes must prove themselves as athletes first, and sexuality is either marginalized or framed very differently. . . . Therefore, black women historically have been situated outside dominant culture's definition of acceptable (white) femininity, and black womanhood

is viewed very differently. . . . Black women athletes are seen as more athletic than white women, so their femininity is discounted as irrelevant" ("Textual Portrayals of Female Athletes: Liberation or Nuanced Forms of Patriarchy?," *Frontiers: A Journal of Women Studies* 26, no. 2 [2005]: 140).

30. John Lisec and Mary G. McDonald, "Gender Inequality in the New Millennium: An Analysis of WNBA Representations in Sport Blogs," *Journal of Sports Media* 7, no. 2 (Fall 2012): 153–78.

31. Janet S. Fink, "Using Athletes as Endorsers to Sell Women's Sport: Attractiveness vs. Expertise," *Journal of Sport Management* 18, no. 4 (2004): 350–67.

32. Cooky et al., "It's Not about the Game"; John M. Sloop, "'This Is Not Natural': Caster Semenya's Gender Threats," *Critical Studies in Media Communication* 29, no. 2 (2012): 81–96; Katherine L. Lavelle, "'Plays Like a Guy': A Rhetorical Analysis of Brittney Griner in Sports Media," *Journal of Sports Media* 9, no. 2 (Fall 2014): 115–31.

33. David J. Leonard, "Dilemmas and Contradictions: Black Female Athletes," in *Out of Bounds: Racism and the Black Athlete*, ed. Lori Latrice Martin (Santa Barbara, CA: ABC-CLIO, 2014), 213.

34. Mary G. McDonald, "Queering Whiteness: The Peculiar Case of the Women's National Basketball Association," *Sociological Perspectives* 45, no. 4 (2002): 382.

35. Sarah Banet-Weiser, "Hoop Dreams: Professional Basketball and the Politics of Race and Gender," *Journal of Sport & Social Issues* 23, no. 4 (1999): 405.

36. Banet-Weiser, 405.

37. "NCAA Demographics Database," NCAA.org: The Official Site of the NCAA, n.d., https://www.ncaa.org/sports/2018/12/13/ncaa-demographics-database.aspx.

38. See McDonald, "Queering Whiteness"; Mary G. McDonald, "Mapping Whiteness and Sport: An Introduction," *Sociology of Sport Journal* 22, no. 3 (2005): 245–55; Lavelle, "'Plays Like a Guy.'"

39. Jennifer L. Hanis-Martin, "Embodying Contradictions: The Case of Professional Women's Basketball," *Journal of Sport & Social Issues* 30, no. 3 (2006): 269.

40. Katie Barnes, "Jonquel Jones and the Untold Story of the WNBA's Reigning MVP," ESPN, June 22, 2022, https://www.espn.com/wnba/story/_/id/34109460/jonquel-jones-untold-story-wnba-reigning-mvp.

41. Risa F. Isard and E. Nicole Melton, "Does Sport Media Raise Her Name? Examining Intersectional Representation in Media Narratives," *Sport, Business and Management* 12, no. 3 (September 2021): 305–22.

42. Mirin Fader, "Sylvia Fowles's Final Ride and the Last Days of a Legend," *The Ringer*, August 11, 2022, https://www.theringer.com/wnba/2022/8/11/23301315/sylvia-fowles-minnesota-lynx.

43. John F. Borland and Jennifer E. Bruening, "Navigating Barriers: A Qualitative Examination of the Under-Representation of Black Females as Head Coaches in Collegiate Basketball," *Sport Management Review* 13, no. 4 (November 2010): 407.

44. Gloria T. Hull, Patricia Bell-Scott, and Barbara Smith, eds., *All the Women Are White, All the Blacks Are Men, but Some of Us Are Brave: Black Women's Studies* (Old Westbury: Feminist Press, 1982).

45. Scholars such as Stanley I. Thangaraj and Nicole Willms have done this within Asian American communities in their books *Desi Hoop Dreams: Pickup Basketball and the Making of Asian American Masculinity* (New York: NYU Press, 2015) and *When Women Rule the Court: Gender, Race, and Japanese American Basketball* (New Brunswick, NJ: Rutgers University Press, 2017).

46. bell hooks, "Choosing the Margin as a Space of Radical Openness," *Framework: The Journal of Cinema and Media* 36 (1989): 19.

47. Moya Bailey, *Misogynoir Transformed: Black Women's Digital Resistance* (New York: New York University Press, 2021), 19.

48. Bailey, 19.

49. Willa Bennett, "Layshia Clarendon on Bravery, Top Surgery, and the Future of the WNBA," *GQ*, December 16, 2021, para. 12, https://www.gq.com/story/layshia-clarendon-year-of-the-brave.

50. Bennett, para. 26.

51. Ben Pickman, "The Return and Rebirth of AD," SI.com, December 29, 2022, https://www.si.com/wnba/2022/12/29/ad-long-covid-identity-new-york-liberty-daily-cover.

52. Legacy Russell, *Glitch Feminism: A Manifesto* (Brooklyn: Verso, 2020), loc. 108–10, Kindle.

53. Russell, 4.

54. For more on the relationship between race, gender, and dunking, see Yago Colás, "What We Mean When We Say 'Play the Right Way': Strategic Fundamentals, Morality, and Race in the Culture of Basketball," *Journal of the Midwest Modern Language Association* 45, no. 2 (2012): 109–25; Layshia Clarendon, "Layshia Clarendon: 'It's Not about Dunking. It's about the System,'" espnW, April 1, 2016, http://www.espn.com/espnw/voices/article/15112298/layshia-clarendon-says-lower-rims-not-answer; Davis W. Houck, "Attacking the Rim: The Cultural Politics of Dunking," in Boyd and Shropshire, *Basketball Jones,* 151–69.

55. Cheryl Cooky and Michael A. Messner, *No Slam Dunk: Gender, Sport and the Unevenness of Social Change* (New Brunswick, NJ: Rutgers University Press, 2018), 4.

56. Raka Shome and Radha Hegde, "Culture, Communication, and the Challenge of Globalization," *Media, Culture & Communication* 19, no. 2 (2002): 174.

57. Thomas L. Friedman, *The Lexus and the Olive Tree: Understanding Globalization* (London: Picador, 2000), xvii; John Bale and Joseph A. Maguire, eds., *The Global Sports Arena: Athletic Talent Migration in an Interdependent World* (Newcastle, UK: University of Keele, 1994).

58. Shome and Hegde, "Culture," 174.

59. Toby Miller, Geoffrey Lawrence, Jim McKay, and David Rowe, *Globalization and Sport: Playing the World* (Thousand Oaks, CA: SAGE Publications, 2001), 31.

60. Aleš Sekot, "Sport Mobility in a Changing Europe: A Global Aspect," *European Journal for Sport and Society* 1, no. 2 (2004): 113.

61. Joshua I. Newman and Mark Falcous, "Moorings and Movements: The Paradox of Sporting Mobilities," *Sites*, n.s., 9, no. 1 (2012): 38–39.

62. Newman and Falcous, 40.

63. Newman and Falcous, 51.

64. Bale and Maguire, *The Global Sports Arena*, 18.

65. Anima Adjepong, "'Periodically I Pondered Over It': Reading the Absence/Presence of Women in *Beyond a Boundary*," in *Marxism, Colonialism, and Cricket: C. L. R. James's "Beyond a Boundary*," ed. David Featherstone, Christopher Gair, Christian Høgsbjerg, and Andrew Smith (Durham, NC: Duke University Press, 2018), 123–36.

66. Bale and Maguire, *The Global Sports Arena*, 18.

67. Patricia Hill Collins, *Black Feminist Thought* (New York: Routledge, 2000); Audrey Macklin, "Particularized Citizenship: Encultured Women and the Public Sphere," in *Migrations and Mobilities: Citizenship, Borders and Gender,* ed. Seyla Benhabib and Judith Resnik (New York: New York University Press, 2009), 276–303.

68. Macklin, "Particularized Citizenship," 276.

69. For detailed data collection information, see the "Note on Sources."

70. Mikki Kendall, *Hood Feminism: Notes from the Women That a Movement Forgot* (New York: Penguin Random House, 2020), xx.

71. Rosalie Rolón-Dow, "Critical Care: A Color(Full) Analysis of Care Narratives in the Schooling Experiences of Puerto Rican Girls," *American Educational Research Journal* 42, no. 1 (Spring 2005): 104.

First Quarter. "Betting on Ourselves"

1. *144* (ESPN Films, 2021), 27:18, https://vimeo.com/552923319.

2. *144*, 00:39.

3. Roopali Mukherjee and Sarah Banet-Weiser, *Commodity Activism: Cultural Resistance in Neoliberal Times* (New York: New York University Press, 2012), 53; Aimee Meredith Cox, *Shapeshifters: Black Girls and the Choreography of Citizenship* (Durham, NC: Duke University Press, 2015), 9.

4. Nasha Smith, "ESPN's '144' Documentary Shows Exactly Why the WNBA Is So Important," *Forbes*, May 13, 2021, para. 17, https://www.forbes.com/sites/nashasmith/2021/05/13/espns-144-shows-exactly-why-the-wnba-is-so-important/.

5. Bill Nichols, *Introduction to Documentary*, 3rd ed. (Bloomington: Indiana University Press, 2017), 26.

6. Greg Braxton, "'The Last Dance' Started a Flood of Sports Docs. And the 'Danger of Oversaturation' Is Real," *Los Angeles Times*, June 14, 2023, para. 15, https://www.latimes.com/entertainment-arts/story/2023–06–14/the-last-dance-netflix-espn-hbo-showtime-prime-video-apple-tv-sports-documentaries.

7. Braxton, para. 21.

8. Nicole R. Fleetwood, *On Racial Icons: Blackness and the Public Imagination* (New Brunswick, NJ: Rutgers University Press, 2015), 84.

9. Dunja Antunovic and Andrew D. Linden, "'Powerful Lessons' in Women's Sport: ESPN's *Nine for IX* Series," *Journal of Sport and Social Issues* 44, no. 6 (December 2020): 534–49; Dawn Heinecken, "The Heart of the Game: Girls, Sports, and the Limits of 'Empowerment,'" *Journal of Sport and Social Issues* 45, no. 3 (June 2021): 251–71.

10. Nichols, *Introduction*, 12.

11. Samantha N. Sheppard and Travis Vogan, introduction to *Sporting Realities: Critical Readings of the Sports Documentary*, ed. Samantha N. Sheppard and Travis Vogan (Lincoln: University of Nebraska Press, 2020), 4.

12. Ian McDonald, "Situating the Sport Documentary," *Journal of Sport and Social Issues* 31, no. 3 (August 2007): 212, https://doi.org/10.1177/0193723507304608.

13. Ian McDonald argues that "sport documentaries are key to placing sports in their social context and in the process reveal that sport is more than simply about the performance on the field of play" (222).

14. "History," WNBPA, n.d., https://wnbpa.com/about/history/.

15. Nneka Ogwumike, "Bet on Women," *Players' Tribune*, November 1, 2018, para. 15, https://www.theplayerstribune.com/articles/nneka-ogwumike-wnba-cba-bet-on -women.

16. Ava Wallace, "Thanks to New WNBA Labor Deal, Kristi Toliver Is No Longer an NBA Coach Making $10,000," *Washington Post*, January 27, 2020, https://www .washingtonpost.com/sports/2020/01/27/kristi-toliver-rule-wnba-cba/.

17. Brooke Baldwin, *Huddle: How Women Unlock Their Collective Power* (New York: Harper Business, 2021).

18. Ogwumike, "Bet on Women," para. 48–49.

19. "Women's National Basketball Association: Collective Bargaining Agreement," January 2020, https://wnbpa.com/wp-content/uploads/2020/01/WNBA-WNBPA -CBA-2020–2027.pdf.

20. Angeline Jane Bernabe, "WNBA Players Will Receive 6-Figure Salary, Child Care Benefits in New Collective Bargaining Agreement," *Good Morning America*, January 14, 2020, https://www.goodmorningamerica.com/living/story/wnba-players -receive-figure-salary-child-care-benefits-68261850.

21. Baldwin, *Huddle*, 176.

22. Baldwin, 3.

23. Baldwin, 3.

24. Baldwin, 181.

25. Bernabe, "WNBA Players."

26. Baldwin, *Huddle*, 181–82. She also wrote, "Every athlete I spoke to (all of whom were leaders in their players associations) told me about the disruption caused to their physical regimens. No one wants to take off three or four days of work to, as [soccer star Megan] Rapinoe put it, 'fight with our employer about our job.'"

27. "Statement on Coronavirus & College Athlete Health," National College Players Association, February 29, 2020, https://www.ncpanow.org/releases-advisories/ statement-on-coronavirus-college-athlete-health.

28. Kyle Boone, "2020 NCAA Tournament Games to Be Played without Fans in Attendance Due to Threat of Coronavirus," CBS Sports, March 11, 2020, https://www .cbssports.com/college-basketball/news/2020-ncaa-tournament-games-to-be-played -without-fans-in-attendance-due-to-threat-of-coronavirus/.

29. @ShamsCharania, Twitter, March 11, 2020, https://twitter.com/shamscharania/ status/1237913057596026881?lang=en.

30. @wojespn, Twitter, March 11, 2020, https://twitter.com/wojespn/status/ 1237914166285008896.

31. "Coronavirus: NCPA Calls for Immediate Suspension of All Sports Activities," National College Players Association, March 12, 2020, https://www.ncpanow .org/releases-advisories/coronavirus-ncpa-calls-for-immediate-suspension-of-all -sports-activities; ESPN Staff, "'It Was Like a Movie': What Led the NCAA to Shut Down Competition," ESPN, March 17, 2020, https://www.espn.com/mens-college -basketball/story/_/id/28908157/inside-unprecedented-48-hours-shut-ncaa-sports.

32. Bradford William Davis, "There's an Essential Difference between 'Essential Workers' and Athletes," New York Daily News, May 28, 2020, para. 14, https:// www.nydailynews.com/sports/more-sports/ny-essential-workers-20200528 -q4xutdeocrhz3hsldoczzouxsa-story.html.

33. 144, 5:16.

34. "Acting Secretary Wolf Signs Exemption Allowing Entry of Certain Foreign Professional Athletes in the U.S.," Department of Homeland Security, May 22, 2020, para. 2, https://www.dhs.gov/news/2020/05/22/acting-secretary-wolf-signs-exemption -allowing-entry-certain-foreign-professional.

35. Azadeh Erfani, "Closing the Border Was an Illegal, Racist Distraction from a Failed Covid-19 Response. Then, It Became Indefinite," National Immigrant Justice Center, June 22, 2020, https://immigrantjustice.org/staff/blog/closing-border-was -illegal-racist-distraction-failed-covid-19-response-then-it-became.

36. Kim Kelly, Fight Like Hell: The Untold History of American Labor (Atria / One Signal Publishers, 2022), 313.

37. 144, 5:26.

38. Ari Chambers, "WNBA Players, Former Sparks GM Penny Toler Speak Out about WNBA Proposed Plan," The Next, June 9, 2020, para. 13, https://www .thenexthoops.com/features/wnba-players-former-sparks-gm-penny/.

39. 144, 4:38.

40. Paul Davis and Charlene Weaving, "COVID-19: Lip Gloss and the Threat to Women's Sport," in Philosophy, Sport and the Pandemic, ed. Jeffrey P. Fry and Andrew Edgar (London: Routledge, 2021), 230.

41. 144, 6:45.

42. 144, 24:02.

43. *144*, 24:52.

44. *144*, 10:58.

45. Davis and Weaving, "COVID-19," 222.

46. *144*, 29:52.

47. The Care Collective, *The Care Manifesto: The Politics of Interdependence* (New York: Verso Books, 2020), 30.

48. *144*, 22:44.

49. Robin D. G. Kelley, "Playing for Keeps: Pleasure and Profit on the Postindustrial Playground," in *The House That Race Built*, ed. Wahneema Lubiano (New York: Random House, 1998), 206, Kindle.

50. Danielle Young, "Watch: Is Double Dutch a Traditionally Black Sport?," *The Root*, August 11, 2017, para. 1, https://www.theroot.com/watch-is-double-dutch-a -traditionally-black-sport-1797683127.

51. Stephanie Carter, "Why Double Dutch Is the Original #BlackGirlMagic Sport," *Mater Mea*, n.d., https://matermea.com/why-double-dutch-is-the-original-blackgirl magic-sport/.

52. Kelley, "Playing for Keeps," 207.

53. Renee Nishawn Scott, "Taking On the Light: Ontological Black Girlhood in the Twenty-First Century," *Girlhood Studies* 15, no. 1 (Spring 2022): 2.

54. "WNBA Announces a 2020 Season Dedicated to Social Justice," WNBA, July 6, 2020, https://www.wnba.com/news/wnba-announces-a-2020-season-dedicated-to -social-justice/.

55. *144*, 14:23.

56. Doug Feinberg, "WNBA Withdraws Fines for Teams That Wore Black Protest Shirt," *South Florida Times*, July 28, 2016, para. 4, https://www.sfltimes.com/news/ wnba-withdraws-fines-for-teams-that-wore-black-protest-shirts.

57. Feinberg, para. 11.

58. Scoop Jackson, *The Game Is Not a Game: The Power, Protest, and Politics of American Sports* (Chicago: Haymarket Books, 2020), 22–23.

59. Patricia Hill Collins, *Black Feminist Thought* (New York: Routledge, 2000), 254.

60. African American Policy Forum, WNBPA press conference, July 30, 2020.

61. Interview with Sydney Colson, Zoom, October 22, 2020.

62. Sarah J. Jackson, Moya Bailey, and Brooke Foucault Welles, *#HashtagActivism: Networks of Race and Gender Justice* (Cambridge, MA: MIT Press, 2020), 60.

63. "On Views of Race and Inequality, Blacks and Whites Are Worlds Apart," Pew Research Center, June 27, 2016, https://www.pewresearch.org/social-trends/2016/06/27/ on-views-of-race-and-inequality-blacks-and-whites-are-worlds-apart/.

64. Lisa B. Spanierman, "White Guilt in the Summer of Black Lives Matter," in *Guilt: A Force of Cultural Transformation*, ed. Katharina von Kellenbach and Matthias Buschmeier (Oxford: Oxford University Press, 2022), 50.

65. Spanierman, 51. Spanierman's work broadly considers white guilt as a complex phenomenon that receives the ire of both conservative and liberal folks: "In these

instances, white guilt interferes with critical reflection about racism because whites get mired in feeling individually blameworthy for racism. Interestingly, both the liberal and conservative critiques implicate the avoidance of appearing racist; in the conservative critique, the impetus is external (i.e., manipulation by BIPOC), whereas in the liberal critique, the impetus is internal (i.e., I want to think of myself, or at least appear, as a good person)" (44).

66. Sirma Bilge, "Intersectionality Undone: Saving Intersectionality from Feminist Intersectionality Studies," *Du Bois Review* 10, no. 2 (2013): 405.

67. Bilge, 420, 407.

68. *144*, 47:28.

69. *144*, 47:44.

70. Brittany Farr, "Witnessing an Absent Presence: Bringing Black Feminist Theory to Traditional Legal Archives," *Black Scholar* 52, no. 4 (October 2022): 64–75, https://doi.org/10.1080/00064246.2022.2111676.

71. Chris Bengel, "Atlanta Dream Players Respond to Letter from Co-owner Kelly Loeffler, Which Objected to WNBA's Activism," *CBS Sports*, July 10, 2020, para. 7, https://www.cbssports.com/wnba/news/atlanta-dream-players-respond-to-letter-from-co-owner-kelly-loeffler-which-objected-to-wnbas-activism/.

72. Elizabeth Williams, "How the WNBA Helped Flip Georgia Blue," *Vox*, January 11, 2021, para. 7, https://www.vox.com/first-person/22221250/georgia-election-results-senate-warnock-ossoff-wnba-elizabeth-williams.

73. *144*, 52:27.

74. Mikki Kendall, *Hood Feminism: Notes from the Women That a Movement Forgot* (New York: Penguin Random House, 2020), 255–56.

75. Kendall, 258.

76. Claudia Harmata, "WNBA Players Wearing T-Shirts Supporting Senate Opponent of Atlanta Dream Owner," *People*, August 5, 2020, para. 8, https://people.com/sports/wnba-players-wearing-t-shirts-supporting-senate-opponent-of-atlanta-dream-owner/.

77. *144*, 17:15. This form of organizing reflects what Crenshaw herself writes: "Although racism and sexism readily intersect in the lives of real people, they seldom do in feminist and antiracist practices. And so, when the practices expound identity as a woman or person of color as an either/or proposition, they relegate the identity of women of color to a location that resists telling" ("Mapping the Margins: Intersectionality, Identity Politics, and Violence against Women of Color," *Stanford Law Review* 43, no. 6 [1991]: 1242).

78. *144*, 28:53.

79. *144*, 29:36.

80. *144*, 31:00.

81. *144*, 31:59.

82. *144*, 30:44.

83. *144*, 32:49.

84. *144*, 35:25.

85. Samhita Mukhopadhyay, "Doing the Work While Doing the Work," *The Nation*, July 11, 2023, para. 5, https://www.thenation.com/article/society/social-justice -trauma-healing/.

86. *144*, 36:39.

87. *144*, 37:16.

88. *144*, 38:48.

89. Fleetwood, *On Racial Icons*, 110.

90. *144*, 34:23.

91. Ben Carrington, *Race, Sport and Politics: The Sporting Black Diaspora* (London: Sage, 2010), 176–77.

92. *144*, 39:33.

93. Ewa Jasiewicz, "Strikes Are Healing," *Healing Justice London* (blog), January 24, 2023, https://healingjusticeldn.org/2023/01/24/strikesarehealing/.

94. *144*, 40:57.

95. *144*, 42:35.

96. *144*, 55:58.

97. Catherine Rottenberg and Lynne Segal, "What Is Care?," Goldsmiths Press, n.d., para. 5, https://www.gold.ac.uk/goldsmiths-press/features/what-is-care/.

98. Jamie K. McCallum, "How the Pandemic Changed the Landscape of U.S. Labor Organizing," *In These Times*, November 17, 2022, https://inthesetimes.com/article/ essential-workers-covid-pandemic-union-labor-strike.

99. Kelly, *Fight Like Hell*, 27.

100. Kimberly Foster, "Daniel Holtzclaw, Police Sexual Assault, and the Terror of Being Uncared For," *For Harriet*, November 9, 2015, http://www.forharriet .com/2015/11/daniel-holtzclaw-police-sexual-assault.html.

101. Grace Clement, *Care, Autonomy, and Justice: Feminism and the Ethic of Care* (Boulder, CO: Westview Press, 1998), 3.

102. Clement, 3.

103. The Care Collective, *The Care Manifesto*, 6.

104. See Katie Johnston, "For Women of Color in Care Work, Says New Report, Inequities Abound," *Boston Globe*, September 1, 2022, online ed., sec. D1, https:// www.bostonglobe.com/2022/09/01/business/women-color-care-work-racial -economic-inequities-abound-report-shows/; Jamila K. Taylor, "Structural Racism and Maternal Health among Black Women," *Journal of Law, Medicine & Ethics* 48, no. 3 (n.d.): 506–17; Victoria Masterson, "Health and Social Care's Gender Pay Problem," World Economic Forum, August 4, 2022, https://www.weforum.org/agenda/2022/08/ gender-pay-gap-health-care/.

105. Joan C. Tronto, *Caring Democracy: Markets, Equality, and Justice* (New York: New York University Press, 2013), 1.

106. Tronto, 36.

107. *144*, 1:09:16.

108. *144*, 1:11:00.

109. Bridget Read and Angelina Chapin, "What Really Happened with the Breonna Taylor Grand Jury?," *The Cut*, October 27, 2020, para. 1, https://www.thecut.com/2020/10/breonna-taylor-grand-jury-what-really-happened.html.

110. @jemelehill, Twitter, January 6, 2021, https://twitter.com/jemelehill/status/1346718884624179200?s=20.

111. @LaChinaRobinson, Twitter, January 6, 2021, https://twitter.com/LaChinaRobinson/status/1346818079767076868?s=20.

112. @diamonddoesit1, Twitter, January 6, 2021, https://twitter.com/diamonddoesit1/status/1346850173272682503?s=20.

113. Marie Solis, "Black Women 'Saved America' from Roy Moore—Now Vote Them into Office, Say Political Activists," *Newsweek*, December 15, 2017, para. 6, https://www.newsweek.com/thank-black-women-vote-office-political-activists-748619.

114. Marie Solis, "Doug Jones Won Because of Black Women Trying to 'Save America,'" *Newsweek*, December 13, 2017, para. 5, https://www.newsweek.com/who-voted-doug-jones-black-women-supported-democratic-senate-candidate-98-746358.

115. @Lexiebrown, Twitter, January 6, 2021, https://mobile.twitter.com/lexiebrown/status/1346856653178736647?lang=en.

116. Joshua Chambers-Letson, "The Body Is Never Given nor Do We Actually See It," in *Race and Performance after Repetition*, ed. Soyica Diggs Colbert, Douglas A. Jones Jr., and Shane Vogel (Durham, NC: Duke University Press, 2020), 272.

117. Samantha N. Sheppard, *Sporting Blackness: Race, Embodiment, and Critical Muscle Memory on Screen* (Berkeley: University of California Press, 2020), 15.

118. Sheppard, 2.

119. Sheppard, 117.

120. Joshua Myers, *Of Black Study* (London: Pluto Press, 2023), 15.

121. Myers, 15.

122. Kimberlé Crenshaw, postscript in *Framing Intersectionality: Debates on a Multifaceted Concept in Gender Studies*, ed. Helma Lutz, Maria Teresa Herrera Vivar, and Linda Supik (Farnham: Ashgate, 2011), 222.

123. Chandra Talpade Mohanty, *Feminism without Borders: Decolonizing Theory, Practicing Solidarity* (Durham, NC: Duke University Press, 2006), 5.

124. Chambers-Letson, "The Body," 272.

125. *Shattered Glass: A WNBPA Story*, documentary (Tubi, 2024), 00:38, https://tubitv.com/movies/100014374/shattered-glass-a-wnbpa-story.

126. *Shattered Glass*, 1:21.

127. Jennifer McClearen and Mia Fischer, "Maya Moore, Black Lives Matter, and the Visibility of Athlete Activism," *Velvet Light Trap* 87 (Spring 2021): 64.

128. McClearen and Fischer, 67.

129. Evan Brody, "Documenting Difference: Gay Athletes of Color, Binary Representation, and the Sports Documentary," in Sheppard and Vogan, *Sporting Realities*, 63–88.

130. Fleetwood, *On Racial Icons*, 81.

131. Emily Plec and Shaun M. Anderson, "Protest and Public Memory: Documenting the 1968 Summer Olympic Games," in Sheppard and Vogan, *Sporting Realities*, 113.

Second Quarter. Translating Timeouts

1. Mark Falcous and Joseph Maguire, "Future Directions: Sporting Mobilities, Immobilities and Moorings," in *Sport and Migration: Borders, Boundaries and Crossings*, ed. Joseph Maguire and Mark Falcous (Abingdon: Taylor and Francis, 2010), 277.

2. "U.S.-Russian Relations," Center for Strategic & International Studies, n.d., para. 1, https://www.csis.org/programs/europe-russia-and-eurasia-program/archives/us -russian-relations.

3. Jim Banks, "H.R. 6422—Putin Accountability Act," Pub. L. No. H.R. 64222 (2022), https://www.congress.gov/bill/117th-congress/house-bill/6422/text?r=12&s=2.

4. Joseph Maguire and John Bale, "Introduction: Sports Labour Migration in the Global Arena," in *The Global Sports Arena: Athletic Talent Migration in an Interdependent World*, ed. John Bale and Joseph Maguire (London: Frank Cass Publishers, 1994), 4.

5. I am happy to report that the bag inexplicably appeared at Kazanochka's gym a few days after I arrived with everything accounted for.

6. Seungbum Lee, "Global Outsourcing: A Different Approach to an Understanding of Sport Labour Migration," *Global Business Review* 11, no. 2 (2010): 154.

7. Lee, 155.

8. Joshua I. Newman and Mark Falcous, "Moorings and Movements: The Paradox of Sporting Mobilities," *Sites* 9, no. 1 (2012): 46.

9. Joseph Maguire, "Blade Runners: Canadian Migrants, Ice Hockey, and the Global Sports Process," *Journal of Sport and Social Issues* 20, no. 3 (1996): 335–60.

10. Jonathan Magee and John Sugden, "'The World at Their Feet': Professional Football and International Labor Migration," *Journal of Sport & Social Issues* 26, no. 4 (November 2002): 429.

11. Magee and Sugden, 434.

12. Magee and Sugden, 431–34.

13. Jody Avirgan and Keith Romer, "The Spy Who Signed Me," *30 for 30*, n.d., https://30for30podcasts.com/episodes/the-spy-who-signed-me/.

14. Avirgan and Romer.

15. James Riordan, *Sport in Soviet Society: Development of Sport and Physical Activity in Russia and the USSR* (Cambridge: Cambridge University Press, 1977).

16. Riordan.

17. Alexander Sunik, "Russia in the Olympic Movement around 1900," *Journal of Olympic History* 10, no. 3 (2002): 46–59.

18. Riordan.

19. Hall of Fame basketball player Cynthia Cooper writes in *She Got Game: My Personal Odyssey* (New York: Warner Books, 1999): "America had boycotted the 1980 Olympics in Moscow; the Soviet Union had responded by boycotting the 1984 Olympics in Los Angeles. The Soviet Union had won gold in 1980 with the Americans absent; America had won gold in 1984 with the Soviets absent. Which was the better team? Everyone in the sport wanted to know. The teams had been like two heavyweight boxers avoiding a title fight. When the big test finally came, it was scheduled on the Soviets' home court [for the 1986 FIBA World Championships]. In the eyes of many who followed women's basketball, that fact alone made America the underdog. Team USA would beat the Soviet Union 108–88 in the FIBA World Championship final" (91).

20. Adele Marie Barker, "The Culture Factory: Theorizing the Popular in the Old and New Russia," in *Consuming Russia: Popular Culture, Sex, and Society Since Gorbachev*, ed. Adele Marie Barker (Durham, NC: Duke University Press, 1999), 12–46. This also happened when I visited a visa submission center in West Hollywood specializing in the paperwork required by Russia. Because of the holiday, I received a gift with the purchase of processing my tourist visa, a cookbook titled *CCCP Cookbook*. Containing over sixty recipes from the Soviet period, ranging from the meals of the proletariat to those of the elite, with classic cultural cuisine sprinkled in, the cookbook offers a historical lens of Soviet culture through food and reflects the nostalgia that remains for many in Russia today. One reviewer describes the book's target audience as a "post–Cold War generation [who] grows up intrigued by a period which many older than them would rather forget." Olga Syutkin and Pavel Syutkin, "Cold War Cuisine: Notes from the CCCP Cookbook," New East Digital Archive, October 9, 2015, para. 1, https://www.new-east-archive.org/features/show/4745/soviet-food -stories-cold-war-cuisine-cccp-cookbook.

21. *Love and Basketball* (YouTube, New Line Cinema, 2000), https://www.youtube .com/watch?v=exvoKmpCwXE.

22. *It REALLY Ain't Fo' Errybody / Overseas Women's Basketball Pros and Cons Part 1* (YouTube, 2016), https://www.youtube.com/channel/UC6oE8wxSah5sXLWX boseHxQ.

23. Joseph Maguire, "American Labour Migrants, Globalization and the Making of English Basketball," in Bale and Maguire, *Global Sports Arena*, 238.

24. Lee, "Global Outsourcing," 156, 158.

25. Munene Mwaniki, *The Black Migrant Athlete: Media, Race, and the Diaspora in Sports* (Lincoln: University of Nebraska Press, 2017), 2.

26. Ben Carrington, *Race, Sport and Politics: The Sporting Black Diaspora* (London: Sage, 2010), 2.

27. For more, see Jane Mayer, "How Russia Helped Swing the Election for Trump," September 24, 2018, https://www.newyorker.com/magazine/2018/10/01/how-russia -helped-to-swing-the-election-for-trump; Kara Lynch, *Black Russians* (Third World Newsreel, 2001); *Being Black in Russia* (BBC, 2018), https://www.bbc.com/news/av/

world-europe-44253936/world-cup-2018-being-black-in-russia; Harry Haywood, *Black Bolshevik: Autobiography of an Afro-American Communist* (Chicago: Liberator Press, 1978).

28. Chamique Holdsclaw, *Breaking Through: Beating the Odds Shot after Shot* (Chamique Holdsclaw LLC, 2012), 205.

29. Holdsclaw, 208.

30. Aleš Sekot, "Sport Mobility in a Changing Europe: A Global Aspect," *European Journal for Sport and Society* 1, no. 2 (2004): 113.

31. Watching Nneka help Cierra up reminded me of a similar scene I witnessed years ago in Barcelona, Spain, at an FC Barcelona men's basketball game. During a heated exchange between a Black FC Barcelona player and an opposing player of Spanish descent, I saw the Black player on the opposing team step in the midst of the altercation and pull the FC Barcelona player to the side to avoid a quickly escalating situation. In that moment it seemed that his focus was to ensure that a fellow Black athlete didn't cause a melee or risk injury rather than siding with his teammate, the Spanish player.

32. @E_Williams_1, Twitter, December 11, 2017.

33. Kate Fagan, "Diana Taurasi's Decision to Sit Out Should Affect WNBA Salaries," ESPN.com, February 3, 2015, http://www.espn.com/wnba/story/_/id/12272036.

34. Howard Megdal, "Breanna Stewart Shows the Toll of Pro Women's Basketball's Never-Ending Grind," *New York Times*, April 21, 2019, https://www.nytimes.com/2019/04/19/sports/breanna-stewart-achilles-wnba.html.

35. Jahmal Corner, "Becky Hammon Defends Decision to Play for Russia," Reuters, July 31, 2008, para. 12, https://www.reuters.com/article/lifestyle/becky-hammon-defends-decision-to-play-for-russia-idUSN30505308/.

36. Corner, para. 25.

37. Avirgan and Romer, "The Spy Who Signed Me."

38. Cooper, *She Got Game*, 112–13.

39. Christopher Faulkner, Gyozo Molnar, and Geoff Kohe, "'I Just Go on Wi-Fi': Imagining Worlds through Professional Basketball Migrants' Deployment of Information and Communication Technology," *Journal of Sport and Social Issues* 43, no. 3 (2019): 211.

40. "Griner Cut but OK after Knife Attack in China," ESPN.com, November 4, 2014, https://www.espn.com/wnba/story/_/id/11821972/brittney-griner-cut-ok-knife-attack-china-agent-says.

41. Instagram, May 13, 2021, https://www.instagram.com/p/COo792TNuQA/.

42. "Remarks by President Biden on the Release of Brittney Griner," the White House, December 8, 2022, https://www.whitehouse.gov/briefing-room/speeches-remarks/2022/12/08/remarks-by-president-biden-on-the-release-of-brittney-griner/.

43. Nicholas Casey, "When a Prisoner Swap Is a Rorschach-Test," *New York Times Magazine*, December 9, 2022, https://www.nytimes.com/2022/12/09/magazine/griner-bout-swap-putin.html.

44. Derek Shearer, "To Play Ball, Not Make War: Sports, Diplomacy and Soft Power," *Harvard International Review* 36, no. 1 (2014): 53–57, 57.

45. Shearer, 56.

46. Phil McCausland and Curtis Bunn, "What Brittney Griner Likely Faced in Russian Penal Colony," *NBC News*, December 8, 2022, para. 9 https://www.nbcnews.com/news/us-news/griner-russian-penal-colony-difficult-prisoners-say-rcna54180.

47. Tracie Hunte et al., "Russia's Long Played with U.S. Racial Politics. Brittney Griner Is the Latest Example," *It's Been a Minute*, NPR, August 12, 2022, https://www.npr.org/2022/08/12/1117141677/russias-long-played-with-u-s-racial-politics-brittney-griner-is-the-latest-examp.

48. Patrick Koenigs, "New Mural Calls Attention to Americans Held Abroad as Loved Ones Say, 'This Doesn't Go Away,'" *ABC News*, July 20, 2022, https://abcnews.go.com/Politics/mural-calls-attention-americans-held-abroad-loved/story?id=87135301.

49. Brad Dress, "New Mural in D.C. Features Faces of Brittney Griner, Other Americans Detained Abroad," text, *The Hill* (blog), July 21, 2022, https://thehill.com/homenews/state-watch/3567704-new-mural-in-d-c-features-faces-of-brittney-griner-other-americans-detained-abroad/.

50. Jenn Hatfield, "New Brittney Griner Mural Has Mystics' Fingerprints on It," *The Next*, July 23, 2022, para. 9, https://www.thenexthoops.com/wnba/washington-mystics/dc-mural-brittney-griner-wrongful-detainees-georgetown-bofhc-washington-mystics/.

51. Ben Morse and Jill Martin, "Brittney Griner Says She'll 'Never Go Overseas Again' to Play Unless It's for the Olympics after Being Detained in Russia," *CNN*, April 27, 2023, https://www.cnn.com/2023/04/27/sport/brittney-griner-press-conference-phoenix-mercury-spt-intl/index.html.

52. Raka Shome and Radha Hegde, "Culture, Communication, and the Challenge of Globalization," *Media, Culture & Communication* 19, no. 2 (2002): 175.

53. Alexa Philippou, "Police Report Details Griner Incident at Airport," ESPN.com, June 12, 2023, https://www.espn.com/wnba/story/_/id/37842850/police-report-details-brittney-griner-incident-dallas-airport.

Third Quarter. Mission Equity

1. Erica L. Ayala, "Athletes Unlimited Basketball Tips Off Inaugural Season in Las Vegas," *Forbes*, January 26, 2022, https://www.forbes.com/sites/ericalayala/2022/01/26/athletes-unlimited-basketball-2022-tips-off-in-las-vegas/. The 2023 player executive committee was comprised of Natasha Cloud, Sydney Colson, Ty Young, Kirby Burkholder, and Lexie Brown.

2. Joe Walsh, "New Texas Law Requires Pro Sports Teams to Play National Anthem," *Forbes*, June 16, 2021, https://www.forbes.com/sites/joewalsh/2021/06/16/new-texas-law-requires-pro-sports-teams-to-play-national-anthem/. This law is a direct

response to the NBA's Dallas Mavericks briefly removing the national anthem from their pregame production.

3. "The Creation of Athletes Unlimited: From a Christmas Eve Dream to Reality," Athletes Unlimited, September 2, 2020, para. 5, https://auprosports.com/read/the -creation-of-athletes-unlimited/.

4. Jonathan Soros, "A New Way to Scale Social Enterprise," *Harvard Business Review*, April 15, 2021, para. 1, https://hbr.org/2021/04/a-new-way-to-scale-social -enterprise.

5. Athletes Unlimited also boasts a star-studded advisory board that includes notable athletes, executives, and media members such as Taylor Rooks, Kevin Durant, Caroline Wozniacki, and Jessica Mendoza.

6. Jon Kraszewski, "Pittsburgh in Fort Worth: Football Bars, Sports Television, Sports Fandom, and the Management of Home," *Journal of Sport & Social Issues* 32, no. 2 (2008): 139–57.

7. Tegan Alexandra Baker, "Long-Distance Football Fandom: Emotional Mobilities and Fluid Geographies of Home," *Social & Cultural Geography* 22, no. 2 (2021): 189–205.

8. "Athletes Unlimited Public Benefit Corporation Report," Athletes Unlimited, March 2022, https://auprosports.com/wp-content/uploads/2022/04/AthletesUnlimited _PBC_Report.pdf.

9. "Sustainability," Athletes Unlimited, accessed November 13, 2023, https:// auprosports.com/sustainability/.

10. For more on greenwashing, see Toby Miller, *Greenwashing Sport* (New York: Routledge, 2018); Natasha Brison, "Spotting 'Greenwashing' in Sports," Global Sport Matters, April 19, 2022, https://globalsportmatters.com/business/2022/04/19/sports -greenwashing-how-to-spot-it-faq/.

11. Jon Patricof and Jonathan Soros, "Letter from the Co-founders of Athletes Unlimited, 2023," Athletes Unlimited, February 1, 2023, para. 18, https://auprosports .com/read/letter-from-the-founders-2023/.

12. Clare Brennan, "Athletes Unlimited Offers WNBA Players a Domestic Home for the Offseason," *Sports Illustrated*, February 17, 2023, https://www.si.com/ wnba/2023/02/17/athletes-unlimited-basketball-wnba-offseason.

13. W. G. Ramirez, "Air Hearn Reflects on Her Rise and Growth on the Basketball Court," Athletes Unlimited, April 2, 2024, para. 6, https://auprosports.com/read/ air-hearns-rise-and-growth-on-the-basketball-court/.

14. Ramirez, para. 10.

15. *All on the Table* (YouTube, 2022), episode 1, https://www.youtube.com/ watch?v=RBf8pZ-R2ZA.

16. *All on the Table*, episode 1.

17. *All on the Table*, episode 2, https://www.youtube.com/watch?v=aCPqLu35AE0.

18. "Athletes Unlimited Public Benefit Corporation Report," 5.

19. Whereas other AU leagues offer #BecomingUnlimited, a program designed to highlight BIPOC stars across predominantly white sports such as softball, volleyball,

and lacrosse, basketball is unique in AU's offerings as the only majority-Black league. Because of this, several other aspects of the season seem to operate a bit differently in terms of its political and cultural offerings.

20. "Athletes Unlimited Public Benefit Corporation Report," 21.

21. Brennan, "Athletes Unlimited."

22. Athletes Unlimited, "AU Pro Basketball Unveils Full 2024 Broadcast Schedule," Athletes Unlimited, February 23, 2024, https://auprosports.com/read/athletes-unlimited-pro-basketball-unveils-full-broadcast-schedule/.

23. *All on the Table*, episode 2.

24. Paula L. McGee, "Feminist Theology, Identity, and Discourse: A Closer Look at the 'Coming Out' of Sheryl Swoopes," *Feminist Theology* 19, no. 1 (September 2010): 54–72, https://doi.org/10.1177/0966735010372168; Samantha King, "Homonormativity and the Politics of Race: Reading Sheryl Swoopes," *Journal of Lesbian Studies* 13, no. 3 (July 2009): 272–90, https://doi.org/10.1080/10894160902876705; Lisa Doris Alexander, "'Raindrops on a Window': Race and Sex and the Framing of the Sheryl Swoopes Narrative," in *A Locker Room of Her Own: Celebrity, Sexuality, and Female Athletes*, ed. David C. Ogden and Joel Nathan Rosen (Jackson: University Press of Mississippi, 2013), 124–45.

25. Michela Musto, Cheryl Cooky, and Michael A. Messner, "'From Fizzle to Sizzle!': Televised Sports News and the Production of Gender-Bland Sexism," *Gender & Society* 31, no. 5 (October 2017): 575, https://doi.org/10.1177/0891243217726056.

26. Ayala, "Athletes Unlimited Basketball."

27. James Blake Hike, "An Athlete's Right to Privacy Regarding Sport-Related Injuries: HIPAA and the Creation of the Mysterious Injury," *Indiana Health Law Review* 6, no. 47 (2009): 58.

28. Hike, 66.

29. Hike, 75.

30. *All on the Table*, episode 1.

31. *All on the Table*, episode 1.

32. "Athletes Unlimited Public Benefit Corporation Report," 2.

33. Paul Lee, Kevin Westcott, and Suhas Raviprakash, "Women's Sports Gets down to Business: On Track for Rising Monetization," Deloitte Insights, December 7, 2020, https://www2.deloitte.com/xe/en/insights/industry/technology/technology-media-and-telecom-predictions/2021/womens-sports-revenue.html.

34. Liz Elting, "Going for Gold: Women's Sports Are Profitable—When Brands, Media and Broadcast Buy In," *Forbes*, July 12, 2023, para. 2, https://www.forbes.com/sites/lizelting/2023/07/12/going-for-gold-womens-sports-are-profitable-when-brands-media-and-broadcast-buy-in/?sh=575a773d125d.

35. Michael R. Littenberg, Emily J. Oldshue, and Brittany N. Pifer, "Delaware Public Benefit Corporations—Recent Developments," *Harvard Law School Forum on Corporate Governance* (blog), August 31, 2020, https://corpgov.law.harvard.edu/2020/08/31/delaware-public-benefit-corporations-recent-developments/.

36. AU acknowledges this balance in its PBC report: "As the first professional sports league to be organized as a PBC, Athletes Unlimited exists to fulfill the inspirational promise of professional sports while building a thriving business that benefits all our stakeholders" ("Athletes Unlimited Public Benefit Corporation Report," 5).

37. "Athletes Unlimited Public Benefit Corporation Report," 22.

38. Aaron C. T. Smith and Hans M. Westerbeek, "Sport as a Vehicle for Deploying Corporate Social Responsibility," *Journal of Corporate Citizenship* 25 (Spring 2007): 44.

39. Tim Breitbarth, Stefan Walzel, and Christos Anagnostopoulos, *Governance and CSR Management in Sport* (Bradford, UK: Emerald Publishing, 2015), 245, http://ebookcentral.proquest.com/lib/uoregon/detail.action?docID=2030578.

40. Michael Serazio and Emily Thorson, "Weaponized Patriotism and Racial Subtext in Kaepernick's Aftermath: The Anti-politics of American Sports Fandom," *Television & New Media* 21, no. 2 (2020): 151–68; Emily A. Thorson and Michael Serazio, "Sports Fandom and Political Attitudes," *Public Opinion Quarterly* 82, no. 2 (2018): 391–403.

41. Julie DiCaro, "NFL's Breast Cancer Awareness Month More about Style Than Substance," *Sports Illustrated*, October 22, 2015, para. 11 https://www.si.com/the-cauldron/2015/10/22/nfl-breast-cancer-month-deangelo-williams. Previous work by other journalists found that, ultimately, only 8 percent of proceeds from NFL merch sold for cancer advocacy actually goes toward cancer research.

42. SI Wire, "Steelers' RB Fined for 'Find the Cure' Eye Black," *Sports Illustrated*, October 28, 2015, https://www.si.com/nfl/2015/10/28/pittsburgh-steelers-deangelo-williams-fined-eye-black-breast-cancer.

43. DiCaro, "NFL's Breast Cancer," para. 19.

44. Nina Totenberg and Sarah McCammon, "Supreme Court Overturns Roe v. Wade, Ending Right to Abortion Upheld for Decades," NPR, June 24, 2022, https://www.npr.org/2022/06/24/1102305878/supreme-court-abortion-roe-v-wade-decision-overturn.

45. "Abortion Laws by State," Center for Reproductive Rights, accessed November 15, 2023, https://reproductiverights.org/maps/abortion-laws-by-state/.

46. Philip Elliott, "Pete Buttigieg on LGBTQ Rights: 'I Don't Think Anything Is Safe,'" *Time*, June 12, 2023, para. 4, https://time.com/6286592/pete-buttigieg-interview-lgbtq-rights/.

47. Elliott, para. 7.

48. William Melhado and Alex Nguyen, "Texas Lawmakers Pursued Dozens of Bills Affecting LGBTQ People This Year. Here's What Passed and What Failed," *Texas Tribune*, March 6, 2023, https://www.texastribune.org/2023/03/06/texas-legislature-lgbtq-bills/.

49. Brian Lopez, "Texas Has Banned More Books Than Any Other State, New Report Shows," *Texas Tribune*, September 19, 2022, https://www.texastribune.org/2022/09/19/texas-book-bans/.

50. Michelle Smith, "Column: NCAA Choices Don't Factor in Choice," *The Next*, November 23, 2022, https://www.thenexthoops.com/features/column-ncaa-chooses-final-four-sites-without-regard-to-choice/.

51. Amira Rose Davis, "Sixty Years Ago She Refused to Stand for the Anthem," *Zora*, September 26, 2019, https://zora.medium.com/sixty-years-ago-she-refused-to-stand-for-the-anthem-cf443b4e75c7.

52. Michael Butterworth, "Sport and the Quest for Unity: How the Logic of Consensus Undermines Democratic Culture," *Communication & Sport* 8, no. 4–5 (2020): 460.

53. Michael Silk, "The Phallus and the Pariah: The Cultural Politics of the Post-9/11 Sporting Body," in *Sport and Militarism: Contemporary Global Perspectives*, ed. Michael Butterworth (London: Routledge, 2017), 221.

54. Michael L. Butterworth, "The Athlete as Citizen: Judgement and Rhetorical Invention in Sport," *Sport in Society* 17, no. 7 (2014): 879.

55. @T_Cloud4, Twitter/X, October 26, 2023, https://twitter.com/T_Cloud4/status/1717565827594015021.

56. Butterworth, "Sport," 454.

57. *The New Faces of the WNBA* (Togethxr, 2023), https://www.youtube.com/watch?v=9gup1FRgJys.

58. Gaye Theresa Johnson, *Spaces of Conflict, Sounds of Solidarity: Music, Race, and Spatial Entitlement in Los Angeles* (Berkeley: University of California Press, 2013), 12.

59. Johnson, 14.

60. Johnson, 14.

61. Johnson's beat juggling reminds me also of Josh Kun's beautiful metaphor of the crossfade, another music comparison to the crossover.

62. *All on the Table*, episode 2.

63. Ayala, "Athletes Unlimited Basketball."

64. Ayala, para. 16.

65. "Who We Are," para. 2.

Fourth Quarter. You Can't See Me

1. Kate Fagan and Seimone Augustus, *Hoop Muses: An Insider's Guide to Pop Culture and the (Women's) Game* (New York: Hachette Book Group, 2023).

2. Natalie Weiner, "The Week Women's Basketball Took Over Dallas," *D Magazine*, April 3, 2023, https://www.dmagazine.com/sports/2023/04/the-week-womens-basketball-took-over-dallas/.

3. Emily Caron, "LSU's March Madness Victory Caps Record-Setting Women's Tournament," *Sportico*, April 3, 2023, https://www.sportico.com/leagues/college-sports/2023/lsu-championship-march-madness-records-ratings-viewership-1234718192/. According to the NCAA, the two Division I semifinal games on Friday were ESPN's two most-viewed men's or women's college basketball games ever on

ESPN+. Additionally, the 2023 Women's Final Four broke the all-time attendance record, with two sellouts. The women's tournament as a whole set an attendance record of 357,542. See Justin Whitaker, "Leaving a Lasting Imprint at 2023 Men's and Women's Final Fours," NCAA.org, March 21, 2023, https://www.ncaa.org/news/2023/4/4/features-leaving-a-lasting-imprint-at-2023-mens-and-womens-final-fours.aspx.

4. Henry Bushnell, "Inside NCAA Basketball's Gender Inequities and How They Were Exposed in 2021," Yahoo Sports, March 14, 2022, para. 6, https://sports.yahoo.com/ncaa-basketball-gender-inequities-2021-exposed-march-madness-162712173.html.

5. Bushnell.

6. @sedonaprince, "Let me put it on Twitter too cause this needs the attention https://T.Co/toDWKL2YHR," Twitter, March 19, 2021, https://twitter.com/sedonaprince_/status/1372736231562342402.

7. @dawnstaley, "#WHATMATTERS https://T.Co/QTQzCwbnZT," Twitter, March 20, 2021, https://twitter.com/dawnstaley/status/1373064039211876358.

8. Bushnell, "Inside NCAA," para. 25.

9. Rachel Bachman, Louise Radnofsky, and Laine Higgins, "NCAA Withheld Use of Powerful 'March Madness' Brand from Women's Basketball," *Wall Street Journal,* March 22, 2021, https://www.wsj.com/articles/march-madness-ncaa-tournament-womens-basketball-11616428776; Bushnell, "Inside NCAA."

10. The second phase of Kaplan Hecker & Fink's review focuses on other sports underneath the NCAA umbrella and can be reviewed here: https://kaplanhecker.app.box.com/s/y17pvxpap8lotzqajjan9vyye6zx8tmz.

11. Kaplan Hecker & Fink, LLP, "NCAA External Gender Equity Review Phase I: Basketball Championships," August 2, 2021, 2, https://kaplanhecker.app.box.com/s/6fpd51gxk9ki78f8vbhqcqhob00950xq.

12. Kaplan Hecker & Fink, 3.

13. Kaplan Hecker & Fink, 7.

14. Associated Press, "Lawmakers Rip Emmert, Demand More Progress on NCAA Equity," *USA Today,* March 15, 2022, para. 2, https://www.usatoday.com/story/sports/ncaaw/2022/03/15/lawmakers-rip-emmert-demand-more-progress-on-ncaa-equity/49939795/.

15. National Collegiate Athletic Association v. Alston, Supreme Court of the United States, June 21, 2021, https://supreme.justia.com/cases/federal/us/594/20-512/case.pdf.

16. Harvard Law Review, "Sherman Act—Antitrust Law—College Athletics—NCAA v. Alston," *Harvard Law Review* 135, no. 1 (November 2021): 471.

17. National Collegiate Athletic Association v. Alston, 1.

18. Senate Bill 5, 82nd Oregon Legislative Assembly, 2023 regular session, https://olis.oregonlegislature.gov/liz/2023R1/Downloads/MeasureDocument/SB0005/Introduced.

19. James Crepea, "Proposed Oregon College Athletes Bill No Longer Includes Royalty Payments from 'Merchandising' Deals," *The Oregonian / OregonLive*, May 19, 2021, para. 4, https://www.oregonlive.com/sports/2021/05/proposed-oregon-college-athletes -name-image-likeness-bill-no-longer-includes-royalty-payments-from-merchandising -deals-after-ncaa-president-tells-sen-courtney-it-would-make-athletes-ineligible-as -employees.html.

20. Michelle Brutlag Hosick, "NCAA Adopts Interim Name, Image and Likeness Policy," NCAA.org, June 30, 2021, https://www.ncaa.org/news/2021/6/30/ncaa-adopts -interim-name-image-and-likeness-policy.aspx.

21. "Name, Image, and Likeness: International Student-Athletes," Office of the General Counsel, para. 2, accessed November 16, 2023, https://generalcounsel.uoregon .edu/name-image-and-likeness-international-student-athletes.

22. Ryan Allen and Krishna Bista, "Talented, Yet Seen with Suspicion: Surveillance of International Students and Scholars in the United States," *Journal of International Students* 12, no. 1 (2022): 175, https://doi.org/10.32674/jis.v12i1.3410.

23. This relationship's origins are most frequently traced to Theodore Roosevelt and college football. For more, see John J. Miller, *The Big Scrum: How Teddy Roosevelt Saved Football* (New York: Harper, 2011).

24. *PostGame: (Iowa) Dawn Staley, Aliyah Boston and Raven Johnson News Conference 03/31/23*, 2023, emphasis mine, https://www.youtube.com/watch?v=gKyL4gQj3Vw.

25. *PostGame*.

26. @inyourlife, "Preach Coach!! Yesss Reiterate the Assignment of Character, Accountability and Responsibility to These Media Reporters and Others That Have Racist Issues. Well Done. Love You Coach [Staley]!! Keep It Going 😰 🖤 💯 🙏 🔥" (YouTube, March 31, 2023), https://www.youtube.com/watch?v=gKyL4gQj3Vw&lc=UgxZ8XT qcwCybH23U7R4AaABAg.

27. @nworafairley4888 (YouTube, March 31, 2023), https://www.youtube.com/ watch?v=gKyL4gQj3Vw&lc=UgygXamLFJdGW_hhpmR4AaABAg.

28. Patricia Hill Collins, *Black Feminist Thought* (New York: Routledge, 2000), 69.

29. Moya Bailey, *Misogynoir Transformed: Black Women's Digital Resistance* (New York: New York University Press, 2021), 5.

30. Akilah R. Carter-Francique and Michelle F. Richardson, "Controlling Media, Controlling Access: The Role of Sport Media on Black Women's Sport Participation," *Race, Gender & Class* 23, no. 1/2 (2016): 7–33; Stacy Landreth Grau, Georgina Roselli, and Charles R. Taylor, "Where's Tamika Catchings? A Content Analysis of Female Athlete Endorsers in Magazine Advertisements," *Journal of Current Issues and Research in Advertising* 29, no. 1 (Spring 2007): 55–65; Risa F. Isard and E. Nicole Melton, "Does Sport Media Raise Her Name? Examining Intersectional Representation in Media Narratives," *Sport, Business and Management* 12, no. 3 (September 2021): 305–22; Katherine L. Lavelle, "'Plays Like a Guy': A Rhetorical Analysis of Brittney Griner in Sports Media," *Journal of Sports Media* 9, no. 2 (Fall 2014): 115–31.

31. For more on the Imus incident, see Cheryl Cooky, Faye L. Wachs, Michael Messner, and Shari L. Dworkin, "It's Not about the Game: Don Imus, Race, Class, Gender and Sexuality in Contemporary Media," *Sociology of Sport Journal* 27, no. 2 (2010): 141.

32. Bailey, *Misogynoir Transformed,* 1.

33. Yaron Steinbuch, "Rutgers Women's Basketball Coach Offers Condolences to Don Imus' Family," *New York Post,* January 1, 2020, para. 10, https://nypost.com/2020/01/01/rutgers-womens-basketball-coach-offers-condolences-to-don-imus-family/.

34. Steinbuch, para. 13.

35. Rachel Treisman, "How a Hand Gesture Dominated a NCAA Title Game and Revealed a Double Standard," NPR, April 3, 2023, https://www.npr.org/2023/04/03/1167704651/angel-reese-caitlin-clark-you-cant-see-me-gesture.

36. Treisman.

37. Bailey, *Misogynoir Transformed,* 2.

38. *LSU National Championship Postgame Press Conference—2023 NCAA Tournament,* 2023, https://www.youtube.com/watch?v=sWfGZiy_yF8.

39. *LSU National Championship.*

40. @gabunion, Instagram, April 5, 2023, https://www.instagram.com/p/CqokVRwJo6l/.

41. Victoria Hernandez, "Iowa Star Caitlin Clark Defends Angel Reese amid Criticism, Speaks on Invitation to White House," *USA Today,* April 4, 2023, para. 6, https://www.usatoday.com/story/sports/ncaaw/2023/04/04/caitlin-clark-speaks-angel-reese-criticism-white-house-invitation/11599712002/.

42. Alisandra Puliti, "Introducing 2023 SI Swimsuit Model Angel Reese," Swimsuit | SI.com, May 8, 2023, https://swimsuit.si.com/swimnews/introducing-2023-si-swimsuit-model-angel-reese.

43. ESPN News Service, "Bidens Clarify National Champ LSU's White House Invitation," ESPN.com, April 3, 2023, para. 5, https://www.espn.com/womens-college-basketball/story/_/id/36058616/jill-biden-wants-national-champ-lsu-runner-iowa-white-house.

44. Brett Siegel, "'True Champions and Incredible Patriots': The Transformation of the Ceremonial White House Visit under President Trump," *Journal of Emerging Sport Studies* 2 (2019): 5.

45. ESPN News Service, "Bidens Clarify," para. 8.

46. *Dormz | Angel Reese & Flau'Jae Johnson* (YouTube, 2023), https://www.youtube.com/watch?v=eMMPm9ozofo.

47. Sam Joseph, "Iowa Hawkeyes Break Attendance Record in Historic Game at Kinnick Stadium," CNN, October 16, 2023, https://www.cnn.com/2023/10/16/sport/iowa-basketball-ncaa-attendance-record-spt-intl/index.html.

48. *Crossover at Kinnick,* episode 1, https://hawkeyesports.com/news/2023/10/05/crossover-at-kinnick-ep-1/.

49. *Crossover at Kinnick,* episode 3, https://doi.org/10/16/crossover-at-kinnick -ep-3/.

50. *Crossover at Kinnick,* episode 3.

51. "Gamecocks and Irish to Make History in Paris," University of South Carolina Athletics, April 12, 2023, para. 4, https://gamecocksonline.com/news/2023/04/12/ gamecocks-and-irish-to-make-history-in-paris/.

52. Pete Iacobelli, "An NCAA First as Women's Basketball Powers No. 6 South Carolina, No. 10 Notre Dame Play in Paris," *AP News,* November 5, 2023, para. 21, https://apnews.com/article/paris-basketball-staley-notre-dame-gamecocks-ivey -7bcfb1df88e296583ccac4b00b68eeea.

53. *Crossover at Kinnick,* episode 3.

54. ESPN PR [@ESPNPR], "Fans tuned-in for #NCAAWBB Championship Sunday on ESPN! 🏀 #SECWBB Championship | 2M viewers 🏀 #Pac12WBB Championship | 1.4M viewers 🏀 #ACCWBB Championship | 679,000 viewers The most-watched SEC, Pac-12 & ACC Championship games for ESPN platforms https://T.Co/htf2dYduMe," Twitter, March 12, 2024, https://twitter.com/ESPNPR/status/1767677969604997611; Margaret Fleming, "Women's Basketball Conference Tourneys Set Attendance, TV Marks," *Front Office Sports* (blog), March 13, 2024, https://frontofficesports.com/ womens-basketball-conference-tourneys-set-attendance-tv-marks/.

55. ESPN News Service, "6 Ejected in SEC Title Game after South Carolina–LSU Tussle," ESPN.com, March 10, 2024, para. 5, https://www.espn.com/womens-college -basketball/story/_/id/39702299/6-ejected-sec-title-game-south-carolina-lsu-tussle.

56. ESPN News Service, para. 18.

57. For more on the impact of this fight on the NBA and professional sports arenas, see David J. Leonard, *After Artest: The NBA and the Assault on Blackness* (Albany: SUNY Press, 2012); David J. Leonard and C. Richard King, eds., *Commodified and Criminalized: New Racism and African Americans in Contemporary Sports* (Lanham, MD: Rowman & Littlefield, 2012).

58. Mark Puleo, "LSU Coach Kim Mulkey Threatens Legal Action against the Washington Post in 4-Minute Tirade," *The Athletic,* March 23, 2024, https://the athletic.com/5363936/2024/03/23/kim-mulkey-lsu-washington-post/.

59. Ben Bolch, "Commentary: UCLA-LSU Is America's Sweethearts vs. Its Basket-ball Villains," *Los Angeles Times,* March 29, 2024, https://www.latimes.com/sports/ ucla/story/2024–03–29/ucla-lsu-america-sweethearts-versus-basketball-villains.

60. Bolch.

61. Thomas Schlachter, "LA Times Edits Article and Apologizes after Drawing the Ire of LSU Coach Kim Mulkey," CNN, April 1, 2024, https://www.cnn.com/ 2024/04/01/sport/la-times-kim-mulkey-lsu-article-spt-intl/index.html.

62. Danny Davis, "Vic Schaefer Explains Why Texas Played Sunday despite the Court's 3-Point Line Issue," *Austin American-Statesman,* March 31, 2024, para. 13, emphasis mine, https://www.statesman.com/story/sports/college/longhorns/womens -basketball/2024/03/31/texas-longhorns-basketball-coach-vic-schaefer-reacts-to -moda-center-court-issues-with-3-point-lines/73162666007/.

63. Following the NC State / Texas game, I walked to a bar near Moda Center to process what had happened and look for more answers regarding the three-point line and other coverage of the game. I was approached by a local NBC reporter, who asked me if I had watched the game and if I knew anything about the controversy or women's basketball in general. I told him that I did happen to know a small amount, and when he asked if I would be willing to discuss it for the 11:00 news, I promptly went outside and offered a condensed version of this entire chapter.

64. Rebecca Cohen, "Racial Slur Was Used against University of Utah Women's Basketball Team, Coeur d'Alene Detectives Say," *NBC News,* April 4, 2024, para. 12, https://www.nbcnews.com/news/sports/racial-slur-was-used-university-utah -womens-basketball-team-coeur-dale-rcna146332.

65. Dave Zirin, "Coaching Great Dawn Staley Defends Trans Athletes," *The Nation,* April 10, 2024, para. 4, https://www.thenation.com/article/society/dawn-staley-trans -athletes/.

66. @jemelehill, "Jemele Hill on X: 'This was a terrible moment for Gregg Doyel, a journalist I've known practically since I first started reporting professionally. Obviously something that never would have been said to a male athlete. I said this some time ago, but another upside of Caitlin Clark's popularity is . . . ' / X," Twitter, April 18, 2024, https://twitter.com/jemelehill/status/1780971139147403578.

Overtime. The Game Is Grown

1. Karen Crouse, a *New York Times* sports reporter, wrote a commentary piece in an issue of *Communication & Sport* responding to the findings of Cheryl Cooky, Michael A. Messner, and Robin H. Hextrum, "Women Play Sport, but Not on TV: A Longitudinal Study of Televised News Media," *Communication & Sport* 1, no. 3 (2013): 203–30, and asked, "When the Dodgers cannot keep up with the web traffic of the Lakers in Los Angeles, how are the Sparks going to make inroads?" ("Why Female Athletes Remain on Sport's Periphery," *Communication & Sport* 1, no. 3 [2013]: 238).

2. *Arthur Jafa + Greg Tate in Conversation: Love Is the Message, the Message Is Death,* 2016, https://vimeo.com/209649169?embedded=true&source=video_title &owner=10357612.

3. "Playa Society WNBA Black History Every Game T-Shirt," Playa Society, accessed October 28, 2023, https://www.playasociety.com/products/playa-society-wnba-black -history-every-game-t-shirt.

4. "About Playa Society," Playa Society, accessed October 28, 2023, https://www .playasociety.com/pages/about-playa-society.

5. Obi Anyanwu, "Is the WNBA a Missed Fashion Opportunity?," *Women's Wear Daily,* October 11, 2021, para. 34, https://wwd.com/feature/wnba-fashion-opportunity -1234969505/. Her description of getting dressed reminds me of Cheryl Miller's comments on dress detailed in the prologue of this book.

6. C. Riley Snorton, *Black on Both Sides: A Racial History of Trans Identity* (Minneapolis: University of Minnesota Press, 2017), 2.

7. Snorton, 59.

8. Snorton, 9.

9. Chris Liakos and Maya Szaniecki, "UN Slams France's Decision to Ban French Athletes' Hijabs at 2024 Olympics," CNN, September 26, 2023, https://www.cnn.com/2023/09/26/europe/un-hijab-olympics-intl/index.html.

10. Liakos and Szaniecki, para. 6.

11. Paul Eid, "Balancing Agency, Gender and Race: How Do Muslim Female Teenagers in Quebec Negotiate the Social Meanings Embedded in the Hijab?," *Ethnic and Racial Studies* 38, no. 11 (2014): 1902.

12. "Laws of the Game" (Zurich, Switzerland: FIFA, July 2007), https://www.fifa.com/mm/document/affederation/federation/laws_of_the_game_0708_10565.pdf.

13. See Jesse Dougherty, "After Playing All Season, Maryland Girl Held out of Basketball Game for Wearing a Hijab," *Washington Post*, March 13, 2017, https://www.washingtonpost.com/sports/highschools/after-playing-all-season-maryland-girl-held-out-of-basketball-game-for-wearing-a-hijab/2017/03/13/63fe82be-0767-11e7-8884-96e6a6713f4b_story.html.

14. Matthew Weaver, "Burqa Bans, Headscarves and Veils: A Timeline of Legislation in the West," *The Guardian*, May 31, 2018, https://www.theguardian.com/world/2017/mar/14/headscarves-and-muslim-veil-ban-debate-timeline; Morgan Lowrie, "Quebec Women Who've Worn Niqabs Discuss Controversial Neutrality Bill: 'It's Part of Who I Am, My Identity,'" *National Post*, October 22, 2017, https://nationalpost.com/news/canada/quebec-women-whove-worn-niqabs-discuss-provinces-controversial-neutrality-bill; Marianne Levine, "Supreme Court Rules against Abercrombie in Hijab Case," *Politico*, June 1, 2015, https://www.politico.com/story/2015/06/ambercrombie-fitch-hijab-case-supreme-court-ruling-118492.

15. Manal Hamzeh, "Jordanian National Football Muslimat Players: Interrupting Islamophobia in FIFA's 'Hijab Ban,'" *Physical Education and Sport Pedagogy* 20, no. 5 (2015): 519.

16. Hamzeh, 519.

17. Gayatri Chakravorty Spivak, "Can the Subaltern Speak?," in *Colonial Discourse and Post-colonial Theory: A Reader*, ed. Patrick Williams and Laura Chrisman (New York: Columbia University Press, 1993), 66–111.

18. Mirjam Swanson, "NCAA Tournament: Diaba Konaté, a Symbol of Joy for UC Irvine, Can't Play Basketball in France," *Orange County Register*, March 20, 2024, para. 24, https://www.ocregister.com/2024/03/20/ncaa-tournament-diaba-konate-a-symbol-of-joy-for-uc-irvine-cant-play-basketball-in-france/.

19. @athleteally and @layshiac, "Tomorrow marks 100 days until the #Paris2024 Olympics, and yet we still haven't seen a response from @ffbb_officiel and @fiba about their discriminatory ban on French women's basketball players who wear hijab. Join @wnba player and Athlete Ally Ambassador @layshiac in calling for basketball to truly be a space for all. Learn more: change.org/BasketForAll #BasketPourToutes [ID: a photo of Layshia Clarendon with a quote from them that says, 'No one should

have to choose between honoring their faith and playing the sport they love, and it's heartbreaking and unacceptable that Muslim women in France are being forced to make that choice']," Instagram, April 16, 2024, https://www.instagram.com/p/C500B-3uJ5x/.

20. Chandra Talpade Mohanty, *Feminism without Borders: Decolonizing Theory, Practicing Solidarity* (Durham, NC: Duke University Press, 2006), 2.

21. Raka Shome and Radha Hegde, "Culture, Communication, and the Challenge of Globalization," *Media, Culture & Communication* 19, no. 2 (2002): 178.

22. Shome and Hegde, 180.

23. Shane Laflin, "From Spain to Storrs: Top Recruit Sarah Strong's Personal Path to UConn," ESPN.com, April 6, 2024, para. 8, https://www.espn.com/womens-college-basketball/story/_/id/39882596/top-recruit-sarah-strong-commits-uconn.

24. @jewellloyd, "No need to hesitate, just know singing the jingle is the right move! @statefarm #ad," Instagram, April 16, 2024, https://www.instagram.com/reel/C51G2apPX2e/.

Index

COURTNEY M. COX is an assistant professor in the Department of Indigenous, Race, and Ethnic Studies at the University of Oregon and the co-director of The Sound of Victory, a multi-platform digital humanities project.

The University of Illinois Press
is a founding member of the
Association of University Presses.

Composed in 10.5/14 Minion Pro
with Myriad Pro display
by Lisa Connery
at the University of Illinois Press
Manufactured by Sheridan Books, Inc.

University of Illinois Press
1325 South Oak Street
Champaign, IL 61820–6903
www.press.uillinois.edu